Research in information systems

A handbook for research supervisors and their students

BUTTERWORTH-HEINEMANN INFORMATION SYSTEMS SERIES

Series Editors

Professor David Avison, BA, MSc, PhD, FBCS
Department of Information Systems and Decision Sciences
ESSEC Business School
BP 50105 Avenue Bernard Hirsch
95021 Cergy-Pontoise
FRANCE
Email: Avison@essec.fr

Professor Guy Fitzgerald, BA, MSc, MBCS
Department of Information Systems and Computing
Brunel University
Uxbridge Middlesex UB8 3PH
UK
Email: Guy.Fitzgerald@brunel.ac.uk

This is a new series under the Elsevier Butterworth-Heinemann imprint which will provide a medium for quality publications in the information systems field. It will also provide continuity with the McGraw-Hill IS series, which has been discontinued. The new series of texts is aimed at first degree and postgraduate students, and the global research community in information systems, computer science and business management. IS is multi-disciplinary. Where formerly emphasis was placed on the technological aspects which remain significant, it now stresses the importance of, and the links to, the business environment particularly, in regard to the social and organisational aspects. If you have a book proposal for this series, please contact either of the Series Editors.

Research in information systems

A handbook for research supervisors and their students

Edited by

David Avison, ESSEC Business School, Paris

and

Jan Pries-Heje, IT University, Copenhagen

ELSEVIER
BUTTERWORTH
HEINEMANN

AMSTERDAM • BOSTON • HEIDELBERG • LONDON • NEW YORK • OXFORD
PARIS • SAN DIEGO • SAN FRANCISCO • SINGAPORE • SYDNEY • TOKYO

Elsevier Butterworth-Heinemann
Linacre House, Jordan Hill, Oxford OX2 8DP
30 Corporate Drive, Burlington MA 01803

First published 2005

British Library Cataloguing in Publication Data
A catalogue record for this book is available from the British Library

ISBN 0 7506 66552

For information on all Elsevier Butterworth-Heinemann
publications visit our website at http://www.books.elsevier.com

Printed and bound in Great Britain by Biddles Ltd, Kings Lynn, Norfolk

Working together to grow
libraries in developing countries

www.elsevier.com | www.bookaid.org | www.sabre.org

ELSEVIER   BOOK AID International   Sabre Foundation

Table of Contents

Preface

The time spent doing a PhD can be the most stimulating period of your life. Attempting to contribute something original to society is surely the most exciting challenge possible. It is also a gateway to an academic career. Supervising PhD students can be even more exciting because of the multiplier effect: you share in all their glory. Both supervisor and student can receive so many rewards. On the other hand it can also be a lonely experience. The supervisor–student relationship can be full of animosity. There can be many 'lows' and many students don't finish. It can seem a waste of time.

This book is intended to help supervisors and PhD students get the most out of the experience and avoid the negatives. There are chapters covering the likely events and challenges on the way so that you will be prepared. These chapters cover the role of the student and the role of the supervisor in these stages so that the supervisor–student relationship can run smoothly and happily. There are chapters covering the practical issues such as finance and those related to doing a PhD whilst also working in industry, teaching or raising a family. Supervisors also get involved in many of these issues. More social aspects such as ethical, gender, sexual and cultural issues are also covered. Academic questions such as 'what constitutes a discipline?' (in this case information systems), 'what constitutes originality?' and 'what constitutes quality' are addressed. There are also two chapters covering quantitative and qualitative research methods. We also look at and compare different models for PhD programs, including those from the USA, UK, Latin countries and Scandinavia.

In many universities, it seems to be assumed that academics with a PhD will somehow 'know' how to supervise. This is far from the case. This book might well be used as a basis for a course training research supervisors. It will also be an important resource for courses supporting PhD students.

The topic is vital to PhD supervisors and their students and there is presently no alternative book available relating to information systems research, for although the book is relevant to other disciplines, particularly in the social sciences, management and computer science, the examples used come from the field of information systems. The book is written by experts: leading international academics in the field of information systems. All these authors have had wide experience of research supervision over many years in many countries.

The book is also full of individual experiences. Two chapters relate to individual experiences of research supervision in the USA and the UK, but there are many vignettes throughout that shed light on particular and personal experiences in context. Many of these have been written by PhD students themselves.

We also wish you, the reader, to be active in your reading. There are five Parts to the book: Reflections, Supervisor–student relationship, Social and practical issues, Academic issues and PhD models. We introduce each Part with a series of questions for both the supervisor and the PhD student so that the reader can ensure the chapters following address his or her needs.

The origins of the book stems from many strands. The first is our long experience of supervising research in information systems. We have had successes and failures, and we have always felt that it would have been useful to have such a book available to guide us through the difficult times. The book helps to address the question 'what do other people do in these circumstances?'. Second, we have also had much experience as members of faculty in various PhD consortia. It has seemed to us that problems revealed by research students on these occasions reflect more on problems with their supervisor and the supervisory process than to problems of the researchers themselves. Just like their students, supervisors do need support as well.

We also felt that such a book should not reflect our experiences alone. Research programs and experiences differ between countries, universities, departments, supervisors and research students. The book needed to reflect this diversity. In 2003 we held a supervisors' workshop in Athens under the auspices of the International Federation of Information Processing (IFIP) Technical Committee 8 (David Avison is vice-chair and Jan Pries-Heje secretary of this group). The need to address this issue was obvious with over 50 turning up in Athens. Most of the chapters are written by some of those attending the meeting, all leading international researchers and experienced research supervisors in the field of information systems.

The first audience for the book is therefore research supervisors and would-be research supervisors, especially in the field of information systems and related domains. To supervise means to have the direction and oversight of the research of others. Why would anyone want to do that? Well, one answer is that research is a fascinating and intellectually stimulating task which is hard to do alone. Further, if you are also a member of faculty with teaching and administrative responsibilities, it may be more feasible to lead the research of more junior colleagues and research students than to do it yourself. This leadership position might be feasible because with seniority often comes the possibility of getting research funding. Junior researchers typically have much more time to dedicate to research but less experience and maybe less opportunity for funding or industrial contacts.

Mirrors have always been fascinating to humans and reflection of oneself is always exciting. By supervising PhD students you can have the pleasure of seeing some of your habits, methods, tools and practices mirrored in the work of your PhD students. The pride and joy you feel when your PhD students are doing well is inestimable. Finally, it can simply be a step in your career. In many countries you cannot become a full professor before you have supervised a number of PhD students successfully.

But this book is also aimed at PhD students and potential PhD students. Why do a PhD? Satisfying your intellectual curiosity is often at the core of the answer. The process of finding a topic, defining a research question and then making every endeavor possible to answer it in a satisfactory way is certainly a process that can challenge and stimulate your curiosity.

However, there may be other good reasons for wanting to do a PhD. Training your mind to handle difficult, complex and sometimes extremely challenging research problems is an important part of your training as a PhD student. Often you become part of an academic community when becoming a PhD student. But at the core of a PhD is your potential contribution to knowledge in the area or the topic you have chosen. Finally, a PhD is now an essential prerequisite for becoming a full member of faculty at a university.

There are many aspects to the subject, so we have split the book into five parts. The first consists of two reflective personal accounts from research supervisors in the United States and Europe. Gordon Davis has had enormous experience, and his chapter covers the basic issues seen from his perspective. It provides an excellent introduction to the book. In each chapter we have asked authors to provide personal stories as vignettes illustrating the issues discussed through examples. David Avison's chapter is unusual in that it consists almost entirely of such stories, a kind of confessional account. Although not generalizable, of course, it does give a 'feel', at least through one career, of the concerns of being a research supervisor.

Part II discusses the relationship between the PhD student and the supervisor. This is complex, and in Chapter 3, Richard Baskerville and Nancy Russo describe aspects of the relationship and different relationships through the use of metaphors: project, process, magic, journey, adventure, child, marriage, student, survival test, apprentice and servitude. In Chapter 4

Ramiro Montealegre and Duane Truex concentrate on the role of the supervisor in this relationship. In Chapter 5, Duane Truex, Ramiro Montealegre, David Avison and Cherie Long look at various aspects of the relationship, including balancing competing requirements of the supervisors and students and pressures that result, and they emphasize the emotional as well as academic aspects as they argue for holistic advising.

Part III looks at wider issues of research supervision, such as: the divided loyalties of doing PhD research with other responsibilities (Björn Lundell, Cathy Urquhart and Jan Pries-Heje), financial issues (Frantz Rowe and Jan Pries-Heje), ethical issues (Robert Davison), gender issues (Anita Greenhill and Lynette Kvasny), sexual orientation (David Wilson) and diverse cultures (David Avison, Muhammadou Kah, Jainaba Kah and Abimbola Soriyan). Research students are diverse in so many ways, and these chapters explore aspects of this diversity. Indeed there is no such thing as a typical PhD student (nor a typical PhD supervisor for that matter!).

Part IV, on the other hand, looks at academic issues. First there is a discussion about the discipline of information systems (Steve Elliott and David Avison), then the perennial issues of quality and originality are discussed (Jan Pries-Heje and David Avison), followed by two chapters which look at choosing appropriate research methods, a vital concern in information systems where the choices are many. Detmar Straub, David Gefen and Marie-Claude Boudreau look at quantitative approaches and David Avison and Michael Myers look at qualitative approaches.

Finally, in Part V we look at models for the PhD in different countries. The US model is covered by Duane Truex and Cherie Long, the UK model by Guy Fitzgerald, the Latin model by João Alvaro Carvalho and Frantz Rowe and the Scandinavian model by Karlheinz Kautz. Of course, models vary greatly even within a country, so in each case we are looking at one instance along with a discussion of variances. It is readily evident that we can learn much from the practice of each other.

We sincerely hope that this book helps to make your supervising experiences and your experiences as a research student exciting and successful.

David Avison and Jan Pries-Heje
Houilles, France

Acknowledgements

We wish to thank all those who participated in the first IFIP TC8 Supervisors' Workshop in Athens, Greece in June 2003, in particular those who formed teams to address particular topics as these suggestions inspired many of the chapters herein: Carl Adams, Kim Viberg Andersen, Chris Atkinson, Chrisanthi Avgerou, Richard Baskerville, João Alvaro Carvalho, Gordon B. Davis, Robert Davison, Guy Fitzgerald, Bob Galliers, Anita Greenhill, Rudy Hirschheim, Debra Howcroft, Pertti Jarvinen, Karlheinz Kautz, Julie Kendall, Ken Kendall, Mikko Korpela, Cherie Long, Björn Lundell, Nathalie Mitev, Ramiro Montealegre, Björn Erik Munkvold, Anja Mursu, Michael Myers, Mike Newman, Niki Panteki, Ray Paul, Isabel Ramos, Helen J. Richardson, Dewald Roode, Frantz Rowe, Markku Sääksjärvi, Steve Sawyer, Ann Séror, Duane Truex, Cathy Urquhart, Dave Wainwright, Edgar Whitley, David W. Wilson, Bob Wood and Trevor Wood-Harper. Angeliki Poulymenakou and Mavra Chadjidimitriou played a major role in helping us organize the event.

Chapters have been refereed by authors of other chapters and many of those attending the supervisors' workshop (what a critical resource!). They also provided some of the vignettes (histories shown as boxed and shaded in the text). So this book reflects a great team effort. The following colleagues also provided particular help in individual chapters: Serge Baile, Bob Barbour, Robert Reix, Suzanne Rivard and Jacques Trahand.

But most of all, we thank all our research students, past and present who have been an inspiration for this book. In particular, we wish to thank the following who provided vignettes used in the book: Lesley Axelrod, Yogesh Dwivedi, Gallina I. Hansen, Nikolaj Hansen, Bettina Törpel, Maryati Yusof and Jasni Zain.

David Avison and Jan Pries-Heje

Part I: Reflections

We start with two chapters which are personal accounts from experienced supervisors reflecting on what supervision is about. Gordon Davis discusses the various issues related to supervising and makes suggestions to supervisors on how to deal with these issues, advice which he summarizes as ten recommendations to supervisors. David Avison's piece is more of a confessional, providing a series of histories based on his experience of supervising.

We think it important to read actively. We will suggest questions that you might consider as you read through the chapters in each of the five Parts of the book. There are different questions for supervisors and students, but also role-play the other person. In that way you will get a feel for the whole process.

If you are a supervisor: you may like to consider your own motivation. Why do you want to supervise? Why are the accounts from the United States and Europe so different? Where do you stand on the issues discussed? Consider the four underlying issues that Gordon Davis discusses:

1　How can you help to surface the doctoral program assumptions in your university?
2　What is the motivation of your PhD students?
3　How would you characterize your own supervision style?
4　How do you cope with different student needs for advice and supervision?

What do you think may be particularly different about an academic life for those starting their career now, as against 30 years ago when David Avison started his? Should he have supervised PhD students despite not having a PhD himself? Read the email that David was sent by Michel. How would you react to such a letter? What do you think happened? How could David have prevented such an unhappy situation?

If you are a PhD student: have you considered your own motivation? Why do want a PhD? Do you like teaching, as it may be required along with researching? What will be your research contribution and how do you make sure it is enough? What will be your research method? Read the resources for doctoral dissertation research mentioned by Gordon Davis.

Look at the various personal histories that David Avison discusses. What would you have done differently if you were the student in each case? For example, how do you stand regarding Jeremy's ethical dilemma which might have cost him his PhD? Have you any say at your university regarding the choice of external examiner? What are the stories of your colleagues who started their PhDs a year or more before you? When do you plan to go to doctoral consortia and conferences? What are the most appropriate for you in each year of your program? Are you already planning papers to submit?

1

Advising and Supervising

Gordon B. Davis

1.1 Introduction

When I had my first doctoral student, I realized very quickly that I didn't know how to be a good supervisor. I had the experience of being a PhD student myself working with a supervisor. I had casual, incomplete, unorganized observations of other supervisors. But there were no models of supervision that I knew about. Advice was anecdotal and incomplete. As with many knowledge work processes, there was an implied assumption that completing a doctoral program and doctoral thesis qualified a professor to be a good supervisor. In fact, as I learned over time, some professors have good instincts and naturally do good supervising. However, most seem to learn through a trial and error process. Indeed, some never seem to learn to be good at it.

My view is that professors can learn supervision skills by following some systematic supervising processes. This chapter codifies some of my observations from being on well over a hundred doctoral thesis committees and being the principal supervisor for thirty or so doctoral theses. I summarize lessons I learned both by mistakes I have made or observed and by successes.

I recognize some difficulties with lessons learned or codified experience. The advice that emerges specifies what should be done (because it has worked) and how it should be done. The advice does not take into account philosophical differences among supervisors or the psychological resistance a supervisor may have to normative advice. Like all such codified experience, the lessons learned are a starting point for building good supervision skills rather than being a perfect recipe. Because the chapter codifies my experience, it does not deal with all conditions (even though I have experienced a wide variety in different countries), but it does provide a good basis for a supervisor to examine his or her supervision for possible improvement. I have learned from both good and bad supervising experiences. I hope that others will profit from my lessons learned.

1.2 An overview of the advice on supervising

This section clarifies terminology and provides an overview of the advice. Terminology may vary in different countries but the underlying problems are the same. To avoid using multiple terms, I will use the following terms to apply to the thesis supervisory function being performed and the objective of the supervision process:

- *Thesis* and *dissertation* are used interchangeably to refer to the doctoral thesis or doctoral dissertation produced and defended by a doctoral candidate. The thesis results from significantly independent work by a doctoral candidate. It is a *contribution* to knowledge.
- *Doctoral candidate* historically refers to a person who has demonstrated a readiness to do a doctoral thesis and therefore admitted to candidacy (probably after some examination procedure). As will be explained, students in many doctoral programs may be considered doctoral candidates during preparatory work. Although this distinction is important in some systems, from the standpoint of this chapter, a doctoral candidate is one who is in a doctoral program and is planning a doctoral thesis.
- *Supervisor* is used to refer to the doctoral student advisor or supervisor. The function is assumed to be essentially the same. *Supervision* refers to the process of providing guidance, advice, and quality assurance for a

doctoral student during two stages of a doctoral program: doing preparatory work prior to a thesis and writing a thesis.

The process of building expertise in advising a doctoral student begins with understanding four underlying issues: doctoral program assumptions, motivations for a doctorate, supervisor styles, and student need for supervision. The first issue is the underlying assumptions about a doctoral program: the two major assumptions are an entry-level doctorate or a mid-career doctorate. The second issue is the student or program motivation for a doctorate. These motivations range from recognition or prestige to a career requirement, with a number of variations of these two extremes. The third issue is different supervising styles. At the extremes, these range from a very strong master–apprentice model to a hands-off model. There are many variations between these extremes. Each supervising style has advantages and disadvantages, depending on the student and the problems being studied. The fourth issue is differences in student need for advice and supervision. At the extremes, these needs range from the need for very close direction and supervision to the need only for general direction and supervision. With basic understanding of these issues, a supervisor can begin to develop a preferred personal style and can make decisions about variations in supervision to suit a particular student or problem.

Given an understanding of the four basic issues of program assumptions, student motivations, supervising styles, and student needs, a supervisor should be familiar with, and apply some basic concepts about, doctoral supervising and some useful procedures. These concepts and procedures will help in achieving good results. Three basic concepts relate to the definition of contribution required for an acceptable thesis, supervisor competence to supervise a given thesis, and appropriate methodology. The contribution concept defines the essence of a thesis. Supervisor competence is a quality assurance concept to ensure a process that provides quality in supervision and advice, either by operational competence or review competence. The methodology concept relates to whether a methodology is appropriate for the problem and powerful enough to yield a contribution to knowledge.

Understanding underlying issues and concepts about supervision are not sufficient. Good program procedures are needed and a supervisor needs to apply good procedures. Good supervision procedures will tend to help produce good theses (assuming the student is receptive to good advice). Some important procedures to be implemented as part of a doctoral program or by doctoral supervision are: a broad introductory seminar, a student career plan that defines the role of the thesis in his or her career, a regular workshop for faculty and doctoral students to discuss presentations and papers, and an introduction of doctoral program information and doctoral student productivity aids. Other supervision procedures such as topic analyses to consider alternative theses, a formal thesis proposal, a thesis project plan, a formal or informal thesis proposal defense, and progress documentation are discussed later in this book and in a short monograph (Davis and Parker, 1997) on managing the doing of a doctoral thesis.

1.2 Four underlying issues important to supervising doctoral students

Not all doctoral programs are the same. Not all theses are based on the same assumptions. A thesis supervisor may impose certain values and standards without considering alternatives. From my experience, I have found it helps me to communicate my supervising experience if I make sure that research students I am mentoring have a shared understanding with me of four issues that I believe underlie differences in doctoral programs. These are doctoral program assumptions, motivations for a doctorate, different supervising styles, and differences in student needs for advice and supervision.

Underlying issue one: Doctoral program assumptions

Discussions of supervising are sometimes unproductive because the doctoral program assumptions are not surfaced. I was in a doctoral program with one set of assumptions, but I spent time in Europe with doctoral students who were in programs with different assumptions. At the risk of oversimplifying, I found it useful to define two alternative assumptions for the purpose and conduct of a doctoral program. I term these mid-career doctoral program and entry-level doctoral program.

- *A mid-career doctoral program* goes back to the historical development of doctoral programs in Europe. A person, who had engaged in teaching or research and demonstrated good scholarly abilities, probably including publications, could seek a doctorate as recognition of scholarly attainment. Given this general condition, the focus of the doctoral program is not on preparatory work but on the thesis. Any preparatory work is based on individualized counseling to fill gaps in knowledge in order to achieve an acceptable thesis. The thesis supervisor is critical to this individualized process. The doctoral candidate may not be in residence at the university. The process places significant emphasis on a final quality control check with external examiners.

- *An entry-level doctoral program* rests on the implied assumption that the doctorate is a credential for beginning a career as a researcher or academic. This is the most common situation in my experience in the USA and other countries. The degree is usually a requirement for entry into an academic career. Students entering a doctoral program may have little or no experience in teaching or research. The doctoral program is designed to prepare them for a career. Therefore, there is a fairly structured set of courses on a range of research methods, discussion of important literature and examples of research in the field of study, and review of important literature and examples of research in one or more underlying disciplines that support research in the field of study. The supervising and mentoring process usually includes strong advice to students on seminars to take, specification of assignments that demonstrate progress in a doctoral program, and criteria for examinations or other evidence of readiness to proceed with a thesis. The program for an individual doctoral candidate is therefore a combination of core subjects and experiences plus individually tailored learning. A typical supervisory arrangement consists of a committee process to evaluate readiness to do a thesis and a committee of four or five faculty members to evaluate the thesis. The committee is headed by a supervisor who takes a significant leadership role. It includes three or four other faculty members with diverse backgrounds and skills. The choices of committee members are based on the ability to assess the thesis proposal, give advice, and evaluate the results.

The two assumptions do not hold perfectly in practice. I am familiar with a doctoral program that has all the external appearance of a mid-career program, but many individual supervisors in the university essentially establish conditions that fit entry-level students. There is a world-wide trend to entry-level doctoral programs, primarily because they fit the majority of students. However, there are students who fit best with a mid-career program. In my experience and from discussions with graduates, there are significant problems when the student is entry-level and the program is mid-career.

> A young student with little business experience and no experience in doing independent scholarly work entered a doctoral program based on a mid-career doctorate. His doctorate did not prepare him well for a scholarly career, and he expressed disappointment with the mismatch between his needs and the doctoral program he chose.

On the other hand, I have advised some mid-career persons not to do an entry-level doctorate and to seek a mid-career program. Those who have followed this advice have found it worked very well.

> A man with a business career in consulting and other supervisory activities retired early and started teaching. He used his background to assist him in doing scholarly work, including research. He found a mid-career doctoral program an excellent fit with his background and his ability to work without close supervision.

A related issue is the length of time it takes to complete a doctorate. There are large variations within universities as well as between universities, so my comments of length are calibrated to high quality programs in information systems (or related subjects) in good universities. Ignoring preparatory activities, a typical thesis takes the equivalent of 12 to 18 months of full-time work. The average time for United States and Canadian doctoral students in entry-level programs (including the thesis) is between four and five years. In the United States, as reported by the National Science Foundation, this time has been increasing steadily during the past 25 years.

There are four reasons for this increase in time: first, the depth and quality of preparation have improved; second, students entering the job market are expected to have evidence of teaching ability; third, students entering the job market are expected to have demonstrated an ability to write and submit articles for publication; and fourth, theses must be completed before taking a position. The latter condition means effectively that students who are a few months behind schedule must wait many months before the next academic recruiting period.

Underlying issue two: Motivations for a doctorate
When I started as an academic, I thought that students working on doctorates all had the same motivation, namely to be scholars engaged in teaching and research. I have found that the real reasons for doing a doctorate are varied. I have been on examining committees in other disciplines and have found a variety of motivations. They affect the design of doctoral programs in different fields and certainly influence the selection of topics, acceptable research methods, and supervising processes. Even within doctoral programs in a given field or discipline, students may have different motivations. Without trying to look at all motivations, four examples from my experience illustrate this point:

- *Requirement for a scholarly career.* Under current and expected academic conditions in academic institutions, a doctorate involving good preparation for a scholarly career is a condition for employment. A well-constructed doctoral program provides preparation that enhances academic career potential.

In the doctoral program in information systems at Minnesota, we emphasize this motivation, and the program is built around this assumption.

- *Requirement for a career as a practitioner.* There are many careers that require a doctorate as a condition of credentials to practice or provide significant economic incentives for those who have doctorates. I have been on committees in which the person getting the doctorate will receive an increase in compensation (without regard to the value of the doctorate in the employment).

I worked closely with a woman getting a doctorate in psychology, and her motivation was to be in a private counseling practice.

- *Evidence of intellectual competence.* Consultants and those in similar knowledge-work occupations may find their careers enhanced by doctorates because the degree provides evidence of intellectual ability.

I was on the thesis committee of a consultant doing a degree in philosophy. The thesis was not related to his work career, but it was evidence of his intellectual competence.

- *Evidence of scholarly achievement.* Those who have been involved in research and related scholarly activities may wish to obtain a doctorate as evidence of their work. Although there are examples of great scholars who do not have doctorates, I have observed that many wish they had obtained the credential.

The motivation of a scholarly career is the dominant basis for many doctoral programs. For the MIS doctoral program at the University of Minnesota, we clearly make that our objective. An entry-level program is very consistent with this motivation. Other doctoral programs seem to support consulting as a basis for doctoral work. Certain programs in the university have professional qualification as the basis for a doctorate, and it is reflected in the design of the programs. I have observed doctoral programs in departments where program objectives and student motivations are varied. One department prepared students for either scholarly careers or professional careers requiring a doctorate as a credential. The mixed objectives may have been one reason they did not do a good job of either.

Underlying issue three: Supervising styles
For the purposes of discussion, it is useful to identify five supervising styles. These are illustrative, but I have known supervisors I would classify in each of the five styles. The five styles are ordered from strong, detailed supervision to hands-off *laissez faire* supervising. Each style has strengths and weaknesses. A supervisor may shift his or her style somewhat depending on the student, but I think it is difficult for a supervisor to be equally effective in all styles.

- *Strong master–apprentice style.* In this style, the supervisor is the master. The student works as an apprentice on problems selected by the master (often on research grants obtained by the supervisor). Assuming a competent master for thesis supervisor, the advantages are significant reduction in the time for the student to formulate a problem, strong guidance and direction in doing the work, and development of specific skills for the type of problem being worked on with the master. Even assuming a competent master, there may be severe disadvantages. The student may be given strong direction but may not develop an ability to formulate research and conduct it independently. The research methods may be limited. The focus on the master's problem may becloud the apprentice student's understanding. The sciences, where the master–apprentice style is very prevalent, routinely expect graduates with doctorates to take post-doctorate appointments. In part, this may be a response to the narrow focus of master–apprentice doctoral training. Of course, the master–apprentice style may be very bad if the master is not a good researcher or is exploitive in his or her handling of doctoral students. On balance, the master–apprentice style fits best the condition of a relatively immature, inexperienced student who needs strong direction. It also fits with well-defined, funded streams of research. This is not my natural style, but I have colleagues who do it very well and train their students well; on the other hand, I have evidence from observing colleagues and from talking with recent graduates that the style can result in exploitation and poorly trained graduates.

> We interviewed a graduating student who was working on a part of a very interesting funded project. Unfortunately, the student had no understanding of the large project because all his efforts were directed at a small part of the research.

- *Collegial master–apprentice style.* Limited domain supervising. This is a less restricted concept than strong master–apprentice. The supervisor is willing to supervise on problems that are within the scope of his or her research and methods within his or her skill set. The set is not restricted by the supervisor's current research activity or research funding. The problems may be selected by the student as long as they fit within the general domain of expertise. This style puts more responsibility on the student than the master–apprentice style, but the student thesis must fit within the existing knowledge of the supervisor. I have seen this work well when both the professor and the doctoral student were interested in a problem and the professor had sufficient expertise to provide good guidance.

- *Collegial development style.* Extended domain supervising. This supervising style includes not only the domain of the supervisor's current or past research but is extended to areas in which the supervisor has an interest and is willing to invest in becoming reasonably proficient. There is a joint learning experience; the supervisor starts with more experience, but both are learning the details of the thesis research area. This style fits a supervisor who is willing to expand his or her research competence; it fits a student who is willing to engage in a joint learning experience. It fits very well for a thesis that opens up a new or fairly new area of research. However, I have seen this supervising style fail when the supervisor was not willing to make the investment to be competent.

> The stream of group decision support research at Minnesota began by this type of advising. A student had an idea, and an advisor was willing to invest in becoming proficient enough to be a good mentor.

- *Guidance and suggestion style.* General supervising over a range of problem domains. Some supervisors have good skills at problem identification and problem formulation over a range of problems and research methods. They conceptualize well and are good at 'sense making'. This style works best with students who are willing and able to take initiative and take responsibility for learning the research domain and the appropriate research methods. The student gets good general guidance and good evaluation of the thesis but usually does not get detailed feedback and detailed mentoring of methods. It is not very good for immature students who need more detailed guidance. I have had some very good supervising experiences with this style with mature students who took initiative. I was able to apply my comparative advantage in mentoring them, but they took responsibility for learning the research domain and methods.

> A student did a simulation that examined the effects of design decisions on the life cycle costs of computer systems. I was familiar with simulation and the general principles being applied, so I could offer good suggestions, but the student had much better knowledge of the characteristics being modeled.

- *Passive hands-off style.* In this *laissez faire* style, the supervisor takes the role of a general quality control reader. The student must take the initiative to define a problem, decide on a research method, develop a research plan, and so forth. The supervisor responds to student plans and initiatives with some suggestions, but the responsibility is almost entirely with the student. Given a competent supervisor who gives good suggestions in response to student initiatives and plans, the advantages are that the student develops independent skills at formulating problems and planning research. The disadvantages are that the student may meander from problem to problem and take too long to do a thesis. Under these conditions, a student may not develop good skills and may drop out of the program. For fairly mature students with an ability to take initiative, this style may work well. It has significant danger with a PhD project for which the student does not have the necessary background for doing a good thesis or the supervisor is unable to do reasonable quality review. For immature students, it is likely to be a disaster. In general, I do not like to operate in this mode.

The five supervising styles are summarized in Table 1.1. The advantages and disadvantages of each are summarized in Table 1.2. The two extremes of strong master–apprentice style and passive hands-off style have significant risks but may work well under appropriate conditions. The middle three styles are less extreme. Supervisors can develop styles that are not at the extremes, based on their preferences, the maturity of students they supervise, the availability of funding, and so forth. Probably the extremes should be avoided, but one style does not fit all supervisors and one style does not fit all students. For example, a supervisor may use a collegial master–apprentice style with many students but change to a collegial development style for other students. For a very mature student who demonstrates good competence, a supervisor who prefers a collegial master–apprentice style of detailed supervising within restricted domains may be willing to change supervising style to a guidance–suggestion style. In any situation, a supervisor should identify his or her own strengths and weaknesses, identify both a preferred style as well as alternative styles he or she can do, and evaluate his or her ability to supervise different students. For example, as indicated earlier, I prefer a guidance and suggestion style, but I have adapted to situations requiring a collegial master–apprentice style and a collegial development style. I have avoided supervision requiring a strong master–apprentice style or a passive hands-off style.

Table 1.1 *Five supervising styles*

Style	Supervisor role and behavior	Student role and behavior
Strong master–apprentice style	Supervisor is master. Supervisor has a well specified domain of expertise and set of problems within it.	Student is an apprentice working for the supervisor. Student works on supervisor's problems.
Collegial master-apprentice style	Supervisor is expert who limits supervising to problems that are within scope of his or her research skill set but will work on student's problem.	Student develops a problem within supervisor's domain and skills and works under the supervisor to develop the research plan and procedures.
Collegial development style	Supervisor is senior colleague who will respond to student research problem and extend his or her supervising domain to include new problems and new skills.	Student takes initiative to introduce new problem that requires new skill set and works as a junior colleague with supervisor in joint development of new domain.
Guidance and suggestion style	Supervisor is a senior colleague who gives good general guidance over a wide range of problems and methods but does not have personal skill in all of them.	Student is an independent, junior colleague who takes initiative for presenting problems and research plans for discussion and guidance. Student develops required skills.
Passive hands-off style	Supervisor has quality control role and responds only to requests or documents and performs only general quality control review.	Student is an independent researcher who takes initiative for developing problem, developing skills, and presenting research plans for general review and approval.

One reason for classifying supervising styles is to help new supervisors to understand their own experience and to build upon their own abilities and preferences. It helps in building more confidence in supervisors, so that they can better adapt to the needs of the students and the conditions of the academic institution.

Table 1.2 *Advantages and disadvantages of different supervising styles*

Supervising style	Advantages	Disadvantages
Strong master–apprentice style	Supervisor is heavily involved and gives expert direction for research activities. Student learns how to do research within supervisor's domain.	Student works on supervisor's problems and within supervisor expertise and may not develop independence.
Collegial master–apprentice style	Supervisor knows the research domain and a set of research methods and can give expert advice on them. Student can take initiative in formulating problem and working with supervisor.	Student is limited to supervisor research domain and supervisor research skills. Student may be constrained to do work that is not within his or her long term research plan.
Collegial development style	Supervisor and student develop together to explore new domain and new research methods. Student develops independence within relationship.	Risk of exploring new research area that does not work. Risk that necessary development of both supervisor and student does not occur or occurs unevenly.
Guidance and suggestion style	Student is able to develop independent research and research management skills while receiving guidance and suggestions. The student may research a broad range of topics and employ broad range of methods.	Student may not get expert advice from supervisor on many issues, so student must search for expert advice. Student has significant responsibility for research quality and management of process.
Passive hands-off style	Student is able to act independently with little interference from supervisor. Student can work on problems of his or her choosing.	Student may make serious mistakes because of lack of advice and suggestions. Student may flounder and not complete on timely basis.

As coordinator of the information systems doctoral program for a number of years, I have heard from students who were frustrated with a master–apprentice supervising style because they were not given enough freedom to develop themselves; I have observed other students who had hands-off supervisors who complained that they couldn't get any advice or direction; other students were very happy with the same supervisors. This suggests a supervisor can do two things to be more effective: the first is to develop a preferred supervising style and communicate this to prospective supervisees; the second is to adapt somewhat to the different needs of students.

Students also need to understand preferred supervising styles of potential supervisors. Students can evaluate their maturity and level of skill. They can evaluate their need for close monitoring and supervision versus fairly loose monitoring. Such self-examination can lead to a useful dialog with potential supervisors. It can lead to clarity relative to expectations by both student and supervisor.

Underlying issue four: Different student needs for advice
There are significant differences in the maturity and confidence of doctoral students relative to the process of selecting a thesis topic, selecting a research design and research method, and managing the process of research and write up. To illustrate the range of students, needs for advice and supervision, three archetypes will be described.

- *Immature, unconfident student.* Although the student may have requisite tools and skills to do research, the ability to work independently is not well developed. The student looks to the supervisor for a problem, strong mentoring, and strong, detailed supervision. The student views the supervisor as 'big daddy.'
- *Somewhat mature, somewhat confident student.* Preparatory work leading to the thesis has helped the student be somewhat confident, but the student still needs moderately detailed direction to get going and moderate supervision during the process. The student views the supervisor as a 'mentoring' colleague.
- *Very mature, confident student.* Preparatory work and experience leading to the thesis has prepared the student to be quite independent. The student recognizes need for guidance and supervision, but the need is at a fairly general level. The student can take general guidance and apply it well. The student views the supervisor as a 'senior' colleague.

Understanding how students differ in their needs may help a potential supervisor not to accept supervisor assignments that he or she cannot do well. It may help a supervisor to modify a preferred supervising style to fit the needs of a student. Table 1.3 summarizes the likely fit and outcomes from supervising styles for the three different student archetypes. The table does not account for adjustment and compensating behaviors by students and supervisors. Neither does it suggest outcomes that must occur, but rather outcomes that are likely in the absence of adjustments and compensating behaviors (from students and supervisors). In other words, students and supervisors may adjust for the apparent lack of fit and compensate in various ways to achieve satisfactory results.

Table 1.3 *Supervising styles and likely outcomes for student archetypes*

Supervising style	Likely fit with student archetypes
Strong master–apprentice style	Good fit with immature, unconfident student. 'Do what I do' provides clear direction. Possible good fit with somewhat mature, somewhat confident student, but the style creates some stress between heavy direction of supervisor and initiative and independence of somewhat mature student. Likely stress and conflict between this style and the independence of a very mature, confident student
Collegial master–apprentice style	Some stress but a workable fit with immature, unconfident student because some initiative is required. Fairly good fit with somewhat mature, somewhat confident student because it provides boundaries for what is expected and allows some independence. Some stress from this style for mature, confident student because of constraints on what can be done by student.
Collegial development style	Stressful for immature, unconfident student because of need for significant student initiative. Good fit with somewhat mature, somewhat confident student because it builds confidence through development interactions. Reasonable fit and reasonably low stress for very mature, confident student if supervisor and student are compatible relative to problems and methods.
Guidance and suggestion style	Very stressful for immature, unconfident student because of vagueness of process and need for initiative that may exceed capacity of novice. Stressful but workable relationship for somewhat mature, somewhat confident student because of high initiative required from student. Good fit and reasonably low stress fit for very mature, confident student who is given much freedom and good feedback.
Passive hands-off style	Likely disaster for supervising relationship with immature, unconfident student because not sufficient guidance. Stressful relationship between supervisor with this style and somewhat mature, somewhat confident student because of insufficient feedback. This style may work for a very mature, confident student but introduces risks because of lack of clarity in expectations.

1.4 Basic concepts for thesis supervising

There are a number of concepts that are important in thesis supervising. Three that are especially significant are: contribution required for a doctoral thesis, supervisor competence for a specific thesis topic, and thesis research methodology.

Contribution required for a doctoral thesis

One of the important roles of a supervisor is to work with the student so that the latter can meet university requirements for a doctorate qualification. There are significant variations within a university and among universities regarding specifications for an acceptable thesis. However, there are some reasonable general guidelines. Individual departments or fields of study may make the general guidelines more specific.

- *Contributes to knowledge.* The role of university research is to create knowledge. A thesis should contribute to this role. The contribution to knowledge may be modest or profound, but this is the important test of a thesis. Some possible ways to think about contribution are given later in this section.
- *Demonstrates independent scholarly ability of student.* A student receiving a doctorate should have reasonable ability as a scholar. The thesis should therefore demonstrate this ability. It should not be just the ability to do what a supervisor says but ability to take initiative and be reasonably independent. For some research, the contribution to knowledge of the thesis itself may be modest, but the research process demonstrated in the thesis indicates development of a capable, independent scholar.
- *Demonstrates quality in use of appropriate research methods.* There is quality if accepted methods are used appropriately. Methodology may sometimes be used as a contribution to knowledge if new methods are applied and demonstrated to be useful.
- *Communicates the problem or objectives, process, results, and meaning of the research.* The thesis should communicate clearly to a reader with an appropriate scholarly background. The reader should be able to assess the quality of the research by reading the thesis.

It is simpler and more meaningful to discuss some general concepts that define contribution rather than making rules that measure contribution. Some general ideas are the following:

- *Based on significant question, problem, or hypothesis.* The thesis should tackle an interesting problem (that is amenable to research). It should be an original work that explains, solves, or adds proof or disproof to the question, problem, or hypothesis. The focus of the contribution may be data analysis, interpretation, design, or concept development.

- *Based on and guided by meaningful concepts or theory.* Theory may come from the field of information systems, but theory may also come from other fields.
- *Provides new or improved evidence.* Existing beliefs may be weakly supported by evidence or argument. There may be conflicting opinions and beliefs. The existing evidence may be contradictory. The thesis makes a contribution if it adds evidence, helps resolve conflicting beliefs, or strengthens the reasoning either supporting or disproving beliefs.
- *Employs new or improved methodology to do analysis or interpretation.* Existing analysis may be incomplete. New or improved analysis includes improved or more complete data, comparative analysis, longitudinal analysis, or application of new or different analytical methods. The new or improved methodologies should be shown to add to knowledge.
- *Develops new or improved concepts or theories.* Existing concepts or theories for a problem may be weak. A thesis that explains and supports a new or improved concept or theory makes a contribution.
- *Develops and demonstrates new or improved design of conceptual or physical artifact.* This is often termed 'design science.' The contribution may be demonstrated by reasoning, proof of concept, proof of value added, or proof of acceptance and use.

A supervisor should also provide practical guidance to the student in evaluating thesis topics. The research should be interesting, theory-based, and make a contribution to knowledge. It should also meet feasibility and career criteria. These are discussed later in this book and in Davis and Parker (1997).

I have had potential students, who have just completed a challenging, interesting project in industry or government, ask if that project could be a thesis. After discussing the contribution to knowledge, theory that could be applied in an analysis of the case, and similar questions, they have not pursued the project as a thesis. Perhaps a development project can be a thesis, but very few projects are suitable. The reasons they are not suitable are generally because they do not make a contribution to knowledge other than actually doing something that everyone knows can be done and at least conceptually how to do it.

An example from my consulting career was a project to design and program a computer model to assist in planning a finance subsidiary for a company. The model could be done easily today with a spreadsheet processor (such as Excel), but in 1961 it required significant work to formulate and program the set of statements to examine the alternatives in the planning model. In other words, the project implemented something that was conceptually well understood. It took significant effort and the results were useful, but there was no conceptual contribution. It did not add to our knowledge of planning or evaluating projects. Note, however, that the project could have become the basis for an interesting investigation about human-computer model interaction in a planning process, and this might have become a doctoral thesis.

Supervisor competence for a specific thesis topic

A supervisor should give good advice, give good direction, and be able to judge the quality of work being performed for a thesis. That means that supervisors are constrained in the problems and methods they can supervise well. It may be useful to distinguish between operational competence and review competence.

- *Operational competence* means the supervisor can do everything well that the student has to do. A master–apprentice or master–colleague type supervisor needs good operational competence, especially with immature students.
- *Review competence* means that the supervisor can understand (or develop understanding) sufficient to give good advice and make good judgments about the thesis. Some supervisors have a broad perspective and are very good at review competence; given a thesis proposal and research plan, they can do a very good job of evaluating the project and making good suggestions. They may not be good with operational advice. Note again the need for matching supervisor competence (operational and/or review) with the maturity level of the student.

My personal view is that review competence is sufficient for good supervising. A supervisor does not always have to be an expert when presented with a proposal where his or her competence is not strong. In such cases, a supervisor who is collegial and open to learning new skills should be willing to invest in learning in order to work with a doctoral student.

In one case I observed, a faculty member chose to invest in a new area of research in order to be a good, collegial supervisor. The result was very good for the student and allowed the faculty member to mentor a number of students in the same area of research. The question in such cases concerns the commitment of the faculty member to invest in this way.

Supervisor competence may be an important factor in student selection of a research area and a thesis topic. Unless a student has good skills and confidence, the tendency is to gravitate to the supervisor who can provide adequate mentoring and quality assurance. In one case, a student did thesis research in an area outside of her long term interest because of the lack of supervisor competence in her department for the area of her interest.

The question of supervisor competence to supervise a student for a problem may have different outcomes depending on whether there is a single supervisor model or a committee. The traditional mid-career doctorate typically has one supervisor. This places significant responsibilities on the supervisor to either not advise on problems where his or her competence is insufficient or to make a strong commitment to build competence. Because the traditional mid-career doctorate places the quality control on external examiners after the thesis is completed, a supervisor with insufficient competence may lead a student to do a thesis that will not be accepted.

The committee model common with entry-level doctoral programs provides a basis for good supervising without relying on a single supervisor. There are still conditions for success. The committee must have a good mix of appropriate skills and be willing to provide good advice and mentoring. The supervisor must invest enough to make sure the committee structure provides the requisite guidance and advice. Another advantage of the committee structure is the ability to have a collegial contract (not a legal contract) based on a thesis proposal. Weaknesses can be spotted early and appropriate advice given.

Thesis research methodology
There are a number of alternative research methodologies that may be applied. Jenkins (1985), at the 1984 Manchester Conference of IFIP 8.2, defined thirteen methodologies (ranging from strongest to weakest in terms of hypothesis testing):

- Mathematical modeling
- Experimental simulation
- Laboratory experiment
- Free simulation
- Field experiment
- Adaptive experiment
- Field study
- Group feedback analysis
- Opinion research
- Participative research (action research)
- Case study

- Archival research
- Philosophical research

The thirteen methodologies focus on obtaining data and interpreting the results. Many theses take a different approach that has been termed *design science*. In design science research, the researcher builds an artifact (algorithm, computer program, analytical method, prototype, theory or set of concepts, etc.). The artifact is a contribution if it adds to knowledge. The issue with design science artifacts as contributions is how to evaluate them. In some fields, the artifacts may be evaluated in terms of simplicity and/or elegance of design; in other fields, the artifacts must be supported by evidence that they yield improved results, are deemed useful by those who apply them, etc. Two references that explain the nature of design science, especially within the context of information systems are March and Smith (1995) and Hevner et al. (2004).

The IS program at Minnesota has had a few design science theses. The evaluation usually centers on proof of concept and evidence of usefulness. The differences of opinion on evaluation of design science research are illustrated by a thesis I chaired on an IS development methodology. The methodology had good conceptual foundations (a necessity). For evaluation, I insisted on a proof of concept and some test of usability. The student therefore taught the methodology to a group, had them use it, evaluated their performance, and collected their reactions. Members of the thesis committee, in the final oral, focused on a different method of evaluation. They wanted evidence from peer review of the methodology by means of articles submitted to conferences and/or journals and accepted for publication. I prefer proof of concept and evidence of usability, but others may prefer peer acceptance of innovation, elegance, or other attributes.

Another thesis committee on which I served was for a student in Philosophy. The proposed thesis was a code of ethics for computer consultants (based on Aristotle's ethical reasoning). The student was building an artifact (a code of ethics) based on a body of knowledge (theory) about ethics. The question was how to evaluate the results. The Philosophy Department was satisfied with an evaluation based on the quality of reasoning employed to build the code. I argued for a test of feasibility (could a small sample of consultants understand the code and evaluate it as useful in practice).

Minnesota information systems doctorates have had a higher frequency of experiments and field studies than the average for these types of studies in the field of information systems. Our approach has tended to emphasize hypothesis testing based on data. Case studies have tended to be used for insight into the problem domain and for understanding of data. For example, I always urge researchers who are collecting data using questionnaires or other instruments to do a small number of in-depth interviews to get insight into how respondents understood the questions, the issues, and why they responded the way they did. These interviews aid the researcher in interpreting the quantitative results.

Conceptually, the question of methodology is simple. The methodology should fit the problem, so that a contribution is achieved. But problems may be amenable to different research approaches and different methodologies. The concept of methodology choice can involve several criteria. These are: the role of methodology in achieving a contribution, methodology choice relative to a long term research career, fit with student skills and interests, and fit with supervisor skills and interests.

- *Methodology and contribution.* The research methods should be powerful enough to support a contribution to knowledge.
- *Methodology choice relative to a long term research career.* If all things were equal, it would make sense for a student to use positivist, hypothesis testing methods early in a career in order to develop skill and familiarity with traditional methods of data collection and analysis. These skills support supervising, reviewing, and evaluation in a research career. Interpretive methods tend to require more maturity and therefore are often best done at a second stage of research in a research stream. Of course, all things are not equal, so the objectives of learning both positivist and post-positivist methods may need to be achieved in a different way.
- *Fit with student skills and interests.* Some methods depend on specialized skills or strong backgrounds in economics, mathematics, statistics, etc.
- *Fit with supervisor skills and interests.* A supervisor can usually develop adequate skill to evaluate almost any methodology, but to give expert advice may be difficult.

1.5 Four procedures for a good doctoral program and good supervising

This chapter has focused on my observations and my experiences. I have organized the results into advice, but I have also explained conceptually why I believe the advice will be useful. I could have focused on concepts and not discussed procedures or practices, but I believe that both conceptual understanding and good supervising procedures are required.

This section will emphasize four procedures that I believe are vital to a good doctoral program and good supervising: an introductory IS research seminar, a student career plan as part of the seminar, a regular workshop for discussion of research papers, and providing students with resources on doctoral programs and doctoral student productivity aids. I believe these procedures are among the most important things a group of faculty members can do to improve the general climate for good supervising. This is especially true of the career plan and the regular discussion workshops. They have evolved from suggestions from faculty members, my own experience, and my observation of good practice. Note that two of these procedures, an introductory information research seminar and a regular workshop depend to a great extent on the doctoral program; the other two procedures, a student career plan and productivity aids, may work best in the context of a seminar but they can be implemented by a supervisor without participation by other faculty members.

Introductory information systems seminar
I found in the early days of the Minnesota doctoral program in information systems that faculty members did not generally favor an introductory seminar that surveyed the field and its research. They felt that such seminars lacked depth and focus. After several attempts, I was able to establish an introductory seminar that was highly rated by the students and supported by the faculty.

The format of the seminar evolved to cover three objectives:

1   Introduce students to the domain of information systems as an academic discipline and have them read and discuss a sampling of classic literature and articles that summarize important topic areas. Since subsequent seminars were more specialized, this was the best opportunity to discuss research frameworks, classic articles, history, and summaries of areas not covered by other seminars.
2   Introduce students to the research interests and areas of competence of the faculty members with whom they might have an opportunity to work. The faculty members were presented as potential supervisors and committee members. Each faculty member assigned readings from his or her own research and perhaps classic readings from the topic area. This feature of the seminar helped the students to become acquainted with faculty members in the first semester of their doctoral studies, and faculty members to get acquainted with the new students in the context of their research. The format was important in gaining faculty support for the course.
3   Start the students in a process of developing a 10-year research plan to become a world class scholar. An example is given as Table 1.4. Of course, not every student will become a world class scholar, but the

planning process is designed to help them plan for it. This has had a very important impact on students in helping them to clarify their interests and identify their thesis topic. Because of its importance, the plan will be discussed in more detail.

Table 1.4 *Abbreviated example of 10-year research plan*

Section/Topic	Description and activities	Outputs
Define broad area of interest within the domain of information systems in organizations	Within the broad domain of use of information and communications systems within organizations, I am interested in the way that these systems impact on the productivity of workers at all levels. This is a broad area of interest that can be researched using individuals, groups, or organizations. Performance data can come from secondary economic data, organizations, and individuals. Data can come from experiments with groups or individuals.	
Define your research stream within broad area of interest	My research stream is on the effect of IT-based systems on individual productivity of knowledge workers (defined as personnel whose jobs primarily involve human mental work to generate useful information). Knowledge workers access data, use knowledge, employ mental models, and apply significant concentration and attention. The concepts and theories that may be relevant are from psychology (individual differences and motivation), technology adoption, and organizational sociology (adaptive structuration). The research stream on individual knowledge worker productivity can study the practices and processes of highly productive knowledge workers or collect and analyze data from groups of individuals doing similar knowledge work. Examples of similar knowledge work are software development, accounting analysis, and financial planning. Data for analysis may be collected by organizations, reported by individuals, or obtained by field observations, field experiments, and laboratory experiments.	Student paper summarizing the broad research stream, the significant literature, and concepts that may apply.
Define research projects in research stream with one as doctoral thesis and others as pre-thesis or	*1. Pre-thesis.* Observations and interviews with a sample of knowledge workers in a given domain. Objective is to understand their use of information technology systems and create a tentative taxonomy of system and system use factors affecting productivity. I will look for intuitive work practices present in high	Conference paper Thesis and journal articles

post-thesis	productivity workers versus productive work practices that were taught to them. I will look for differences in adoption and use of system features.	Several articles and conference papers
	2. Thesis. Laboratory experiment with students doing course work in the specified domain with one group doing work without instruction in productivity improvement and an experimental group that is taught productivity improvement skills. The focus of the thesis experiments will be on the effect of training in productivity features.	Major conceptual article
	3. Post thesis. More laboratory experiments to discover the relative effects of individual differences versus training and to relate these to important tasks in the domain. Field studies of knowledge workers in specified domain. Measurements to discover effects of individual differences and effects of system features and training.	
	4. Post thesis. Formulate tentative theory of productivity with systems in knowledge work. Formulate questions to be resolved in order to use the theory in education, on-the-job training and mentoring, and design of knowledge work systems.	
Plan for preparation to be a scholar who spans the field and is expert in a research stream plus preparation for thesis and post-thesis projects	Preparation involves background study in individual differences and effects of training on performance and literature on adoption of innovations and adaptive responses to systems. The initial study will be to get acquainted with the issues in understanding productivity by knowledge workers. Data collection will employ some grounded theory methods, but the objective is to explore with existing theory rather than to build a new theory at this time. Preparation will include some study and review of grounded theory methods. Preparation will include methods for conducting laboratory experiments and related statistical analysis. The thesis experiments will use student subjects in order to do significant experiments with willing subjects in a reasonable time frame.	Papers and projects in courses will, if possible, focus on my research methods and issues.
Time schedule over 10 years for important activities to become a recognized world-class	*Overview of time schedule:* Preparatory courses and doctoral studies courses – 2 years Observations and interviews of a sample of knowledge workers – during the first two years of courses. Conference paper. Lab experiments with students – 1 year	

| scholar in knowledge worker productivity with systems | Completion of thesis and related papers for conferences/journals – 1 year
Three sets of experiments of increasing complexity and related papers and conference presentations – 3 years.
Field experiment with knowledge workers. Papers etc. – 1 year.
Tentative theory of productivity with systems in knowledge work. Papers, conferences – 2 years. | |

Use of student career plan to provide clarity

Most students have an interest in a broad field. As they investigate research in the broad field, they may find many topics of interest. They have difficulty in narrowing their focus. A second problem is selection of a thesis topic. Students often select a topic without considering the implications of the topic for a career. For students with a motivation that requires only a thesis and no further research, the failure to consider long-term implications is not a problem. For those who choose a research or scholarly career, failure to consider the thesis as a part of a career plan may have serious consequences. My use of a career plan to provide clarity about research interests and the role of the thesis in a scholarly, research career has emerged through experience in assisting students to make choices fairly early in their doctoral studies. Although the career plan is presented as a basis for achieving academic tenure, I have found the plan is useful in clarifying research objectives and thesis research questions without being motivated by tenure.

> I participated in a discussion of a research proposal by a student who was having difficulty. The discussion with the student emphasized his lack of a clear research question. His response was, 'I know that, but I don't know how to do it.' I took a different tact and carried him through a planning scenario that emphasized his interest in a general research area and the interesting research questions associated with the general area. I then led him to consider how the project he had proposed fitted into the research stream and should therefore provide evidence and answers to some of the questions. This planning approach seemed to get him out of the difficulty he was having in formulating the research question.

The basic academic career reasoning that motivates this procedure is somewhat based on the typical tenure process in North American universities, but the reasoning can be generalized to a broad range of systems. The career reasoning is:

- When a person with a new doctorate takes a university position, there is a period of five years or so in which to demonstrate scholarly research abilities. Tenure decisions take place typically during the sixth year, but the record that is presented is work that has been done through the fifth year. Published work is given a higher priority than articles in review or work in progress. A faculty member with a new doctorate therefore needs to move rapidly to establish a good research and publication record.

- If a person in a scholarly research track waits until the completion of the thesis to decide on future research, it is difficult to complete sufficient research and have sufficient publications to have a good record for promotion.
- Given an entry level doctoral program of four to five years and time to promotion decision of five years, it makes sense to create a ten-year career plan to build research skills, build a network of colleagues, and build a record of presentations and publications.
- With a ten-year plan, the thesis becomes a major milestone in the plan. It is one of several related research projects. Together, the projects demonstrate research ability and establish a record in a given research topic area. There is synergy in the projects. There is reuse of methods. Projects can build upon prior projects in the research stream.
- With a ten-year plan, a researcher can plan appropriate related study and development of appropriate, useful research skills. The investment is not just for the thesis; it is for the research stream.

Students have difficulty thinking about a ten-year plan, but as they do iterations of the plan, they become more focused and the plan makes sense to them. In our introductory course, we found that a minimum of three iterations with feedback after each plan are required to get the student to appreciate the value of planning. The biggest objection they have to the planning is that they may change their mind, and the plan will not fit. No problem; they know how to create a new plan. The process of planning has four distinct results:

1 Statement of broad area of interest
In working with students, they often name their interests very narrowly. I try to get them to think of narrow interests as instances of a topic area or research stream. As they do so, they see an area of interest emerging. If they name a very broad interest, I ask them to identify some broad streams of research within it. Three examples illustrate broad streams of research:

- *Example a:* Information system development
- *Example b:* Information system management
- *Example c:* Electronic commerce

2 Selection of a research stream that is a subset of the broad area of interest
Within a broad area of interest, a student should be able to define several research streams and select one.

- *Example a:* Within the broad area of system development, a research stream might be information requirements determination
- *Example b:* Within the broad area of information systems management, a research stream might be information system planning
- *Example c:* Within the broad area of electronic commerce, a research stream might be information systems for conducting e-commerce

3 Set of research topics with one defined as the thesis
Ideally, several related topics should be identified with one being identified as a proposed thesis. The other topics will follow soon after. There is an expectation that the topics will build on each other and that there will be synergy in doing the research.

- *Example a:* A set of topics within information requirements determination might focus on eliciting methods. Within the topics on eliciting methods, a thesis topic might be the effect of eliciting methods in achieving correct and complete requirements or perhaps the effect of analyst domain expertise in eliciting correct and complete requirements.
- *Example b:* Within the set of topics on information system planning, thesis research might focus on alignment of business plan and information systems plan. The specific thesis research might be on the effect of type of business on plan alignment, or effect of proposals from the information systems group on the business plan.
- *Example c:* Within the set of topics in the research stream on information systems for conducting e-commerce, thesis research might focus on economic evaluation of applications for conducting e-commerce. For example, a thesis might choose to focus on the economic effect of website characteristics or perhaps the economic effects of being a first mover, follower, etc.

4 Plan for achieving appropriate preparation

This plan includes readings, seminars, small projects, research methods, courses, etc. There should be general preparation to be a broad-based scholar and specific preparation for the type of research to be done. For example, a student with a plan that emphasizes economic models should develop good skills in modeling. A student who plans to study human behavior in the arena of information systems should develop skills in the design of experiments, and a student who plans to collect data about the behavior of management personnel should develop interviewing and survey skills.

> In the introductory seminar I have taught in the first semester of the first year of doctoral studies, the students prepare a ten-year plan. Rob Kauffman, who is taking over the seminar, has added refinements. The students do three iterations. They get detailed feedback and advice on how to distinguish between instances of research and streams of research. The results have been excellent. The students use the plan to guide them in selecting supporting fields, selecting projects in seminars, and writing papers.

The plan also allows for good supervising in the case of significant changes in student objectives. If the research stream changes, the preparation needs to be reviewed.

> Looking back on one of my advising situations in which I was not satisfied with the outcome, the poor result was my failure to recognize that the student changed expectations for the research stream he intended to pursue. The change should have been accompanied by additional coursework and other preparation. Not making these adjustments meant the student entered the job market working on a research stream for which he was not well prepared.

Regular workshop

A regular workshop provides candidates with opportunities to interact with others. In addition to providing both general and specific sources of knowledge and advice, a doctoral student should be provided with opportunities to listen to research presentations by established scholars and other students. They should have an opportunity to present their papers and get comments on content, methods, result, and presentation. A regular workshop or colloquium in which research papers are presented is invaluable.

> The procedure we (and some others) follow in our 70-minute weekly IS workshop is to distribute the paper in advance (post on a website). Those who attend are expected to have read the paper. The presenter makes formal remarks for about 20 minutes. This allows about 50 minutes for questions, responses, and discussion. The tone of the session is critical but positive and supportive. In a typical academic year with 27 workshop sessions, there will be about one-third Minnesota faculty, one-third faculty visitors from other schools, and one-third Minnesota IS doctoral students. This means that, during a doctoral program in IS at Minnesota, a doctoral student will attend well over 100 workshops with a broad cross section of research topics and research methods being discussed. A typical student will have an opportunity to present his or her work more than once.

The idea of the weekly workshop is well known but generally not well defined. The format of the IS workshop at Minnesota has benefited from a variety of inputs. We started the regular weekly workshops when Dennis Severance was a faculty member at Minnesota. Features of the workshop were modeled after a very successful workshop series in accounting at Ohio State University. I believe a regular workshop is vital, so I often discuss it when I talk with doctoral students in visiting other schools or in doctoral consortia. When I discuss the advantages of a weekly workshop, faculty members ask about the difficulty of doing it, and students usually indicate they do not do it at their school. The fundamental problem is getting commitment and making it regular. Both faculty and doctoral students benefit, but doctoral students have the most to gain. Therefore, it may require initiative by doctoral students to get it going and keep it going, in cooperation with those faculty members who are willing to join in the project.

Another valuable opportunity for student development is provided by doctoral consortia. These may be organized by conferences, scholarly organizations, sets of universities, etc. The basic idea is to have students present their work at various stages of development and get feedback from both senior researchers and other students.

Productivity aids

In preparatory seminars and personal advising, I have found it very important and valuable to discuss resources that will help PhD students be productive. Each supervisor probably has some sources that he or she considers useful. Some examples of general knowledge and advice for PhD students that might be useful are the following. The 'starter list' contains both general sources of information to understand doctoral programs and productivity aids for doctoral students, such as endnotes. The productivity aids are very important to introduce early in the supervising process, because the benefits tend to be cumulative.

- *Re-envisioning the PhD.* This is a website from a project to re-examine the PhD and to assemble best practices and best concepts. The site includes interesting or promising practices and resources. The website is: *http://www.grad.washington.edu/envision/*
- *Tomorrow's Professor Listserv.* Sponsored by the Stanford University Center for Teaching and Learning, it posts short articles. Although there is a science orientation in many of the articles, there is thoughtful material on being a doctoral student, entering the job market, etc. The articles are organized under five headings including 'Tomorrow's Graduate Students and Postdocs' and 'Tomorrow's Academic Careers.' The website for more information and for subscribing is: *http://ctl.stanford.edu/Tomprof/*.
- *ISWorld resources.* A very useful source of information and advice is found on *www.isworld.org*. Examples under this service include a repository of experimental tasks, working papers, research ethics, endnotes, resources for doctoral students, etc. Two pages illustrate these resources and advice: *http://www.isworld.org/#research* and *http://www.isworld.org/phd/phd.htm*.
- *Manual of style.* Adopting a style for layout of papers (headings, footnotes, etc.) is a good investment. It reduces effort required immediately and in the future. There are a small number of well-regarded manuals. Examples are the
- *Chicago Manual of Style* (Turabian, 2003) and *APA Publication Manual*, but there are other good ones. The main point is to select one and use it consistently.
- *System for making and filing notes (using a computer)*
- *Reference documentation (end note) software.* Use the software to record references for use in articles and books. The software will format references in any of the major styles. There are also end note libraries for many topics. ISworld.net contains end note libraries that may be useful for researchers in information systems (about 30 at this time): *http://www.isworld.org/endnote/index.asp*.

Other useful procedures to promote completion and quality

A supervisor can promote completion and quality for a thesis by encouraging students to employ some simple methods such as the following (described and illustrated in Davis and Parker, 1997):

- Topic analyses to promote early evaluation of ideas for theses
- Thesis proposal
- Thesis proposal defense (either formal or informal)
- Project time schedule and budget
- Agendas, summaries of meetings, memos on significant decisions, cover memos for chapters, etc.

A supervisor may be invaluable in helping students to maintain momentum and to overcome discouragement and delays. Prompt return of drafts with helpful comments, regular meetings, providing deadlines, and having the student turn in intermediate products for review are all important.

A professor close to retirement who received a doctorate from Minnesota shared with me some notes from his personal history about his supervisor (not me in this case). 'Much of my success in completing it (the thesis) so quickly was because of his (advisor) efforts to give me fast turn around on rough drafts with helpful critical ideas.'

A supervisor can help a student maintain perspective. Spouse and family should not be sacrificed for the sake of a thesis. I had a student drop out of the doctoral program because he felt he could not maintain a good marriage and be a good student. It prompted me to consider the need to discuss the issue and help students to place boundaries on their academic activities. A supervisor may help a student to block out dedicated times for spouse or family and to maintain some balance in his or her life (setting a good example probably helps also).

1.6 Summary

Based on my experience, my advice to a new supervisor (as explained in the chapter) can be summarized as a set of ten recommendations.

1   Clarify in your mind the assumptions governing the doctoral program at your school. Clarify if they are stable or in a process of change. Decide which assumptions you wish to challenge and which you are willing to accept.

2 Clarify in your mind the most important motivations for doctorates among the students who enter your doctoral program. Clarify which of these motivations can be well served within the program.

3 Clarify in your mind the supervising style that is most natural to you (and figure out the one that your supervisor applied to you). Clarify in your mind the range of supervising styles you can do well.

4 Clarify in your mind the needs that students in your program might present to you as a supervisor. Ponder what kinds of students you can work with best and which kinds you might have difficulty working with.

5 Define the advantages you have relative to supervising and relative disadvantages. Clarify in your mind the limits of your knowledge and skill in supervising on different methods and on different topics. Consider the limits on your ability to invest in topics or methods in order to advise on a thesis outside your current limits.

6 Encourage your school or department to have a good introductory seminar that prepares students to be scholars. Participate actively in such a seminar.

7 Participate actively in a regular doctoral student–faculty workshop.

8 Learn and teach procedures to help students manage their thesis research. Examples to teach your supervisees are: topic analyses to consider alternative theses, a formal thesis proposal, a thesis project plan, a formal or informal thesis proposal defense, and progress documentation.

9 Be supportive of students in helping them to develop a 10-year plan to be a world class scholar. Do a retrospective plan for yourself and update it to understand the benefits and limits of such a plan.

10 Develop a supervising approach and style that recognizes individual differences and establishes a collegial environment in which you are not only a mentor to your supervisees but a friend who gives good counsel to supervisees who are trying to become good scholars and yet still 'have a life.'

2

Confessions and Reflections

David Avison

2.1 Motivation

This chapter gives a story of an academic life as seen by the author. Readers are warned that my story is atypical, as all such stories would be. It is, of course, also very subjective and selective, but – I hope – enlightening and fun to read. I tell my story through a mixed-up recollection of experiences I have had with individual research students. I have changed the names of the researchers discussed in the chapter and also changed other aspects to prevent identification. But the stories are fairly truthful, at least from my perspective.

The chapter aims to serve a number of purposes. Its main aim is to provide new academics with a *feeling* of the potential issues, concerns and possible developments in an academic life, with emphasis being placed on research aspects. Of course your academic life will be very different than mine. The discipline of information systems has changed in status and research topics covered (see Chapter 12), and, more generally, the conditions in academic institutions have changed. Even so, I expect you will have similar concerns to many of those discussed in the chapter and have equivalent, though not the same, encounters. As well as discussing aspects of supervision that worked from my own experience, it also describes some experiences that did not work. In other words it is as much about what not to do as what to do.

Experienced colleagues will recognize some aspects of the story in their own careers. On the other hand, my history is largely based in the UK, and Gordon Davis (Chapter 1) provides a view of an academic life in the United States. Further, as is evidenced in Part V, there is no typical PhD in the US, UK or anywhere else; programs differ between particular schools and individuals within it.

I am also of a certain age, race, gender, sexual inclination and class, all of which, along with other factors and experiences, will have had an impact on what I do and how I relate to others. These sorts of issue are discussed fully in Part III. Of course I do not consciously treat people differently because they differ from me in some way, but I wonder how our background affects us all and impacts on others.

A second purpose of this chapter is to give a narrative introduction to the topics of the book and show how they might be important, indeed of great concern, at some time in an academic's career. Here a potential context for these topics is provided. So, there are many references to parts of the book where an issue introduced here is discussed in more detail and more roundly later. But let me start on the story of my life!

2.2 Early academic career

I loved my life as an undergraduate in the social sciences, too much so, as my final degree gained in 1969 was not particularly good and I was unable to get support to do a masters course. I had to get a job and a job in 'computers' apparently paid well. I rose from trainee programmer, programmer, chief programmer, systems analyst to project leader over a period of four years. It was not as much fun as being a student but by the end I had enough savings (and my wife's encouragement) to do an MSc in the applications of computing at North London Polytechnic (now London Metropolitan University). This was the only institution in London offering a practical and applications-oriented masters-level course in computing. It was there that I met my fellow student, Guy Fitzgerald.

At the end of my course in 1974, I applied to be a lecturer in computing at Thames Polytechnic (now University of Greenwich) and was successful. On my first day I met Trevor Wood-Harper who was also spending his first day as a lecturer. Guy and Trevor have become great friends and colleagues of mine and we have published much together.

If this chapter does nothing more than persuade you to value friendships with academic colleagues, then it will have played an important role. Make friends with your fellow researchers and academic staff. Such friendships can be enormously valuable from so many points of view. But be aware also that you will come across academic jealousies and disputes.

My appointment was made in 1974, and it was not unusual for a newly appointed lecturer to lack a PhD at that time in the UK, particularly in the polytechnics, which were mainly teaching institutions. Business experience was considered at least as important in teaching computing, as information systems was known at the time. Many leading researchers and research supervisors of my generation do not have PhDs themselves or, like me, gained their PhDs some years after starting their academic careers and having already supervised PhDs.

It is less common now in the UK for newly appointed academics in IS not to have a PhD, but still common elsewhere. For example, I have been recently supporting some newly appointed academics in Sydney, Australia. These colleagues have many years business experience, are excellent teachers, but wish to research and 'get a PhD' as well as teach.

Part III looks at 'atypical' PhD students, but these are the norm rather than the exception. Most PhD students in many countries do not conform to the 'newly graduated, full time norm' that academics may have expected to supervise. Some may do their research in industry or teach in universities, as Björn Lundell, Cathy Urquhart and Jan Pries-Heje discuss in Chapter 6.

I stayed at Thames Polytechnic for three years. But I wanted to move to a university where research was supported more. It was certainly difficult with a teaching load of 17 hours a week. Despite that I had managed to publish a journal paper and a book covering material given on a master's course, both co-written with my head of department, Tom Crowe, with whom I also keep in contact, though he has been retired for some time. But I wanted to 'do research' and applied for and was appointed as lecturer (assistant professor) at Aston University in their Department of Computer Science.

Looking back, I am a little cynical regarding my motivation because I had little idea about what research was about. I wanted to teach fewer hours, that is for sure, and research was more the price to pay than the carrot. But I did like the idea of having more time to publish. Publishing made me feel good. I confess that I still get satisfaction from seeing my name in print. I did not have any real intention of doing a PhD at that time as it seemed better to spend time on papers than a PhD. It had not occurred to me that the two could be combined. It was therefore a surprise to me that I was soon supervising research students.

Sahed

My first PhD student came to me not long after joining Aston. I would like to think that this was because of my reputation and track record as a researcher. This was far from the truth. It was because Aston was near Sahed's home in Birmingham and I was the only lecturer in information systems there. For much of my career I have worked in departments (computer science and management) where I was the sole IS member of faculty or one of only two or three people. The feeling of isolation is difficult to overcome, though regular attendance at conferences, along with membership of the Association of Information Systems (AIS) and the local national society can help. Of course, the AIS and the national equivalent, the UKAIS, were not around at that time. The feeling of isolation might be even greater for your research students and I encouraged Sahed to attend conferences to meet people.

In Chapter 3, Richard Baskerville and Nancy Russo discuss metaphors for a PhD program. One such metaphor is that of master and apprentice, but my first experience was much more akin to apprentice and apprentice. Gordon Davis has introduced the problems of training supervisors, and this book provides support for this, but I learnt mainly by doing, and sometimes this learning was at the expense of my students. This is not good practice, and I think that supervisors' workshops, that are devoted to discussing the job of supervising IS students, should be regularly available in our domain. Indeed, it was such a workshop, I think the first international one in IS, that inspired this book.

In Chapter 5 the subject of choosing a supervisor is discussed. It is important: a PhD is a minimum three-year relationship, and the stakes are high. Giving up (a phenomenon that is much more common than failing) can be a major blot on someone's life. If Sahed had studied this chapter and the book, he would surely not have made the same choice of supervisor. By the way, research suggests that there is an increasing likelihood of non-completion if the supervisor is going through a divorce, so potential PhD students should check the marital status of supervisors as well as other credentials!

Happily, he was a good student and eventually succeeded, despite many difficulties. This was due to his abilities, not mine. I remember when about to present a conference paper of his work (let me be honest) he walked me round the conference site to calm me down. I guess I now give conference papers in my stride, though I am always nervous, but I will not forget how I felt that first time. Robert Davison discusses joint publication and the ethical issues relating to this in Chapter 8.

I have also sometimes been a poor choice as external examiner for others. An external examiner provides an outsider's view of the thesis and the choice of external is crucial (see Chapter 17). For example, I regard choice and justification of research approach as crucial in PhD research (see Chapter 14 on quantitative methods by Detmar Straub, David Gefen and Marie-Claude Boudreau, and Chapter 15 on qualitative methods by David Avison and Michael Myers), yet on two occasions I have examined students who had no answer to the question: 'what research method did you use?'. It seems they had a job to do and they did it, end of story. I don't think that this is a good training in research nor does it provide essential skills for future research supervisors.

In my view, this is not acceptable in an IS PhD, though it is more common in computer science. It seems to me that research methodology is important in itself, because we need to know what approach was used, whether it was appropriate for the research question pursued and whether it was used appropriately. On the other hand, I am not suggesting there should be a very general overview research methods chapter in the thesis. Like any other chapter, this should be focused towards the approach adopted by the student in the research, showing and justifying its use.

James

My second research student at Aston proved to be much more typical (I think a better word is 'ideal' rather than typical) in that he completed within three years, drove the research, and was an outstanding researcher generally. We had known each other previously as I supervised his undergraduate project. His work (like that of many of my PhD students) centered on action research in an organization. This can be problematic, as Bjorn Lundell, Jan Pries-Heje and Cathy Urquhart make clear in Chapter 6 about serving two masters (the company and the university). But it was not a problem in his case.

Indeed, part-time research is not necessarily detrimental. At Brunel University, where I am part-time research professor, records show that the average time to completion for part-time students is no longer than full-time students, despite assumptions to the contrary. A focused student can spend his or her time more effectively if research and job can be put into separate compartments and the available time for research is used effectively. But in James' case, the work in the organization related to his research, so there was not a problem.

I was told James was gay. I always felt that not discussing this was a barrier. In truth, I felt it was a pity that James himself did not raise the subject – I thought that it would not be appropriate for me. I was concerned that he did not do so because he might think I was anti-gay. I wanted to show my liberal credentials! Nobody knows, however, what are our own deep-seated prejudices. Did it matter in this case? I do not know, but it would have helped me if Dave Wilson's discussion in Chapter 10 had been available at the time. It is, I hope, obvious to readers that a supervisor is more than responsible simply for academic matters and the role calls for sensitivity in many personal issues. But I do not think it appropriate for the supervisor to 'dive in', rather it is best to ask whether there are any problems in time or money management, for example, and see if the student broaches any issue of a personal nature.

In the UK, we have a system of external examiners who interview the student after having read the thesis. James' external examiner was very supportive and full of praise for his work. Indeed there was never a question about the quality and originality of his contribution (see chapter 13), though this has not always been the case in my experience. The external examiner had only one suggestion for James, the inclusion of a paragraph discussing the work of a noted scholar. Coincidentally this proved to be the external examiner himself! Since then, I have ensured that my students include liberal citations of the external examiner. We academics really are terribly arrogant, always wanting praise and respect for our work!

Albert

We have mentioned the potential conflict between research and an industry partner. The more common conflict in my experience is that between the university in terms of demands for teaching and the university in terms of demands for research and this is discussed in Chapter 6. To make ends meet, and finance is frequently a concern of research students (see Chapter 8), Albert did some part-time teaching in the Department. His class contact hours were not high, about three hours of tutorials each week on the same topics.

The problem with Albert was that he loved teaching and discussing issues with students and helping those with difficulties. His office was open all hours to his students, and those of other tutors as well. His research was suffering and in the end I suggested he put a notice outside his office giving his 'opening hours' and these were restricted to two days a week, far more than should have been the case even then. This resulted in him taking nearly six years over his PhD, which should have been completed within three to four years.

Tina

I have always found it strange that a good researcher should be assumed to be a good teacher. Many are, and there can be a 'trickle down' effect as results from research are assimilated into teaching. Tina needed the money gained from teaching to support her part-time PhD, but she got poor feedback from students and began to dread the teaching aspects of the role. Researching and teaching require different skills, and Tina did not carry on as a lecturer after gaining her PhD because of the 'threat' of teaching. Happily, she now has a research post that involves no teaching at a leading UK university.

Mary

Mary was rather different. Although a good researcher doing good research, she was very negative about her own abilities and the likelihood of her getting a PhD. Despite an excellent academic record, she found it difficult to adjust to the life of a PhD student. It is much less organized, of course. I had the impression that she was very depressed at times. Despite me giving her lots of (deserved) praise throughout, she 'gave up' on at least two occasions during the four and a half years that she eventually took for her PhD.

Mary is perhaps more typical of my PhD students than the confident James, though she also completed successfully and has had a very successful academic life since. Again, the external examiner was very complimentary. But as the above examples show, each student is very different and requires different support and perhaps different support mechanisms (different supervisory styles, as Gordon Davis puts it).

Mary had two mock examinations before her actual viva, with colleagues playing the role of examiners, and that helped to build up her confidence. I arrange one as a matter of routine for all my students, and they seem to always perform better in the real viva, having had a 'dry run'. I have heard of others videoing the mock viva so that it is possible to rerun every aspect, and I may try that in the future. I have also heard of an open mock viva, which would be useful for other students, to see what happens. Some departments also put on little 'plays' where experienced staff role-play successful and unsuccessful viva experiences for debate with students afterwards.

Mohamed
The main issue relating to Mohamed was the choice of external examiner. The external was rather aggressive and negative at the 'viva' (though Mohamed did eventually get his PhD following additional work). I was informed later by friends at another university that he had a reputation for being somewhat negative to students who were not 'white'. In Part V we discuss the examination process in the context of different models and in Chapter 11 discuss different cultural and other related issues. Certainly I have been careful since about choice of external examiner, though I have made at least one other mistake (see Jeremy's story below).

Some students do take criticism badly and we need to be sensitive in criticizing and make sure that we praise them where appropriate. But research students need to see that constructive criticism is healthy and necessary to improve their work. I like to give students my own papers after they have been reviewed for the first time. They can see that experienced academics also get criticized, sometimes severely. I ask them for advice on improving my papers. As editor of a journal, I ask them to criticize a paper for which I have the 'professional' reviews of senior academics and to fill in the journal referees' form. I then ask them to read the reviews and see if there critique is similar. In this way, they can see that criticism is normal, criticism relates to the work and not the person, and they also develop their own critical skills. When outside speakers come, I also encourage research students to question the presenter and later discuss their research with him.

Jeremy
Mary's happy result was not the outcome for Jeremy, who was told by the external examiner that the thesis did not contain enough of the examiner's work, and Jeremy needed another year to ensure that it was properly represented. Both Jeremy and I found this inappropriate and unacceptable. It is true that the external's research was relevant to Jeremy's topic, but Jeremy did not think it central. Nevertheless, in this situation, the external examiner obviously has a lot of power. Jeremy decided not to conform and he finished up with an MPhil, rather than a PhD. This is not such a good qualification, and in this example was naturally seen by many as a 'failed PhD' (see Chapter 17).

I have asked myself since on many occasions whether I should have done something different, perhaps arguing for another external examiner. Jeremy, who was a mature student and an academic at another university, did not want this, so I did not force the

> issue. Nor could I persuade him to conform more to the external's requirements in order to get his PhD.
>
> I often think of the issues surrounding this result. I think about questions about ethical values as well as different strategies that I may have adopted. Certainly Jeremy's ethical values were beyond reproach. But they may well have had a negative impact on his career.

Much less important, of course, it also affected *my* self confidence. A student of whom I thought highly, failed to get his PhD. This result reflected negatively on me. Successful PhD supervision is very satisfying indeed, and unsuccessful experiences deeply distressing.

> Henry
> Taking over from another supervisor is in my experience problematical. Henry found me a very poor second to his other supervisor who left to take up a post at another university. It proved difficult for him to adapt to my approach. Practically, I was demanding other things from him. It seemed unfair to him. His obvious disappointment did not make me feel too comfortable either. In some ways the problems that did occur were a result of the fact that his previous supervisor had a different view to me about the role of the supervisor: we had different metaphors for the supervisor–student relationship (see Chapter 3). As a result, the student had a difficult time. But we survived this challenge.
>
> Although the topic of Henry's research was fairly new to me, I did not and do not see that as a major problem. On the contrary I delight in finding out about a new topic, as long as it is within the domain of information systems. I would not take on computer science projects now, though most of the research I supervised in the beginning was computer science rather than IS oriented, and these projects usually contained much programming code.

Although I think it appropriate to take on new topics as part of the learning process, I think it is unwise for students to tackle topics just because they are in vogue. By the time the PhD study is over, they may be out of vogue. Further, my own use of action research was questioned in the early 1980s when I started to use this approach, but later the approach became much more interesting to IS researchers (indeed, Baskerville and Myers (2004) is a special issue of the *MIS Quarterly* on action research). So it is much more important in my view to research and supervise using research methods in areas which interest you and the researcher. Your time will also come (perhaps also 20 years later)!

It is my research students, along with reviewing submissions and attending conferences such as *International Conference in Information Systems (ICIS)* and *International Federation of Information Processing (IFIP)* and editing the *Information Systems Journal,* that have kept me informed of the most recent literature and practice. However, I think all of us in this domain do have a sense of being out of date at times.

I feel much more reticent, however, about supervising research students where their chosen research approach is outside my experience. I think that is much more dangerous, as we only truly understand an approach after having used it in some depth ourselves. I would certainly always ensure there is a colleague very experienced in the approach at hand if I thought this might be a problem. I always refer students using statistical methods to colleagues in the Stats Department as reassurance.

Heidi
Heidi was another student where I became supervisor when the first supervisor left. She was at the stage of preparing drafts of her thesis. I am very meticulous at this stage and Heidi found me over-critical and it was obvious that she did not like my interference. She asked for another supervisor to replace me and of course I accepted this decision.

Again, this was difficult. Having had much experience as an external examiner, I am aware of the negative impression gained from a thesis which has many mistakes, is poorly written, verbose, incoherent in part, and boring to read. I felt that all these criticisms were fair and the thesis needed improving greatly before submission. Otherwise it might fail. I gave a huge amount of detailed criticism and spent a long time commenting on the draft. On the other hand, I was neither saying that Heidi was a poor student nor that her research was poor; in fact I thought the opposite. Unfortunately, she took my criticisms badly and became demoralized.

If I had been Heidi's supervisor since the beginning (or could relive the experience) I would have known how to judge the situation and communicate myself better. I would get my 'praise' message across first, and suggest only that she improves the writing so that the external sees this quality of research that underlies the thesis. But the message I was giving (or at least the message that was received) was totally negative. Another lesson learnt!

Even at this stage, it is difficult to know whether work is good enough. Examiners differ, and some may pass a thesis where others would require further work. I thought that Heidi overvalued her draft. Most students in my experience undervalue their work. A supervisor needs to reassure these students. But it does take experience to know because it is an academic judgment, gained from experience. I often ask what other colleagues think, and this mechanism is routine where supervision is carried out by a team rather than an individual. A view expressed by two or three academics can be more reassuring and better founded. We are not looking for perfection, but a piece of work that is satisfactory.

June and Auguste
Earlier, I discussed Jeremy, a student who finished up with an MPhil. There is another way in the UK that an MPhil is awarded. This is where the student registers for this degree with the intention of doing an MPhil, rather than a PhD, at the beginning. Two students followed this course with me at Aston University and both were successful. Both did a project in industry and the project area was put in the perspective of the literature in the

dissertation. But the project work did not constitute an original research contribution. The demarcation between the two degrees is not particularly well defined in practice and both students had the ability, in my view, to complete a PhD program successfully. But they were not willing or able to make the sacrifices and commitment that a PhD does require.

2.3 Mid career

I supervised many students to PhD at Aston, despite not having had a PhD myself, but the above stories give a flavor of many of the experiences. In the meantime, I had been promoted to senior lecturer (associate professor). Later, I was arrogant enough to think that I should be applying for professorships elsewhere. I was rejected outright a few times but did get a couple of interviews. It was obvious that to get a professorship it would help, at the least, if I had a PhD. That was the major motivation for me, though I did fancy the kudos of having one. I wanted to be called *Dr. Avison;* I wanted my parents to know that I was called Dr. Avison. I wanted to say 'boo' to all those people who had rejected me. Pathetic, isn't it?

David
I sought my PhD with 100% focus. I used previous research work I had done plus some action research I was then doing as the basis of my PhD on IS development. In effect, I was my own supervisor. There is no metaphor in Chapter 3 to describe this relationship, but I guess that readers can think of one or two possibilities. Although this is not generally advised, I had already published a lot, supervised a number of PhD students to successful conclusion, and had the confidence (arrogance you may say) to do it this way. I got my thesis written and successfully examined by two external examiners comparatively quickly and in 1990 was officially *Dr. Avison*. It was not long afterwards that I applied for and got a Chair in IS at the University of Southampton.

The thesis was used as one basis of a book published later. I am troubled by the emphasis placed in so many departments and deans on publishing in a very narrow band of journals. Further, the lack of worthiness, at least as seen by some deans, of publishing books may lead to the demise of the subject. Books are a means of communicating our excellent work to students and the general public, not journal papers, which in truth are read by very few people. Indeed, only *Communications of the ACM,* with a distribution of 85000, is seen directly by many people who may be influenced by IS research. But this also is not placed in high regard by most deans as it is seen as too practitioner focused. Of course, high quality journal papers are also very important, but in my opinion there is undue weight placed on these publications.

Before discussing further experiences as a research supervisor, and also my role at Southampton in providing a research lead for the discipline of IS and in designing and contributing to courses for PhD students, I wish to discuss my role as *external examiner* through some cases. This role is different to that of supervisor. It is meant to be an 'objective' assessment of a thesis by an outsider, to see if it warrants the award of a PhD. The external reads the thesis and contributes to the viva. It is a difficult job.

In this role you are first asked whether you will do it. I like to look at the abstract to see whether the topic area is within my area of competence, or at least whether I think it is. Once the university has agreed that I am sufficiently competent and experienced through looking at my CV, I am sent the thesis. Having read it, I fill in my initial reactions and a date for the viva is agreed. I try to ensure as best as I can that the student is as relaxed as possible at the viva and the 2 or 3 hours consists of a discussion not an interrogation, though the student needs to defend her thesis.

Most occasions are wonderful. It is a joy for me, as an external person, to see what a researcher has done for the past three or so years. Normally I learn a lot, the atmosphere is positive, after all I am out to find out what was achieved, normally a great deal, not to trick the student. It is rare that the student does not pass there and then, subject to only minor corrections.

My questions are focused on two things in the main – other questions spring from this beginning – 'what is your contribution?' and 'can you justify the research approach that you used to make this contribution?'.

I have already mentioned one problem that has occurred, that is the student's lack of interest in and knowledge of the research method and its alternatives. I guess a better tactic for the university department might have been to choose an external examiner who does not think research methods are important in PhD research.

John
Another very unhappy experience occurred when I suggested to John that he had not spent sufficient time at the case study site, nor had enough evidence to justify the claims made about the implications of his 'in-depth' case. I suggested that further time on the field study was required. This was a shock to him and his supervisor who made it very clear that 'I was wrong'.

   This type of situation is very difficult to handle from many points of view, but I applied my best judgment and gave reasons in full. Such a result must be fully justified of course in the external examiner's report. Happily I got the support of the internal examiner. But again, I have worried about it since, even though when he eventually resubmitted, the work was clearly within the required standard and was now an excellent contribution. But 'my best judgment' may not conform to other equally valid judgments. But that is the nature of the process, which is not, at least in my experience, 'scientific' in that sense. Some attempts are made in Chapter 13 to get to grips with the issues of quality and originality, but examining a PhD is a subjective process.

Julian

On another occasion, it was obvious that the internal examiner and I differed greatly about our views on Julian's thesis. Again this was very difficult to handle and the atmosphere at the viva was regrettably not very friendly. How awful for the candidate having to experience this as the culmination of his three years' study and contribution! Happily he did eventually gain his PhD. But the viva was not pleasant for anyone. Interestingly I have not been invited by that university to be external examiner for a PhD since that time!

Nevertheless, these cases of external examining are interesting because they are exceptional. I have been external examiner for around 35 PhDs, and most have been very happy experiences for all concerned. I have also examined in Australia on some occasions where the judgment needs to be made on the thesis alone as there was no viva (at least in the cases that I examined) and in Scandinavia, where the candidate gives her defense to a large audience of family, friends and sometimes enemies. I had to play the role of prosecutor, a role I did not particularly enjoy at the time. Happily, this proved to be a successful defense as well (which presumably means that I lost).

I have also been a member of faculty at many PhD consortia. These are meetings of PhD students together with experienced research supervisors. They usually occur alongside major conferences such as *ICIS, Americas Conference in Information Systems (AMCIS), Australian Conference in Information Systems (ACIS), European Conference in Information Systems (ECIS),* and *UK Conference in Information Systems (UKAIS).* Participation at these events has also been a joy for me. Again, it is a great experience to discuss research with PhD students. The atmosphere has always been in my experience critical but very positive. I have never been to one where the student ratings have not been very high (not always true of my mainstream teaching!). My students also come back invigorated from these events, more confident and motivated. I do recommend supervisors to send their students to one if at all possible. At Brunel University we have a research retreat which performs a similar function, even if internal to only our students. The best students from this retreat are put forward for international PhD consortia.

I also recommend supervisors to act as members of faculty at such consortia. You will also learn a great deal.

Yet attending these PhD consortia over the years was part of the inspiration to organize a supervisors' workshop in Athens and work on this book. I fear any weaknesses in the system detected at such consortia, usually reflect badly on the supervisory process at their home institution. Rarely were there any fundamental problems with the students themselves; in my view we need support for supervisors, not just their students.

I was founding professor of information systems at Southampton. In my inaugural lecture I introduced IS to the university and town so I entitled my talk 'What is IS?'. I had to set and lead a research tradition in IS. I realized that it was difficult to attract research students in a discipline where it was easy at the time for our undergraduate and graduate students to land good jobs. It is not a domain well established in terms of research traditions, yet another reason for this book.

Amongst other attempts to attract students we advertised in the higher education press; we tried to sell the possibility to our own bright students, both undergraduates and on our masters course in IS; we made it clear that we were willing to consider part-time students; we offered bursaries; we applied for research grants, which included financial support for research students (see Frantz Rowe and Jan Pries-Heje's discussion of financing PhD programs in Chapter 7), but good applicants came in slowly. It takes some time to build up a reputation as a research group and build up research. But we certainly succeeded eventually and had many successful outcomes. On the other hand, it is difficult to have a continual supply of PhD students.

Michel
You may want to hear of my less successful experiences? So here is an example. I reproduce below an email sent to me from one very unhappy ex-student of mine, along with my reply:

David
I was looking through some old papers and found one from you when you told me that I had to terminate my studies as my English was very bad and I had several other weak sides. Just to inform what a person with all these handicaps can do I am attaching a list of all the papers I have had published after your verdict. I hope you understand that I felt very bad having you as a counsellor and I hope that you don't treat all your students in the same way. I felt humiliated but I remember that you told me that was your way of handling people. One positive remark – you made me angry and that has perhaps strengthened my motivation for writing these papers.
Still making research
Michel

Hi Michel
Nice to hear from you. Delighted over your success! I am pleased to have formed part of this success, even though you thought it negative at the time, it has obviously spurred you on. Bravo indeed – continue the good work.
David

I think it would be unethical of me to comment on Michel's story at all, apart from saying that this result obviously caused us both distress. I am happy to say that this is the only student I have had where I have terminated the progress to PhD. A very few, however, have given up on their own volition. Giving up can be due to many reasons from a lack of motivation, the temptation of a well-paid job to family pressures. On the rare occasions that this has happened, I have not applied any pressure to stay (though in truth it is a waste of resources) but left the door open to return at any time. Mary was the only person who took up this offer (see her story above).

Theodore

However I had thought another student of mine might end up in failure. The motivation for Theodore concerned his wish to become a 'real' academic as he saw it, along with improved promotion prospects at his university, by having a PhD. But he was a part-time student who was making very poor progress. Every time I saw him he had another interesting topic, partly because he was himself interesting and was fascinated by each avenue he looked at and started to explore. I was very impatient with his lack of real progress. I did not see much in writing, and I wondered if he had writer's block. With Theodore we changed tack after over three years part-time study and wrote a specific program and timetable for him with chapter titles, dates (and also dates by which I would provide feedback). We agreed to part if either of us failed to keep up with this schedule. Neither of us did, and we developed our friendship and have worked well together since. We have produced many papers coming from this work and collaborative research that we worked on later.

The enforced discipline provided by the timetable had a very positive effect. But each student is different, and what worked for Theodore may not work with all students.

Shirley

As is made clear in Chapter 6, part-time study for PhD is difficult. Shirley too was a mature student working for a leading software company. She was very bright and exciting. Yet she gave up. It was a choice between making money and devoting more time to her PhD. We thought her motivation to do a PhD was strong, yet we were wrong and I note that 'making lots of money' was correctly not one of Gordon Davis' underlying issue 2: motivations for a doctorate!

Thomas

Thomas, also a part-time student, spent many years – far too long – on his PhD. It would have been better for everyone to apply a termination mechanism in this case. It was the student himself who made the decision to give up. Although not my student, I knew Thomas personally and the PhD was much more of a pain than a pleasure to him, and the decision to end the process, once taken, was certainly a relief to him (and, I assume, his supervisor). But we can all make the right decision in hindsight.

> **Alex**
> My Department also had a student from abroad whom we saw every three to six months. I remember him very well. However, I felt that we did not help him much with his PhD research when we met. Meetings were not very communicative. When he did spend time with us, he seemed lost and lonely, despite our best efforts, and always seemed glad to leave. We thought many times that we ought to suggest that registration for a PhD should be terminated. Yet somehow he did eventually submit his thesis and he got his PhD. It was a surprise to everyone, none more so than me, but those of us who attended the viva felt it was well deserved. He had been absorbing the advice that we gave him and applied it well to his research and his thesis. Maybe we all need to examine our own prejudices. In this case, unlike Thomas, it would obviously have been a mistake to terminate the process.

Overseas students can have particular problems. Even where there are other researchers around, they can feel isolated because of homesickness, and race or religious differences. At Southampton there was a society for foreign researchers, lecturers and their partners, which was particularly helpful as it provided a network so that support was there when needed.

> **Betsy**
> For Alex, progress seemed to be slow throughout. I am external adviser to Betsy, and she was not unusual in that she made a slow start. However, the reason was not due to lack of focus but that of awaiting approval of her Australian university's ethics committee regarding her research proposal. Her work is in the area of health applications and she is interviewing patients, so applying for approval is not unreasonable. However, delays in convening meetings of the ethics committee and giving feedback set her research back by around 9 months. This has been demotivating, particularly as the long delay was so unexpected.

Publishing with one's research students is a thorny issue. My own practice is to collaborate with my research students as much as possible on joint publications. The paper might be centered on an aspect of the student's PhD research, but it may have my contributions through discussions of the work, planning the paper, writing the paper as well as having some input from my own research. I am likely to be the major player when handling the requirements of referees and associate editors. I believe that I always make an important contribution where my name is on the list of authors. Writing the paper together is more than involvement; it is commitment to the work. On the other hand, for conference papers, I am normally of the view that the authors should be the presenters, if PhD students, and I rarely include my name on these papers. But, as Robert Davison makes clear in Chapter 8, the ethics of this and many other aspects relating to the supervisor–student relationship are not always clear cut.

Heinz and Helen

Many PhD students have become my colleagues and long-term friends. Two *started* the process as colleagues and long-term friends. At Southampton, experienced members of academic staff have the opportunity to submit their PhD by including in their thesis previously published work along with a new introductory chapter that binds the chapters together by discussing the overall theme and contribution. At Aston, where I gained my own PhD, this option was not open to me. Indeed, it is not commonly available in the UK universities. But I am not sure whether I would have chosen this option even so. It is certainly a different experience, though I am not suggesting it is any less worthy.

I have discussed students who have provided some thorny issues during my career at Southampton where I led information systems teaching and research. However, most of my students seem to have had fairly smooth journeys to PhD success, both there and at Aston, though no experience has been without its problems, even disagreements.

But in the final analysis, although we are the supervisors, it is the students' research and their responsibility. Assuming, therefore, students stick to the official regulations, you can advise them but they must make the final decisions.

On the other hand, my advice has, I hope, improved with experience. I am certainly more organized, a skill which is important to supervisors and students alike. Skills can be taught, though it is rare in UK universities for there to be training schemes for research supervisors.

Focused and regular meetings are essential. I think it important that each meeting addresses an important issue. I require students to produce a deliverable at each meeting. It may be a draft conference paper, a critique of someone else's paper or a draft timetable. It can be used to help a student over a particular hurdle, for example, to decide when a literature review is fairly complete and correctly focused, or commenting on an exemplar thesis that might be used to inspire students who do not know what is expected of them. It also ensures that students get into the habit of writing, which has not been natural to most students with whom I have worked.

I am certainly less 'hands off' than I used to be. Demanding a deliverable provides focus and purpose for the meeting. Delivering the thesis might be a long time away, so intermediary goals are essential. However, I try to strike a balance between ensuring students do not flounder and are guided and yet not over controlled so that they can discover things for themselves (see Chapters 1 and 3).

But I hope I am also flexible enough to take account of individual student's needs. I always keep a record of meetings, progress and so on. These records will be useful if something does go wrong. However, although good supervision is to some extent about developing skills in practical situations, other aspects are about the more natural ability to deal with human problems sympathetically and constructively.

2.4 Late career

Students in France need to be successful in a prerequisite masters' level course on research before starting a doctorate (see Chapter 18). At ESSEC Business School, I am at the time of writing involved in designing a new Masters in Research course for future PhD students in management (including information systems), and I am also working on a joint program for information systems students of two Paris universities with ESSEC. However, so far I have not myself supervised students through to a doctorate in France. It is the universities, rather than the grands-écoles, which traditionally supervise doctorates, but this is likely to change and I hope I am one who does some trailblazing.

Gaston
I have, however, examined a French PhD candidate at the Sorbonne. It was a very formal process compared to the English viva, though it was good to share a glass of champagne with the successful candidate afterwards, along with his family and friends. The French have a system of grading the PhD, so that the student can pass, pass with merit or be so meritorious that he passes with the congratulations of the jury! Gaston enjoyed the latter accolade, and so the champagne flowed well.

Guy Fitzgerald and colleagues point out in Part V that there are many differences in PhD programs. My experience in the UK is that we are now providing more and more formal courses to support our PhD students. Guy and I run one such course at Brunel University, where I am part-time research professor. Such courses cover research methods in the main but also practical issues of doing research: using the library, using software, managing your supervisor, preparing the research proposal, how to get published, what happens at conferences, what is the examination process and so on. The large cohort means that we can have many discussions informed by different experiences: the seminars are designed to be participatory. The course is compulsory to first year researchers and I think it is not a coincidence that there has been an increase in the numbers of students completing within three years.

At the end of the course we claim that students should be able to:

1   Demonstrate understanding of qualitative and quantitative research methods in information systems

2   Be able to choose appropriate research methods for their own research topic
3   Analyze and evaluate published research in information systems
4   Prepare a literature review, research proposal and logistical plan
5   Demonstrate organizational, presentational and leadership skills.

It is also the only university where I have been involved which has a substantial PhD program in IS in terms of numbers of students. The environment is excellent for research students as the critical mass means that the students can support each other; it is efficient as well as effective to have a research training program to help them; it is much easier to attract funding; there are excellent facilities; there is a tradition of publishing which encourages others; there are many members of staff available with supervision more of a collective responsibility; there is an excellent program of external speakers; the department is highly rated by the UK government and this reputation attracts more good students to apply. The atmosphere generally is very supportive of research and research students in IS. This is in sharp contrast to my experience at my previous UK universities where I have felt isolated, which is disheartening.

In such an environment we can be much more selective. Students are interviewed where feasible, though this is not always the case for students coming from abroad. In the latter case, the comments from referees are important and I frequently telephone referees to dig a little deeper. I am concerned about motivation, the ability to work independently, some signs of intellectual creativity, and an ability and experience at writing, and communication skills in general.

The chapter and the book have been mainly about relationships. Although latterly we have looked at relationships between researchers in a large research-oriented group, in the main it has been about the relationship between a supervisor and his or her students. In Chapter 3, Richard Baskerville and Nancy Russo discuss various metaphors to understand the nature of supervising PhDs, and the 'marriage metaphor' is one of many that I can relate to. However, although one very experienced and leading information systems supervisor informed an audience of UK academics that most of his female research students fell in love with him, sadly this never happened to me (at least, not to my knowledge).

The same man also suggested that many of his male students 'died' on him. This actually happened to me only a few weeks before writing this chapter. This has touched me greatly, of course. We do get close to our research students, but the term student is such an inappropriate term. They are friends and colleagues and we are doing research together. Our roles in the process are at times ambiguous, but his death has hit me as a personal loss. Although, I guess, an odd and inappropriate reaction, I feel cheated of not being able to support and research further with someone who was going to produce an excellent thesis. He was also great fun to research with.

How would I characterize my supervisory style? In chapter 1, Gordon Davis suggests five basic styles: strong master/apprentice style, collegial master/apprentice style; collegial development style; guidance and suggestion style and passive hands-off style. Later, in Chapter 3, Richard Baskerville and Nancy Russo suggest supervisor as customer, mentor/coach, guide, companion, spouse, teacher, Mother Nature, model and master. Many people identify with only one of these. I can identify with all of them.

My true style is a *contingent* one, because I think that students are different and they require different advisor styles. Further, the same person requires different styles at different times. A research student may be going through a bad patch or a good patch or may need redirecting. There are all sorts of reasons why a different style is needed at different times. As Duane Truex, Ramiro Montealegre and colleagues point out in Chapters 4 and 5, different styles may be appropriate at different stages of the project as well. I would like to be inspirational when we are discussing potential directions for the research, disciplinarian if goals are missed and meticulous when at the writing-up stage. Along with personal crises, there may be crises in progress on the PhD, and the supervisor needs to smooth the emotional stages of the PhD journey as well.

But contingency also has a negative side in my case as well. I also change according to my mood and my style will reflect this at any time. I hope that research students as well as supervisors read this book. If so, remember we are also human and have our weaknesses. I have been guilty of being less than sensitive on many occasions during my PhD supervisory experience, as the quote from email correspondence relating to Michel makes very clear. I fear I may have also seemed patronizing, rude, impatient or even disinterested at times. Over three years I must have made many mistakes. I am only human! But I hope these were rarer than the times I was more positive.

It is paramount through all this to make time for family. They will be making sacrifices whilst you have fun researching or supervising research. Acknowledge this and ensure they are compensated. In Chapter 4 all sorts of potential pressures and crises are raised and some help is provided on how to deal with them. A PhD is an academic qualification, but many issues can be classified as emotional ones, and this is true for the research supervisor as well. Some people have additional pressures and conflicts, some of which are discussed in Chapters 9, 10 and 11.

So I guess that rounds up my biased and fragmented story of supervising PhDs over 25 years. It has been a privilege to carry out this role and be involved in this book. It is a particular privilege to follow on from a chapter by Gordon Davis, who is probably the most experienced and well-respected research supervisor in the discipline and his chapter is proof. But I have already pointed out my own arrogance so I will challenge one of his recommendations. Gordon suggests a ten-year plan for the student. Of course the advice contained therein is very sensible and likely to lead to a well-motivated and successful doctorate and career that follows. But I am concerned at the potential mechanistic nature of such programs. Of course, this will not apply at Minnesota with Gordon Davis and his colleagues. But in lesser hands I fear some conformity and uniformity might lead to dull and unadventurous PhD output in terms of research work, publications and future members of faculty, and this may itself result in a stale and declining discipline. I champion the case for atypical PhDs: *viva la difference!*

2.5 Conclusion

By describing various encounters with research students, this chapter has introduced a number of issues that can occur in the supervisor–student relationship. It suggests that good supervision practice is not natural to academics: good training procedures and workshops will help to ensure that supervisors do not learn at the expense of their students. We have looked at many academic issues, but a supervisor is more than responsible simply for academic matters and the role calls for sensitivity in many personal issues as well. Some students do take criticism badly and we need to be sensitive in criticizing them and we need also to praise our students at every appropriate opportunity. The process of supervision cannot be standardized as each student is very different and requires different support and perhaps different support mechanisms for successful conclusion. Nevertheless, although we are the supervisors, it is the students' research and their responsibility; you can advise them but they must make the final decisions and live by them.

Part II:
Supervisor–Student
Relationship

This second part of the book focuses on the supervisor–student relationship. Chapter 3 by Richard Baskerville and Nancy Russo sees the supervisor–student relationship in terms of different metaphors: as a project, process, as magic, a journey, an adventure, as parent–child, as a marriage, as teacher–pupil, a survival test, as apprentice–master and as servitude. This is followed by two chapters written by Duane Truex and Ramiro Montelegre; one chapter focusing on the role of the supervisor and a second (with David Avison and Cherie Long) on the role of the student.

If you are a supervisor: think about the metaphor that most applies to you and your research students. Are they all the same? Which metaphors apply to each of your colleagues? Have you and your colleagues discussed this with your students? Are you sure the metaphors of the students and their supervisors match?

Consider the key attributes of good mentoring in Chapter 4. Do you adhere to all of these? Is it feasible to do so or do you think this is an 'ideal' that we strive for rather than expect to follow absolutely? Which ones are essential? What is your idea of holistic supervision? In what ways are you hoping to grow in intellectual and emotional maturity through the supervisory process?

How are the competing pressures on the institution, members of faculty and students balanced at your university? How do you support the university in terms of the institutional pressures discussed in Chapter 5? Take a look at Figure 5.1. Do you recognize these emotional stages of a PhD for your students? Do you support your students during their emotional stages of a PhD? How do you impose limits on interfering in their personal lives? In view of all these demands from your PhD students, how do you cope with your own pressures at the same time?

If you are a PhD student: which of the metaphors in Chapter 3 do you find most attractive? Which metaphor best describes the relationship between you and your supervisor? Try to think how it will develop over time? Do you think that the two metaphors used by yourself and your supervisor are compatible?

Take a look at Figure 4.1 on holistic supervision. Try to map your own situation. Where are you now? Do you feel comfortable with own growth process? What pressures are you facing? Can you cope with them alone? Do you feel that maturation process is going well? Do you think your supervisor should involve himself or herself more?

Building networks can be very supportive. How are you doing? Has your supervisor been involved? Is he or she sharing some of his or her contacts and involving you in the networking? Have you attended doctoral consortia where you have an excellent opportunity to broaden your personal network? Do you remember to keep in regular contact with the people you have met?

Consider the section called 'Finalizing' towards the end of Chapter 4. Have you thought about: setting career expectations (what do you expect after the PhD?); establishing market credentials (how good are yours?); introducing yourself to the academic institutional environment (do you know it, or have you kept outside?); finding a position (have you an idea of where and when to look?); and finally, following up after leaving the university (do you discuss this with your supervisor and other colleagues?).

Finally take a look at Figure 5.1. Which emotional stages have you experienced? Do you think it appropriate for your supervisor to get involved? How can this correct level of involvement be maintained?

3

Metaphors for PhD Study

Richard Baskerville and Nancy L. Russo

3.1 Introduction

Perhaps nothing could be more important at the outset of PhD studies than establishing the appropriate, basic framework within which the process of completing the PhD program will proceed. Frequently, however, both the supervisor and the student may wrongly assume that this infrastructure is entirely given by university regulations. In fact, many choices about the instantiation of the process are made by the supervisor or by the student. Metaphors can be used to describe these choices. When these are not explicit or not well understood by both parties, miscommunication may lead to frustration and potentially to a breakdown in the process itself.

Through the use of metaphors, this chapter will help you to clarify and understand the assumptions shared by PhD students and their supervisors. Conflicts between the supervisor's assumptions and the student's assumptions can prove destructive to the process and thereby to the success of the student. Similarly, the nature of the student and the supervisor as individuals may also suggest what metaphors (and incumbent assumptions) could operate successfully in defining the approach to the PhD supervision process.

There are many metaphors that supervisors and students can adopt, either implicitly or explicitly, as critical parts of the PhD study infrastructure. Common metaphors include 'the project,' 'the process', 'the student', 'the journey', etc. These metaphors and others will be discussed in this chapter. Each of these metaphors, and even those not mentioned here, brings a body of assumptions to the roles and the relationship of supervisor and student. Metaphors vary in the degree to which the experience is centered on the supervisor, or the student, or both. Conflict can arise where the supervisor operates under a different metaphor to that of the student, or when a student doesn't grasp the full meaning of the metaphor. In such cases, either the supervisor or the student, or both, may build unspoken expectations that become unfulfilled in the supervisor–student relationship.

As with all such conflicts, this can be avoided by discussing and agreeing appropriate metaphors early in the relationship, that is, the unspoken, implicit relationship should be made explicit. Some common metaphors are summarized in Table 3.1. The table is roughly ordered by the degree to which the experience centers on the student (the first few rows of the table) to the degree to which the experience centers on the supervisor (the last few rows of the table). The metaphors are described in more detail below, and may aid supervisors and their students in identifying and coming to a shared understanding of their relationship and roles in the conduct of the PhD study process.

3.2 Project

Adopting a project metaphor is a quite rational way to frame PhD studies. This metaphor embraces control, management and strategic design of the process for achieving a doctorate. It enables supervisors and students to apply project management concepts, jargon, and techniques to the activities. The overall goal is the completion and achievement of the PhD degree via the production of a thesis. The project metaphor centralizes planning. The infrastructure will usually embrace stages or phases, specified work products, and milestones that demark progress toward degree completion.

Table 3.1 *Summary of Common Metaphors*

Focus	Metaphor	Supervisor Role	Student Role	Benefit	Risk
Student-centered	Project	Customer	Project manager	Short timeframe	Lost Flexibility
↑	Process	Mentor/Coach	The transformed	Future research	Resistance
	Magic	Wizard	Novice	Independence	Little feedback
	Journey	Guide	Traveler	Adaptive	Scope creep
	Adventure	Companion	Adventurer	Depth	Trivial outcome
	Child	Parent	Child	Nurtured maturation	Irreparable differences
	Marriage	Spouse	Spouse	Tacit exchanges	Divorce
	Pupil	Teacher	Pupil	Preserves style	Lost independence
	Survival Test	Mother Nature	Survivor	Student confidence	Sudden failure
↓	Apprentice	Model	On-the-job trainee	Active learning	Supervisor replication
Supervisor-Centered	Servitude	Master	Slave	Research stream	Incompetence

Generally, the project metaphor centers on the student. The supervisor usually undertakes the role of a customer who receives and approves the completed work projects, and the student becomes the project manager as well as the fundamental worker in the project. It is possible to envision a situation in which the supervisor becomes the project manager, directing the work of the student; however, this is not a recommended strategy. In any event, because the metaphor centralizes a project plan, the student will always know what work remains and will be able to estimate quite accurately, based on available information, a completion date.

Benefit: Usually this is a good frame to adopt when time is short, and when the student needs clear guidelines. *Risk:* The approach inhibits flexibility. The scope of the research questions can grow if not controlled.

This creep often arises during the literature search when the student discovers the interconnectedness of scholarly knowledge. For example, a research question about knowledge management can grow as the literature search begins to branch across expert systems, artificial intelligence, intellectual capital, organizational learning, core competence, alliances, and innovation, not to mention knowledge itself. Each of these areas will also spread widely onto other bases.

Alfred was a student in a major urban university in Europe. Betty was a very senior professor and Alfred's supervisor. There was a shortage of faculty in this IS group, which meant that all of the instructors were rather overburdened with teaching. Betty was also head of School, with many administrative duties. Alfred was numbered among twelve other PhD students working with Betty.

Betty's work overload set the tone of the relationship from the beginning. It was very difficult for Alfred to get appointments to see Betty. Betty was often late, had not thoroughly read Alfred's work, and their meetings were punctuated by frequent interruptions. Betty's advice came in hurried snippets uttered quickly before their brief meetings closed. Betty had advised Alfred to submit a paper to a conference, and when this was accepted, she encouraged him to discuss his work face to face with other academics. Alfred soon came to depend on a network of other students and faculty for advice and guidance for his work. As Alfred realized the financial income implications of further delays caused by waiting for guidance from Betty, he decided to make completion speed his top priority. Alfred created an aggressive independent project plan complete with milestone charts and deliverables, and began to operate against this plan without Betty's knowledge.

Alfred and Betty illustrate the project metaphor. Betty simply became Alfred's customer, consuming the draft chapters as these emerged from the research. She didn't really have much time to do more. Alfred began to manage the whole process, including deciding when and how to engage Betty within the constraints he knew her workload imposed. It was a risky strategy, as in the end there were major oversights in the literature review that were only discovered in the oral defense, and endangered the overall contribution. Thankfully, the examining committee was helpful and Alfred got the opportunity to make the necessary revisions after the defense, even though these substantially reshaped the conclusions of the thesis.

3.3 Process

An alternative metaphor for PhD studies is embodied by a learning process metaphor. It aims to enable supervisors to facilitate a transformation in the student, one in which the student acquires a different worldview. The overall goal is for the student to become an academic. The process metaphor centralizes very high-level thinking skills. The infrastructure will usually embrace reading, reflection and critically written papers as the student hones the ability to critically perceive, logically analyze and clearly express original thought.

The supervisor usually undertakes the role as a mentor or coach who presents the student with ever more difficult intellectual challenges until they are ready to undertake a complete and original analysis leading to a significant contribution. The supervisor and student seek to engender a 'transformation' in the student as the student's mind is transformed from 'ordinary' to 'intellectual.' Empirical work is only important for gathering the raw material for analysis. Because the metaphor centralizes the student's thinking skills, the newer student may not know quite how much work remains, but students who have made the transformation will be rather confident about remaining work and completion dates.

Benefit: It usually provides a good foundation for approaching future research. A scholar is created and endures. *Risk:* Some students are not suited to becoming an intellectual (or at least in the same way as the supervisor). They may increasingly resist the guidance (that the supervisor may see as 'profound' and the student may see as 'impenetrable.') If the transformation does not happen, the student may fail or drop out, exhausted.

3.4 Magic

In some cases, it may appear from the outside that the PhD thesis is 'pulled from the hat' after a few years, as if by magic. The student observes and works alongside the supervisor and absorbs the 'tricks of the trade,' and the wisdom of the senior academic. The student hangs around the supervisor until the magic (the spark of genius) emerges in the student, just as it did in the supervisor many years before. Marked by this emergent magic, the thesis appears spontaneously.

This represents a very hands-off approach by the supervisor. The only actual role of the supervisor is that of a model on which the students may reshape themselves. As a model, the supervisor parades before the student the series of amazing episodes by which new knowledge is created. The supervisor might initially work with the student on developing a viable research question and research approach, and then have minimal interaction with the student until the work is finished. At this point the supervisor evaluates the final work to determine if it is ready for public display.

Benefit: The student learns how to work independently to conduct a research project and report the results. This independence means that the student becomes his or her own person, a quite distinct version of academic modeled on, but different from, the supervisor. *Risk:* Few, if any, measures of progress are noted. The student has little guidance along the way, and runs the risk of getting off track and not becoming aware of the misdirection until the very end of the process. In such case, significant rework may be required.

3.5 Journey

Adopting a journey metaphor emphasizes the unique nature of every student and each project. It enables supervisors and students to innovate and reframe PhD work as it evolves over time. The overall goal is to complete the journey and reach a worthwhile thesis. This metaphor centralizes discovery by the student, and the uniqueness of each researcher and each research setting. The stages of study correspond to an explorative trip:

- *Launch,* the beginning stage in which the student must decide in which direction to set out
- *Explore,* the early stage in which the student probes for the boundary between known and unknown knowledge
- *Discover,* the later stage in which the student develops a new contribution to knowledge
- *Return,* the final stage in which the student provides a report (a thesis) that describes the discoveries.

The supervisor usually undertakes the role of a guide who can point the student towards the initial destination and take the student a good distance along on a wilderness trek that the student must inevitably complete alone. Discoveries await the appearance of just the right researcher, with just the right background to completely recognize the value and novelty of the discovery. The supervisor is an experienced leader for the student, helping the student to negotiate the early trials and obstructions, but inevitably setting the student free to reach journey's end on their own. The metaphor recognizes that journeys may be fruitless, and thus PhD studies unsuccessful, simply because the chosen direction led to nothing interesting, a barren wasteland, so-to-speak. Because the metaphor centralizes discovery, the student never knows whether a novel and significant contribution will be found soon along their path, or never at all. Confidence in estimating completion timeframe only appears when the significant and novel contribution is discovered.

Benefit: Journeys are very adaptive enterprises. The student can shift to new directions when the context changes. This is a very flexible framework, perhaps suited most to exploratory research. *Risk:* The issue of scope, particularly having to do with changing research questions over time, can be a problem with this approach. This topic creep often arises as the natural curiosity of the students leads them along the boundary of the unknown. The student may explore many cul-de-sacs on the way. For example, a research question about knowledge management can be reformulated into a more interesting research question about intellectual capital, which in turn can be reformulated into a question about a knowledge economy, which in turn can be reformulated into a question about ethical accounting, etc. Topic creep can also rise late in doctoral studies as a student becomes a world-class expert in the topic area. His or her expertise means that little that they read in their area will be new or interesting. Bored with their central questions, a curious student may not be able to retain focus on any project long enough to complete a thesis and make a serious contribution of their own.

Finally, these journeys can also be exciting experiences. The student or the supervisor may feel it is 'better to travel than to arrive.' In other words, the motive to complete the PhD may be diminished by the excitement of the journey. Either the student or the supervisor may begin working to prolong the experience and avoid completion. Indeed there may even be a fear of final thesis submission, an act that will terminate the journey and seem like an ante-climax.

3.6 Adventure

Adventures are similar to journeys, but an adventure metaphor centralizes the importance of the research process, without an attempt to plan an initial destination. Like journeys, every research project becomes a unique experience that may or may not lead to discoveries. In an adventure, however, the importance falls on the endless quest for knowledge rather than the knowledge itself. Stages and deliverables are less important in this metaphor than activities. PhD research is a quest for a prize, with an object of digging up new knowledge by following clues. The prizes are findings that are not just significant, but revelational discoveries.

The supervisor is an experienced companion for the student, usually demonstrating how to negotiate pathways through the unknown, thereby making the unknown more known. The adventure metaphor centralizes exploration by the student-adventurer. The goal is not discovery, it is discovering. The completion of the PhD becomes a side issue, a by-product of the process that is necessary only to enable further pursuits. Because the metaphor centralizes the act of discovering, neither the supervisor nor the student will seem to care about completion dates, sometimes choosing a random moment of the adventure in which to write up some recent discoveries as a PhD thesis.

Benefit: It is usually a good metaphor for developing extensive depth in the study. Since discovery is centralized, the topic will be explored more completely and thoroughly. *Risk:* There is some risk that the outcome will be insignificant if the exploration doesn't yield a revelation. The adventure may yield a series of trivial discoveries that have little to contribute to thinking beyond the immediate topic area.

Edith was a PhD student in an urban North American university with a prestigious doctoral scholarship won in an internationally competitive process. Florence was a rising assistant professor, and anxious to work with PhD students. Florence dedicated a great deal of time to her teaching responsibilities and struggled to build her teaching record.

After a year of doctoral seminars, Edith felt marginalized and dehumanized by the program. She had been expecting to work closely with important professors, but thus far she felt that she had been herded together with students from other management disciplines with whom she had little in common. The faculty encounters had mostly been rather formal and related only with seminars. Since she was fully funded by her scholarship, she was free from teaching responsibilities, and duties associated with research assistantships, both of which would have provided normal one-to-one exchanges with faculty. She felt alone and was considering leaving the program.

Edith became excited when she heard Florence give a research seminar talk about an electronic commerce research project (in agency theory) that was just starting. She approached Florence and found, at last, the very personal concern that she was seeking. Florence was equally excited about Edith's interest and immediately suggested that Edith join the project. Edith became intensely involved in Florence's project. The two worked continuously on all phases, putting in long hours on campus, and frequently working at Florence's home at nights and on weekends. Edith began to develop interests in the economics of electronic commerce, which Florence encouraged and nurtured. While Florence's project neared completion, the focus of the two scholars turned more and more toward Edith's thesis. Eventually, their collaboration was entirely focused on Edith's work. Beyond just discussing academic theory, research methodology, and the topic, Edith and Florence would often discuss the excitement and joys of academic life, the effects of the extensive work on Edith's family, and future career planning based on Florence's experience. Edith easily completed her thesis, which was regarded within the university as one of the strongest and most innovative in recent times.

Edith and Florence illustrate the adventure metaphor. Edith was energized by the strength that Florence drew from her work, and the central importance that Florence placed on her career. Edith was essentially invited to join Florence as a companion for one adventure, and then the two shifted roles for a second adventure, one in which the adventure belonged to Edith and Florence was the companion. This case was particularly successful, because the adventure led to an outcome that had more than sufficient depth to justify a doctorate.

3.7 Parent-child

This metaphor explicitly acknowledges the maturation process that takes place over the course of PhD study. This approach recognizes that there may come a point, likened to the adolescence phase, when the student (child) rebels against the control of the supervisor (parent). This may take the mild form of questioning the specifics of the research or may be so extreme as to result in the student working outside of the area defined by the supervisor permanently or for some time before reconciling with the supervisor and the project. A good 'parent' understands and accepts that this process is a valuable part of the growing process as a 'child' establishes his or her own unique identity separate from that of the parent.

The role of the supervisor in this approach is to nurture the student and to guide the development of the student from researcher infancy through adulthood. In a healthy relationship of this type, the supervisor not only instills cultural norms and behaviors, but also attempts to guide the maturation of the student into a responsible, independent researcher. The student's role is to absorb the lessons, both explicit and implicit, provided by the supervisor. The supervisor attempts to protect the student from serious injury along the way, but realizes that small bumps and bruises are part of the learning process.

Benefit: The student is allowed to develop his or her own identity as a researcher, with support and guidance along the way. The supervisor watches over the progress of the student, taking a smaller and smaller role as the student reaches the end of the PhD study process. *Risk:* There is a possibility that the rift caused by the rebellion of the student may not be reparable. This would force the student to transfer to another supervisor or to abandon the PhD study.

3.8 Marriage

A marriage or partnership metaphor represents the strong personal relationship between the supervisor and the student. If successful, it grows over quite a long time span and can endure beyond the PhD degree program; perhaps even lasting throughout the student's career. The relationship is much more than an academic one, involving give and take and resulting in benefit to both parties. This metaphor is usually a form of 'intellectual romance.' It is not so much platonic love as it is a Vulcan mind-meld. The relationship between the supervisor and the student is rather intense, and more of an equal partnership than is seen in some of the metaphors. Each party brings unique talents, experiences, or abilities to contribute to the intellectual relationship. The 'marriage' is not just related to completion of the thesis, but includes introduction to the culture, community, and significant individuals. Both parties suffer through the process of bringing up 'the baby' (the thesis).

Initially, the role of the supervisor in this type of relationship is something akin to a dominant spouse, the person in the relationship who knows the answers and usually leads when tough problems arise. Initially, the role of the student is something akin to a subservient spouse who operates autonomously but depends on the supervisor for support with problems. The relationship evolves throughout the study and afterward, perhaps becoming more equal as years pass.

Benefit: The marriage metaphor engenders an ideal setting for exchanging tacit knowledge. The partners grow to know what each other is thinking. Student and supervisor do not necessarily think alike, but each can anticipate the thoughts of the other. In this metaphor, twice the brainpower gets synchronized and applied to a research problem as one unit. *Risk:* Supervisors can grow too close to the student to supervise effectively. There may not be enough detachment. Like any extremely close relationship, dissolution can be rough, very much like a divorce. Nasty passions and possessiveness can envelope the division of the shared intellectual property. Students and supervisors taking this metaphor more literally will face additional risks, perhaps the wrath of the University administrators because of obvious ethical questions (see also Chapter 8)!

> John was a PhD student of Laura and the relationship seemed to be one of teacher and pupil for the first few years. As the research developed, the relationship became more like a marriage. Two years after John gained his PhD, it was a marriage, literally!

3.9 Pupil

Adopting a pupil metaphor manifests the supervisor as a teacher who interacts in a singular fashion with one important student as a pupil. Supervisors will often apply the Socratic method in an individual conversation with a student to help him solve intricate mental puzzles. The overall goal is to create student learning, to expand what the pupil knows. The supervisor 'opens up' the pupil's head, and 'pours in' the knowledge. Where previous metaphors have centralized the student or at least the student–supervisor team, this metaphor shifts emphasis toward the supervisor's importance. The supervisor is active: the student is a follower.

The role of the supervisor is instructional: the teacher. The role of the student is to be a somewhat passive learner: the pupil. The pupil arrives as raw material to be shaped and refined through training. Exchanges are less of a conversation, and more of a lecture: the supervisor talks; the pupil listens. Like school pupils, the student is produced in 'cookie-cutter' fashion from the supervisor's academic factory.

Benefit: The student will usually follow an instructional program preset by the supervisor. Strong and clear familiarity develops with a concise 'style' of research. The research tradition in the program will be reproduced. *Risk:* The pupil metaphor can endanger the independence of the student. Independent development of a research style or intellect is subtly discouraged. The metaphor also promotes research form over function, for example, methodology over contribution. It can be a very limited experience for a future academic.

Charles was a part-time student in a famous, suburban North American university, with a sprawling green campus and somewhat pretentious neoclassical architecture. He was a faculty member at a small, nearby college, nearing tenure, and concerned that the lack of a PhD would mar his chances to retain his current posting. Donald was a rising assistant professor, and anxious to work with PhD students. Donald had a light teaching load and few administrative duties. Charles had taken several of Donald's master's courses and had proven an excellent student. Charles discussed moving toward the PhD, and with Donald's encouragement, applied under a special community program and was accepted.

Donald's own experience had approximated the journey metaphor, and he planned to adopt this approach in supervising Charles. In their initial meetings, he explained to Donald this kind of approach to guiding students through doctoral studies and emphasized the importance of continual forward progress. While Charles readily agreed in the beginning, he had difficulty picking out a way ahead. Charles's teaching responsibilities in his own college absorbed nearly all of his time, and he found that he was not all that keen on spending large amounts of time away from his young family. While Donald kept urging Charles to read this and read that, Charles developed little interest in the proffered readings and began to grow very bored with the process. Charles would ask Donald for guidance about courses to follow, lectures to attend, and writing assignments. Donald continued to keep their meetings brief and to encourage Charles to read more broadly in the field and return for one-on-one scholarly discussions. Eventually Charles became frustrated because he could not find any structure to the studies, and one day, following a meeting with Donald in which he was given yet another reading list, he withdrew his registration without explanation and disappeared without even saying goodbye to Donald.

Charles and Donald illustrate crossed metaphors. While Donald was operating under the assumptions that approximate the journey metaphor, Charles had formed expectations that more closely approximated a pupil metaphor. After all, Charles had been Donald's student before. Although Donald might have tried to explain that their relationship was going to be different, Charles never quite comprehended what this meant. The expectations of both the student and the supervisor were different, and rather incompatible.

3.10 Survival test

The survival test metaphor represents the doctoral process as a series of tests that must be passed and obstacles that must be overcome. The student must be a 'survivor' suffering great travails and surmounting great barriers along the way. There are various pass or fail decisions as the work progresses. The overall goal is to survive as an academic. Some would-be survivors drop out at various stages (as often due to personal factors as to academic ones). Some, however, make it to the end. In this metaphor, the supervisor becomes more centralized, setting up or identifying a series of goals or hurdles that the student must overcome to continue under tutelage. The hurdles may be intensified if the supervisor is faced with an overabundance of students, and seeks a method of weeding out the less determined competitors.

The role of the supervisor is to devise a series of activities that will move the student forward towards completion. These activities may involve the submission of research papers, creation of some artifact, or demonstration of the mastery of some particular topic(s). The supervisor, like Mother Nature, must challenge the student regularly with problems modeled after those normally and regularly faced by 'received' academics. The role of the student is that of the survivor, using wits and craft to prevail over all adversities. In some cases this may even mean physical survival through student poverty, marital discord, and health issues. (These are issues that may be shared with the supervisor!)

Benefit: This metaphor usually builds confidence in the student, and may also build important competence in problem solving at a very high level. The student will learn to confront opposition and overcome adversity. *Risk:* Failure can arise surprisingly fast and unexpectedly. This metaphor can sour the student on academic life. It can lead to frustration and 'burn-out' in the student. It sets up competition rather than cooperation and collaboration between fellow students. It places the student and the supervisor in somewhat antagonistic roles. It can also imbue questionable ethics in the student if survival leads to cheating or 'hard ball' competition.

3.11 Apprentice

The apprentice metaphor represents doctoral study as a process through which the apprentice (student) learns to master the (academic) craft at the feet of a master craftsman (the supervisor). Together the supervisor and the student are a master–apprentice team in which the student learns as the supervisor demonstrates techniques and methods for problem solving within the supervisor's ongoing projects. The overall goal is the creation of a first 'masterpiece' (a PhD thesis). Once this masterpiece is inspected and accepted, the apprentice becomes master and can then begin to take on apprentices as well. The master is centered in this metaphor: the student's work will often have the same look and feel as the supervisor's work. Such students will often seem to have the mark or stamp of the supervisor, continuing after PhD completion to work in the same way, and on related topics, to their supervisor. Because the work centralizes mastery of technique and method, the student will often have a sense for their progress, but their sense of completion will only appear very near the end of their PhD work.

The role of the supervisor is to act as a model of the appropriate academic 'behavior.' Supervisors help students to 'learn by doing.' Students study how the supervisor works, and model their own working styles and habits on their master. In this way, the student's role is that of an 'on-the-job' trainee. The student is assigned various tasks and learns constructively through praise from the supervisor, and also through the supervisor's criticism when tasks are completed poorly.

Benefit: Students benefit strongly from the active learning model (learn by doing). Doctoral study is less threatening, as students gradually work up to the master's level. While the role of the supervisor is centralized, there is less antagonism. Usually the master will prove a benign despot. *Risk:* The doctoral program will closely follow only one model of academic life. There is a strong possibility that the doctoral study merely 'replicates' the supervisor. The new PhD may be seen as merely a poor copy of the original and a risk as an academic recruit. There may be little exposure to diversity in research methods, topics, lifestyles, etc. As 'master craftsman,' perfectionist supervisors may never find satisfaction in the work products of independent-minded students, since these products are less likely to be precisely similar to those of the supervisor.

3.12 Servitude

Under this metaphor, the student will often work for an extensive period on the supervisor's research projects. There is usually a more-or-less explicit agreement that the student will put substantial time (sometimes years) into the supervisor's projects. In some cases, there may be little or no attribution of the student's contribution, regarding them instead as 'coding monkeys,' 'library gofers,' or 'data gatherers' who complete trivial and menial tasks. The goal of the process is to enhance the work of the supervisor. The PhD degree is seen rather as a payment-for-services. Supervisors under this metaphor may proudly proclaim their phalanxes of doctoral students, emblems of sizable research funding and academic fame. The student may be closely supervised at first, but gradually gain increasing independence as the student masters the techniques of research-craft. Ultimately, the student's actual PhD project may be carved as an advanced piece from ongoing projects of the supervisor.

The role of the supervisor is that of a lord and master. The student is a slave. Both parties often accept that the relationship should be a brutal one. Supervisors do precisely that: supervise. Almost all research activity is completed by students, and subject to final compilation and publication by the supervisor (and possibly attributed only to the supervisor). Usually this metaphor does mean that slaves win the protection of their masters, however. For example, the supervisor may appear at the student's doctoral defense and brutally suppress any opposition to the success of the thesis examination.

Benefit: The benefits largely accrue to the supervisor and the research outcomes. Commanding a large party of doctoral students can develop an impressive and coherent research program, achieving both depth and breadth in the research. *Risk:* The ethics of this metaphor are debatable at best. Student thesis work can be trivialized in order to protect the intellectual property of the supervisor. (The supervisor may view the thesis as ideas and discoveries 'given' to the student, and may seek to minimize the value 'lost' by this process.) The metaphor can also be replicating: slaves learn (and sometimes yearn) to be masters.

Graham was a PhD student in a 'new' university in Europe. Some years before, the university had been reformed from a polytechnic, and had impressively grown its image as a major research university. Hilda had been courted away from an 'old' prestigious university and was one of the prize members of the faculty.

When Graham proposed his research, Hilda found him interesting and promising and accepted supervision of his project. Graham felt honored and fortunate in being accepted to work under Hilda. Hilda, however, was quite busy, and delegated functional supervision of her PhD students to other faculty. These were not junior faculty, by any means, but were often the senior faculty members, like Jill, for example, competent researchers who dated from the old polytechnic days but had never developed the reputation of Hilda. Eventually, Graham and Jill began to work on a project that included Graham's thesis area. Hilda would occasionally meet with such teams, and during meetings with Jill and Graham; she would appraise Graham's progress and offer advice. In general, both Jill and Hilda agreed that Graham was making good progress. But when the three met, it was often Jill, rather than Graham, who would make the most forceful arguments about the importance and quality of Graham's work. One day, Graham and Jill engaged in a fierce argument over the validity of a particular statistical operation Jill had suggested for Graham's data. Jill assured him that the operation, and its critical results were absolutely acceptable and the important findings made Graham's thesis a sure bet. Graham strongly disagreed, and eventually the pair met with Hilda to arbitrate. Hilda agreed with Jill. The statistics were fine and the results were a real contribution. Graham completed soon after, but convinced of his own incompetence, he pursued his career without ever submitting a single work for publication consideration. He taught introductory courses in small colleges in various visiting positions.

Graham and Hilda's experience approximates a servitude metaphor. Graham was being driven to build a thesis that satisfied everyone but himself. He was never quite able to operate only on faith in his supervisor's (or any other's) opinion. To a certain extent, Graham became wrongly convinced of his own incompetence by Hilda's PhD-making machinery. It was not clear to him whether the important ideas were his own or Jill's. While others might have accepted the senior opinions and continued to move forward, Graham balked. He completed his PhD without ever really believing he was capable of completing a PhD.

3.13 Choosing the right metaphor

Supervisors and their PhD students rarely *choose* the metaphor that governs their relationships. Rather, the metaphors provide a handy descriptor for understanding and characterizing the many different forms in which such relationships might emerge. The metaphors are also helpful in recognizing a particular supervisor's 'typical' relationship with doctoral students. It lends clarity to the assumptions that govern a supervisor's expectations, as well as what the students might expect.

It can be useful for the supervisor and the student to discuss such metaphors as the student's work progresses. The metaphors imply a balance in the assumptions present in the roles of the supervisor and the student. Examining the operating metaphors can surface crossed-metaphors in which the supervisor's assumptions and expectations are different from those of the student. The metaphors can help surface pathologies in the ongoing relationship. For example, if the supervisor is operating with a servitude metaphor, and the student is operating with a process metaphor, it is unlikely that either will find the relationship satisfying. The student will be seeking coaching and transformational inspiration, while the supervisor is expecting attentive execution of precise instructions.

Other useful observations about the relationship can be surfaced using the metaphors. For example, when a student ceases to make progress, or is progressing too slowly, a review of the operating metaphor can help understand the reasons. For example, if a student is making little headway toward completion, discovering that a 'journey' metaphor is operating may help the supervisor and the student to recognize that the scope of the project is creeping. The metaphor can help focus attention on problems and possible solutions.

Because the metaphors describe relationships, assumptions and expectations, rather than research methods or outcomes, so any of the metaphors are more-or-less suitable for any research method or topic. However, we can certainly recognize some natural affinities between the metaphors and certain research approaches. Metaphors such as the 'journey' or 'adventure' are consistent with exploratory research that develops new theory using problem-oriented approaches like action research or ethnographic techniques like grounded theory. Such approaches seek to build theory from experiential data, and the findings emerge like the discoveries in a journey or an adventure. Metaphors such as the 'apprentice' or 'servitude' are consistent with some design research projects that involve implementation of large-scale, complex systems. Such approaches seek to validate theories constructively, by building and perhaps applying working models. If the project is a large coordinated collection of several PhD studies, the necessary teamwork requires centralized and authoritarian project leadership from the supervisor.

In addition, the nature of the relationship between the supervisor and the student may also be directed somewhat by the type of PhD student. For example, an industrial PhD student – one who is working in industry while working on the PhD – might require a different type of supervision than a full-time student. And a student who is completing a PhD with the intention of taking on an academic career would likely require a different type of supervision than would a student who is undertaking PhD study for the sheer joy of learning, with no intention of becoming a professional researcher.

3.14 Conclusion

Metaphors help to surface assumptions that inhabit PhD study infrastructures. These assumptions are important because they imply roles, benefits and risks in the process. Understanding the metaphors may help to contextualise frustrations, the ups and downs of academic research. The metaphors enable us to highlight problems when assumptions are inconsistent. For example, consider cross-metaphors at opposite ends of the spectrum: a supervisor operating under a project metaphor and a student operating under a servitude metaphor. Neither party is actually taking charge. The student is waiting to be told exactly what to do. The supervisor is nudging the student to manage the study processes. Expectations and needs are unmet and communications will probably break down.

The assumptions surfaced by the metaphors also suggest that success or failure of doctoral students may be defined by the suitability of the prevailing metaphor to the natures of the student and the supervisor. A self-guiding, independent student may succeed gloriously in an environment where the project metaphor prevails, but instantly self-destruct under a servitude metaphor. A full-time student might flourish under a process or an apprentice metaphor, but this metaphor may be unsuitable for a part-time student with practical career goals. It is important not only that the student–supervisor metaphors match, but that the student matches the metaphor. Indeed the supervisor must also match the metaphor. For example, more collaborative kinds of working metaphors, such as adventure, marriage, or student metaphors, may require a more intense commitment by the supervisor. A self-centered supervisor might flourish under a project or servitude metaphor, but never lead any student to completion using a marriage metaphor.

There is room for further work on such metaphors. There are likely to be plenty of other alternatives to the eleven models above. The relationship between the metaphors and detailed structures in the doctoral programs provide an interesting area for exploration. For example, theses can follow a monograph model or be constructed from a series of (published) papers. Do these metaphors operate with equal success across the various thesis structures? Some doctoral programs are highly unstructured, accepting research students whose central task is the production of a near 'earth-shaking' research thesis. Other programs are highly structured, involving a clearly defined and sizable seminar series, perhaps followed by a slightly more modest thesis. The relationship between the success of certain metaphors as guides to researchers and the categorical nature of students also has potential interest. For example, do certain metaphors succeed better for students with work experience or with students whose central goal is a teaching career, or students seeking university administrative careers or part-time students?

Clearly, there are some circumstances when the metaphors should change. When a student has to change supervisors, for example, there may be a need to agree on a mutual, new metaphor. Otherwise, conflicts in the assumption space may lead to a breakdown in the doctoral process. We should also recognize that a failing student might be salvaged with a metaphor change (along with a supervisor change perhaps). This wouldn't necessarily represent a failure of the supervisor or the student, so much as it would represent a metaphor failure or conflict between the nature of the student and the nature of the supervisor. Whenever such a metaphor changes, it seems a very good idea for the parties to discuss the operating metaphor, and any proposed metaphors, since these have a lot to say about the assumptions operating in the relationship.

A PhD study is not usually a linear process. Even though the supervisor and the student may choose to subscribe to a metaphor other than a project metaphor, university regulations will often prescribe certain milestones or work products. Keep in mind that the order and existence of these milestones and work products will vary among academic cultures and geographic regions. Nevertheless, they are part of the overarching structure of the program, and cannot be ignored.

Doctoral work can be a very risky enterprise. It involves a multi-year effort by a student operating in a very independent way. The student is likely to spend years following a program leading to dissertation research, and is at the greatest risk. Often the supervisor must be watchful of the risks that students undertake, being sure that that they understand the risks, and helping them to mitigate the risks wherever possible. Risks arise when students undertake less structured dissertation projects of the discovery type, for example. In these situations, the supervisor's role is to aid the student in identifying research paths that are most likely to provide fruitful results. Supervisors must recognize such risks as scope and topic creep, and help their students to dampen the effect. They must educate students on the need to keep abreast of ongoing research in their areas, in order to avoid any momentary replication. In addition, the supervisor must keep a watchful eye for any political or procedural pitfalls that may await the unsuspecting student. Whereas students should of course be expected to address known risks in their research projects, it is the supervisor who is in the best position to manage higher level risks by giving careful attention to the particular characteristics of the student, the operational metaphor, and the institutional structure and rules and their potential for conflict or failure.

4

Focus on the Supervisor

Ramiro Montealegre
and Duane Truex

4.1 Introduction

In Chapter 3, we looked at the supervisor–student relationship. In the next two chapters, we focus on the roles of the supervisor and student, respectively, emphasizing emotional aspects. Of course, neither chapter looks exclusively on one or the other, they are interlinked, but an emphasis is placed in this chapter on the role of the supervisor.

It is not uncommon to hear the supervision process characterized as training, gate keeping, socialization into a research tradition and community and intellectual grooming. Sometimes one hears of the need to motivate and serve as a role model for the student. But less frequently are members of faculty spoken of as personal change agents, counselors, surrogate parents, or praetorian guards, destined to protect the student from various negative forces. Yet supervisors can find themselves in such roles.

Thus, this chapter explores the role and responsibility that the supervisor plays in *holistic* supervising. It deals with the management of the mentoring relationship in its many forms including the monitoring and, sometimes, intervention into a student's personal life. In so doing we offer a cautionary note. The mentoring process is not static. Indeed it may be cyclical with students rising and falling in various emotional cycles. So just as the student's journey is not static nor wholly predictable, then it is likely that the supervisor's role must be viewed as a dynamic life cycle evolving in real time along with the needs of the student. Thus we do not offer a prescription, but rather some 'rules of thumb' based on our experience as PhD supervisors. This chapter summarizes features and issues often warranting special attention that are common to successful PhD mentoring relationships over time. The goal is to encourage mentoring habits that are in the best interests of both the student and supervisor.

In Greek Mythology *Mentor* was Odysseus's guide and trusted counselor whom Athena later used to school other Greek leaders. Mentoring refers to the role as a trusted counselor or teacher, especially in professional occupational settings. Thus a mentor is someone who takes a special interest in helping another person develop into a successful professional. But mentoring is more than advising and more than managing. It is a personal commitment to managing a relationship with someone undergoing one of life's transformative experiences.

Supervising is both a personal and professional relationship. It develops over an extended period during which a student's needs and the nature of the relationship tend to change. A supervisor should be aware of these changes and vary the degree and type of attention, help, advice, information, and encouragement that she or he provides. It is an emergent relationship in an emergent process.

The Council of Graduate Schools (CGS, 1995) cites Morris Zelditch's summary of a mentor's multiple roles:

> *Mentors are advisors, people with career experience willing to share their knowledge; supporters, people who give emotional and moral encouragement; tutors, people who give specific feedback on one's performance; masters, in the sense of employers to whom one is apprenticed; sponsors, sources of information about and aid in obtaining opportunities; models, of identity, of the kind of person one should be to be an academic.*

In general, an effective supervisor–student relationship is characterized by mutual respect, trust, understanding, and empathy. Good supervisors are able to share life experiences and wisdom, as well as technical expertise.

They are *good listeners, good observers,* and *good problem solvers.* They make an effort to know, accept, and respect the goals and interests of students. In the end, they establish an environment in which students' accomplishments are limited only by the extent of their talent and drive to achieve.

In the realm of information systems, we might say that a good supervisor seeks to help a student master the educational experience, keep a balance between social and technical issues, socialize into the culture of the information systems discipline, and find suitable employment. This relationship typically spans several years and may evolve into a deep friendship. Thus these obligations can extend well beyond formal schooling and continue into or through the student's career. It is an emergent personal process of personal growth for both parties.

4.2 Supervision as an emergent process

Supervising is an evolving process (rather than a sudden relationship) that is cumulative and expansive. While there may be a turning point that can be retrospectively seen as 'clicking' with a student, there is no single point in time when the true relationship forms. The nature of a supervisor–student relationship varies over time with the level and activities of both student and supervisor. In general, however, each relationship must be based on a common goal: to advance the educational and personal growth of the student. It is, of course, a relationship through which the supervisor can also benefit enormously; but the central focus must be the intellectual, educational and personal development of the research student.

This section describes the relationship by listing several aspects of good supervision practice. For this purpose, we adopt a general form of the process comprised of three broad, but distinct, activities as shown in Figure 4.1:

1 **Initiation and proposal** This activity consists of helping the student in initiating a PhD program, finding a topic of study, and preparing the research proposal.
2 **Research and development** This deals with helping the student in becoming socialized into the language, literature and methods of the discipline such that the student can demonstrate mastery of the field as well as conducting the research proposal. In some traditions this activity also involves taking classes and preparing for comprehensive exams. In other settings this can be done through qualifying exams and the

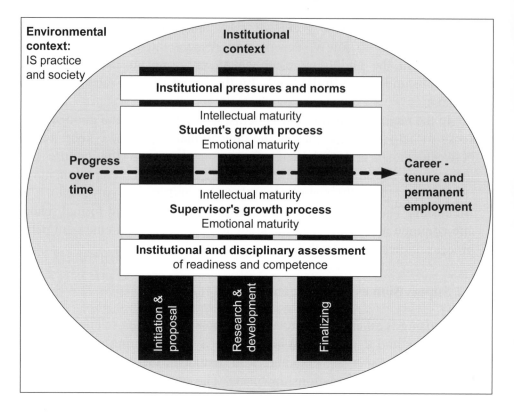

Figure 4.1 *Holistic supervision: balancing institutional and social forces during the PhD process*

publication of papers demonstrating the mastery of core elements in the field.

3   ***Finalizing*** This activity requires helping the student in preparing the thesis and moving on after completing the doctoral thesis.

Of course, supervising students is a dynamic process, dependent on the individuals involved, yet capable of creating a new form of the relationship. There is no single formula for good supervision; styles and activities are as varied as human relationships. However, as will be described below, some key aspects seem to be useful throughout the process, while others are more specific to a particular activity. The list presented here is based on what has worked for different people in different situations. Although these aspects are very important, they are by no means intended to be an exhaustive list of the required skills, nor do we prescribe that to be a good supervisor you need to follow every single aspect. Instead, you should develop a style that is comfortable to you, a style that fits your character, your personality, the situation, and the setting. After all, the PhD is the most individual of degree programs. And while there are many commonalities inherent in the 'doing' of a PhD, the degree still has attributes of a 'one off' project. The recommendations should be taken as broad principles and as an ideal to guide the prospective supervisor. It would be rare for any one supervisor to display all these abilities.

4.3 Key attributes of good mentoring

The following recommendations should be taken as broad principles and as an *ideal* to guide the supervisor. No one supervisor is likely to be perfect at all these!

- *Listen carefully.* A good supervisor is a good listener. Hear exactly what the student is trying to tell you without first interpreting or judging. Pay attention to the 'subtext' and undertones of the student's words, including tone, attitude, and body language. This is especially true, and often more difficult, when the power differential between student and professor is amplified by differences in culture, gender and age. When you think you have understood a point, it might be helpful to repeat it to the student and ask whether you have understood correctly. Through careful 'active' listening, you convey your empathy for the student and your understanding of a student's challenges. When a student feels this empathy and respect, the way is open for clear communication and more effective supervision.
- *Keep in touch.* The amount of attention that a supervisor gives will vary widely. A student who is doing well might require only 'check-ins' or brief meetings. Another student might have continuing difficulties and require several formal meetings a week; one or two students might occupy most of your time. Try through regular contact – daily, if possible – to keep all of your students on the 'radar screen' to anticipate problems before they become serious. E-mail is often useful here. Don't assume that the only students who need help are those who ask for it. Indeed for some students it is difficult to ask for assistance. In some cultures asking for such aid carries a host of cultural burdens and may imply a loss of face. Even a student who is doing well could need an occasional, serious conversation. In any event, a good supervisor will maintain sufficiently frequent contact to know about personal or other problems that could hinder progress and will generally make every

necessary effort to help the doctoral student grow into a mature and productive colleague. Thus in our experience it is useful to schedule regular 'check in' meetings with each student.

- ***Set regular deliverable deadlines.*** Most people are motivated by deadlines. When appropriate, mutually establish deliverables. They may be literature searches, readings germane to a particular topic or simply following a research thread. But keeping deadlines is a skill essential to master as a PhD and tying deliverables to the regular interaction helps in the decomposition of the large task of completing a PhD into more bite sized chunks. It is also advisable to tie the deliverables to some aspect of writing. Reading notes added to a growing *Endnote* library (or similar) or in a subject dictionary, for example, can be invaluable when preparing a thesis proposal or future literature review for an article. It also provides added focus for the supervisor–student meetings and helps the student hone an essential skill.

- ***Build networks.*** Kathy Kram, in her book *Mentoring at Work* (1985), explicitly acknowledges that mentoring relationships occur in a variety of forms and in a variety of strengths, and that students may (and probably do) have more than one such relationship at any given time. Although most mentoring in doctoral programs focuses on traditional forms of supervisory relationships, that is, a single relationship with a student, it is important to recognize that no supervisor can know everything a given student might need to learn in order to succeed. Therefore, students may well benefit from *multiple supervisors* of diverse talents, ages, and personalities. Sometimes a supervisory team works best. Appropriate supervisors could include professionals in industry, other students, more advanced research associates, as well as members of faculty in the same or different fields. You can be a powerful ally for students by helping them build their network of contacts and potential supervisors. Moreover, building a professional network is a lifelong process that can be crucial in developing a satisfying position and career. In those university settings where we are fortunate to host visiting faculty from abroad or our home country, we have a wonderful opportunity to help the student build a network through introductions, colloquia and arranged exchange visits. Similarly, it may be helpful to encourage the student to submit papers to selected conferences so they may begin the process of finding a community of scholars outside the immediacy of the home institution. Be aware, however, that some students can also become confused by different, perhaps mutually exclusive, advice.

- ***Be a role model.*** In a typical relationship the student will also be a keen observer of our own scholarly activities. This provides an excellent opportunity to teach by example. The student should have the opportunity to watch the supervisor in tasks such as writing a paper and nurturing it through the review and publication process. Let them read drafts and the critical remarks of reviews when papers are returned as well as celebrate with the announcements of a manuscript's acceptance. If you are on conference program committees or have journal reviewing or editorial responsibilities, it is an opportunity, when appropriate, for the student to share in reviewing and administrative duties. This will help them learn about community building and good academic citizenship. This principle extends to the whole range of academic activities. Be alert for ways to illustrate ethical issues and choices. The earlier students are exposed to the notion of scientific integrity, the better prepared they will be to deal with ethical questions that arise in their own work. Discuss your policies on grades, conflicts of interest, authorship credits, and who attends or presents a paper at a conference. Use real-life questions to help the student understand what is meant by scientific misconduct: What would you do if I asked you to cut corners in your work? What would you do if you had a boss who was unethical? Most of all show by your own example what you mean by ethical conduct.

It was my practice to meet with my PhD students every week or ten days on average after they had completed the initial stages of reading and mastery with core information systems literature. Given that in the American model we would have had more formal classroom contact as well, these individual meetings became customized and personal sessions in which a range of topics and questions could be explored. After a time, formalities would be dropped, trust is built and from time to time I would have a glimpse into the student's personal realm.

The regular meetings had numerous benefits. But one related to having a regular deliverable. The student would present their own papers or discuss papers that they had read. But the meetings were an essential part of the emerging supervisor–student relationship.

In one case I was meeting with a student whose thesis writing had stalled. The pressure of teaching responsibilities provided a reasonable excuse for the diminished pace of work. I knew that he was working a seven day schedule and that the pressure was, as seems typical at this stage of thesis work, an intense and isolating experience. But I sensed there was more and that it was unspoken. I was careful not to pry because as a foreign student from Asia I knew he valued his privacy. But during one of our weekly meetings the student, a young man in his 30's, read a framed essay I had in my home office. It said in part that '...men make love with their eyes and women make love with their ears.' He asked about this passage and in his asking I sensed that there was a great deal behind the question.

I said that like all generalizations there was some truth in the statement, but that I sensed marriage relationships in the US were different than in other parts of the world. I then asked him what he thought and if things were different elsewhere. He opened up and I learned that the pressure of work and thesis was placing an intolerable strain on his marriage. Being in a foreign country was removed from traditional sources of support. And his isolation was loading the work of managing the family entirely on his wife and leaving her feeling so alone that she was contemplating returning to their country with his children. The possibility was too much for him to bear. But his cultural norms were such that he had to bear the strain in silence. Until now that is.

My own marriage had failed during the thesis stage. I could share from my own experience and talk about the pressure and the difficulty it was causing his family and himself. Together we talked through a plan that began with heartfelt and direct conversation with his wife about the process of completing the thesis. It involved creating a work schedule that actually put family time and relationship time in the schedule so they both knew it too was important, even in the midst of the thesis project. It involved bringing his wife back into the process so she had a better sense of what was required and a better idea of how long it would take to complete. It helped them feel more as partners in the process and thus reduced the isolation.

The story has a happy ending. Perhaps in part due to cultural norms as the supervisor I had the authority to 'suggest' a change in personal schedule and have it considered. This was perhaps also because we had built the trust relationship and I knew the student and his family from previous social engagements. Tending to this emotional strain removed a major obstacle to the student's progress. He finished the first draft of the thesis in four months, while working full time.

- *Be approachable and available.* Some students will feel comfortable approaching their supervisors; others will be shy, intimidated, or reluctant to seek help. A good supervisor can lessen such confusion by getting to know students and being familiar with the kinds of suggestions and information that can be useful.

     Effective supervision need not always require large amounts of time. An experienced, perceptive supervisor can provide great help in just a few minutes by making the right suggestion or asking the right question. For their part, students need to understand the professional pressures and time constraints faced by their supervisors and not view them as merely a means or impediment to their goal. For many members of faculty, supervision is not their primary responsibility; in fact, time spent with students can be time taken from their own research. Students are obliged to recognize the multiple demands on a supervisor's time.

4.4 Phases of the supervision process

In the following we suggest a generalized staged development of the research program over time and draw attention to important issues at each stage. It will need to be adapted for your own research environment in general, and the particular situation (progress, student's personality, etc.), in particular.

Initiation and proposal
When advising during this activity, you might be asked to describe the features of an academic career, and suggest career trajectories. Many students at this stage lack sufficient experience to imagine what kind of work they might do as academics. Don't assume that students know something just because it is obvious to you. One of your goals for students during this activity is to provide a 'map' to the terrain and a 'travelers' guide' to the professional universe that they might some day encounter. Some key supervisor skills include:

- *Assessing the decision to pursue a doctoral program.* Help the potential doctoral student visualize career paths. Some of them, especially if they are the first in their families to attend college, fear they lack the ability or preparation to become scientists. A student might enjoy teaching others and being successful in taking classes without understanding how to conduct research. Remind them that *careers evolve slowly.*

   You can help by posing fundamental questions: What have you most enjoyed in life? What are you good at? What kinds of activities are most satisfying? Do you like abstract problems or hands-on activities? How much schooling do you need to do that? Suggest early exposure to a range of courses, summer research assistant positions, research internship opportunities, or independent research-oriented courses. Encourage them to explore many options by talking with other students at all levels and with professionals about their careers. Potential doctoral students should understand the nature of jobs in academia, and the time and effort involved in a doctoral program.

   A wise colleague once said that: 'completing the PhD has as much to do with emotional maturity as it does with intellectual ability.' By this she meant that the PhD was like the long distance race in which the student needs to be prepared for the long term, multi year journey. Process models for the PhD vary widely from country to country. In some traditions additional coursework and a structured sequence of tasks must be completed before the student is admitted to actual candidacy. In other traditions the students screened for admission are deemed ready enough to begin independent research and begin the process of topic development and thesis research almost immediately and will need little additional formal instruction. In most settings the PhD is not like any other degree acquisition process the student has experienced. Thus we see one of our mentoring roles as helping the student recognize that difference and weather the transition.

- *Assessing the right institution and doctoral program.* If students are ready to make the leap to a doctoral program, encourage them to use the telephone, visit campuses (and university home pages), talk with current students and members of faculty, seek out alumni, attend conferences, and read publications by faculty. Personal meetings with faculty and doctoral students can bring a feel for the profession and provide an excellent foundation for choosing an appropriate learning environment and suitable doctoral program.

  When a new potential doctoral student arrives at your institution for a campus visit it is important to discuss the general process required in your institution. In the more formally constituted programs, such as many in the United States, it is essential to discuss the rules regarding required and elective courses, comprehensive exams, thesis, and teaching. Requirements vary even within an institution. Keep handy your institution's student handbook or course guide for continuing discussions. In the traditions where structured coursework and other formal benchmarks of progress are not part of the process or where the focus may be more akin to an apprenticeship model, it is appropriate to provide examples (perhaps by analogy) of how other successful candidates managed the process. It may be even more critical in these settings to arrange for prospective students to spend time with other students in varying stages of the journey. Whatever your particular tradition it is important for the potential student to have a clear picture of the commitment being made in starting a PhD.

- *Assessing student's potential.* How can you tell whether a student has what it takes to undertake a PhD? The usual indicators for program admission are references, course records, test scores, and success in undergraduate or master level research. But these are poor measures for the degree of commitment or for understanding the student's motivation for pursuing the PhD. Gently probe the student's level of interest. Do you detect the energy of curiosity and motivation? *Pay special attention to motivation*, which might be more important than background in deciding a student's eventual success or failure. Don't be afraid to use your intuition, but beware of letting your own assumptions or biases distort your opinion of a student's potential. This may also be an appropriate time to get a feel for the personal and social support structure the student may have available to them. The time requirements, the multi-phased changes in the candidate's worldview and single-minded focus periodically required by the PhD journey can be difficult on families and relationships. If the student's support system is ill equipped for these stresses, progress may be delayed or aborted midway through.

The rigorous environment of graduate school is not a good place for hesitant students to avoid the 'real world' or to pass time while deciding what to do with their lives. A doctoral program requires high levels of commitment and ability. A doctorate is appropriate for most students who desire research careers, including academic research and industrial research. But a doctorate does not restrict a person to a life in academe. For example, information systems doctorates can be employed in business, consulting, or industry.

- *Conducting a research project.* Whether with you or a colleague, conducting a research project is valuable in helping the student to understand the nature of research better, regardless of the topic. Your institution's research-support office might be a good resource in locating research opportunities as are national disciplinary societies and your own personal contacts. Fortunately, information systems has an excellent infrastructure, with the *AIS* as the international association and local societies like the *UKAIS* and *AIM* (the French equivalent).

Help the student find a well-planned project that interests both of you and that can be completed in a defined period. Work with the student to set up a clear time line for completion of research. Set high but realistic goals; it is obviously very important to select a project that has a good chance of success. Define your own responsibilities, including regular feedback and evaluation. Make connections between course work and the literature.

For committed students, such a project can have an important influence during the rest of their doctoral experience. Do *not*, however, place students in research posts without evaluating their fitness and desire to perform the work. Research that is poorly conceptualized or executed might be worse than no research experience at all. If a student does have a poor research experience, try to explain the reasons. A student who understands the causes of failure is less likely to suffer damage in the doctoral program.

Your broader challenge is to interpret a research experience in the context of the student's total education. The primary purposes of student research during this activity are to master techniques, to learn to think critically, to acquire strategies for problem solving, and to learn the importance of patience and perseverance in the unpredictable context of research.

- *Teaching careful planning and use of time.* Let students know what their responsibilities are and agree on schedules. Suggest breaking a large period of study into smaller periods, 'easing' into it by steps, and setting a time limit for each step. Encourage the student to set aside regular time for planning and also for self-improvement (reflective thought, physical exercise, reading for pleasure, and so on). By monitoring a few obvious indicators, such as grades, you'll be able to detect the symptoms of a problem before it becomes a crisis.

- *Choosing a supervisor.* During this activity, it is also important to help students in choosing a research adviser – and yet some of them exercise less care in this decision than they do in the renting of a house. Encourage students to shop around carefully, to talk to present and former students of the supervisor, and to gain personal impressions through face-to-face interviews. Be sure that a potential student knows your particular style and finds it congenial.

  Students should also be advised to examine the performance of possible supervisors: publication record, financial-support base, reputation, success of recent graduates, recognition of student accomplishments (for example, through co-authorship), and, most important, willingness to spend time with students. Much of this information can be learned directly from the potential supervisor and his or her current and past students.

- *Accepting students.* You might be approached by more than one student about being a supervisor. Bear in mind the responsibilities of saying yes, and examine your other commitments. Handling a large group might be possible with a 'secondary supervisor' network, where senior members of your research group act as mentors to junior members.

  Remind yourself, and students whom you consider taking on, of the importance of personal chemistry. Do you think you can work productively with this person? Can you imagine recommending this student for a job? This is a dynamic and at times intense multi-year commitment. It needs to feel right for both parties. If the relationship doesn't feel right for either party, or if communication is poor, think about helping the student find another supervisor as soon as possible. You might also consider developing the skills that will allow you to work with a more diverse group of students.

Research and development

The broad purpose in this activity is to gain research experience and skills that open new vistas. The cardinal goal should be to help those you supervise to enhance their initiative, independence, and self-reliance. Those who grow accustomed to nurturing support but who have failed to develop independence might be painfully shocked when moving into a position where such support is lacking. Make it clear to your students that they should demonstrate independent research thinking, be productive, have their work reflected on their record, and make sure that someone in a position of authority knows what they are doing and can facilitate their next steps. Some of the key aspects of good supervisory practices include:

- *Choosing a research topic.* Urge the student to do a thorough review of a particular literature of interest and find the gaps within it. Then, the student should think through a research topic within that field – imagine a thesis title, list hypotheses to test and perhaps expected outcomes, and write a full proposal. The title and outcomes might change, but a well-designed planning procedure (perhaps including a public presentation and defense) helps both you and the student toward a common understanding of the project. It also allows other committee members to contribute early in the process. If you approve a topic outside your expertise, recruit a committee member who is an expert. Discuss with the student whether the project meets these conditions; it should interest you as well as the student, permit the student to learn useful skills, serve as the basis for a thesis no matter what the results, and be designed for completion within a reasonable period.
- *Choosing a committee.* Both supervisor and student should participate in choosing a committee. Be sure the group represents a good mix of fields, analytic approaches, expertise, and other qualities. If you as research adviser have a practical bent, a colleague who is a theorist might add good balance. Share with the student any knowledge of personal or political conflicts among potential members which could disrupt a student's progress and morale.

  Some students are tempted to seek members who are unlikely to be critical. You should encourage students to avoid this strategy. The members of a committee should be respected as scholars and have the expertise needed to give thorough research supervision. The student needs committee members who will form the nucleus of a professional network and eventually help the student find employment and a satisfying career path.

- *Teaching careful planning to increase productivity.* Students benefit from writing regular progress reports (preferably in the form of research articles) to clarify their own work, to communicate with you, and to sharpen their writing skills. You might choose to have weekly research-group meetings where students take turns presenting papers and exchanging experiences. Make presentations informal, with time for many questions.

  At the same time, discourage rigid schedules. Remember that every student is unique, and many end up doing things differently – and often much better – than you might have imagined. If a student falls behind, consider that the cause might be exhaustion, unclear direction, lack of commitment, or dislike for the project or persons involved. Some students, through no fault of their own, will require extra time. These include new parents (fathers as well as mothers), those who work part time, students with disabilities and those who return after an off-campus fellowship or other leave of absence, and so on.

  If, after a reasonable period, a student has not shown high aptitude for research, the supervisor should advise a non-research career. This can be difficult if a student has planned a research career, but if you are convinced that a student's abilities are insufficient or are stronger in another field, the kindest course is to say so.

- *Facilitating professional growth.* There are many ways to facilitate students' professional growth in addition to one-on-one counseling. One strategy is to create informal cross-disciplinary groups (such as a group of IS researchers using qualitative methods). Use monthly meetings (with incentives like free food) as forums for discussing such topics as interview strategies, coping with negative reviews, and giving good presentations. Another approach is to organize interdisciplinary seminars with other departments to introduce students (and faculty) to new avenues of inquiry and to colleagues in related disciplines.

- *Mapping academic goals and course work.* In many programs this stage is the time the student rounds out his/her breadth of knowledge in the discipline through required or elective coursework. We paraphrase the essayist Postman (1988) in observing that the knowledge of a discipline largely means knowledge of the *language* of that discipline. For many students formal coursework is an efficient process for acquiring hitherto unfamiliar knowledge. In some traditions deciding what courses or literature bases must be mastered before full admission to the degree is a negotiated process. The student and supervisor, or perhaps even a larger committee, agrees that certain skills must be mastered as a step in the

PhD acquisition process. In either case during this broadening and 'rounding out' activity, students will require different amounts and kinds of attention, advice, information, and encouragement. Often students will not know what questions to ask, what information they need, or what their options are (especially when selecting courses). Some key aspects of good mentoring for this stage include discussing students' interests and goals, and outlining the differences between IS areas might help them decide areas of scholarship. In addition, you can suggest colleagues and doctoral students doing research in those fields who would be willing to talk with them.

For electives, encourage students to take courses that they enjoy or that can lead to new fields of study. The early months of the doctoral program at least offer the opportunity for experimentation with fields of knowledge. Urge the student to seek practical experience using various types of research methods. As their career unfolds, they might work outside their field, outside research, or even outside their native country. However, students need to learn to keep a balance between breadth and depth, since they should develop focus and depth in a specific area of a field where they will become experts.

Finalizing

The students' goal during this activity should be to finish in a timely fashion, and this should be your goal for them as well. It can be tempting to suppose that post-proposal students require little or no supervision. In fact, post-proposal students who might have scant supervision, ill-defined goals, and poor access to a community of peers tend to incur greater risks of isolation and stagnation than graduate students. That is why as much as a third of doctoral candidates who complete course requirements never complete their thesis (Davis and Parker, 1997). It is important to emphasize that during this activity, the supervisor needs to be available and supportive, as many doctoral students feel overwhelmed with the task at hand and uncomfortable with the lack of structure (and deadlines) which they had during their course work. A good mentoring relationship can be crucial to the success of post-proposal students as they develop original research ideas and move toward greater independence and maturity. In addition, be aware that one of the most valuable contributions of the mentor is to help the student find a 'real job.' Several steps need to be executed even before the job search begins. Some of the key aspects of good mentoring practices include:

- *Be aware of the evolving relationship.* In long-term relationships, friendships form naturally; students can gradually become colleagues. At the same time, strive as a supervisor to be aware of the distinction between friendship and favoritism. You might need to remind a student – and yourself – that you need a degree of objectivity in giving fair evaluations. If you are unsure whether a relationship is 'too personal,' you are probably not alone. Consult with the department chair, your own mentor, or others you trust. You might have to increase the supervisor–student distance.

- *Setting career expectations.* This begins with a thorough review of students' experiences and goals. Help students establish their expectations and 'terms of employment.' Set a schedule for follow-up reviews at regular intervals. Career goals, which can change appreciably over time, should be a central topic of these discussions.

- *Establishing market credentials.* In addition to helping students carry out research, a supervisor has the obligation to help them with aspects like designing a good curriculum vitae, preparing teaching and research portfolios, rehearsing interviews, raising grant money, and learning about the current job market.

- *Introduction to the academic institutional environment.* Supervisors can help by making students aware of the nature and dynamics of academic institutional life – an obvious step that is often ignored. Encourage your department or institution to include doctoral students in faculty seminars, retreats, and meetings with speakers. Even through relatively simple mechanisms, such as luncheons and workshops with senior faculty, junior faculty can obtain needed guidance on career goals, ethical behavior, housing and financial issues, collaborative relationships, grant proposal writing, resource people, teaching policies, department politics, personal issues, and criteria for appointment, promotion, tenure, and salary discussions. These gatherings might also provide an opportunity to conduct rehearsal interviews.

One of the danger points in the PhD process in the United States occurs when the student moves from being a PhD student to being a PhD candidate. This is a stage following successful defense of the thesis research proposal and progress to completing the thesis itself. In many US settings at least, this is a stage typically reached after three or four years of preparatory work. And often it is at this stage, commonly referred to being ABD (All But Dissertation), that candidates will accept ABD teaching positions. They will leave the degree-granting environment to work as a member of faculty elsewhere. The lure of salary and the ability to leave the diminished status of PhD student behind is great. But there is, of course, a cost. Academic life is demanding and the transaction costs of getting established, preparing new courses and taking on service demands, along with settling in a new location, competes for available thesis completion time. There are as a result, many ABD faculty; those who were never able to complete the thesis in the allotted time. And it is not atypical for those who do finish to have been delayed a year or more as compared to their expected completion schedule at the time of proposal defense.

Not completing is a costly error. Some institutions void the faculty contract if the degree is not completed by an agreed upon date. The ABD faculty almost always forfeits salary. And there is a negative stigma attached to not finishing.

My own practice has been to encourage students to stay focused and complete the thesis before taking an academic position if at all possible. I have tried to secure funding if normal funding has been exhausted. But financial pressures may make this unrealistic. So at a minimum I have tried to assure that before the student leaves I have at least a complete first draft in hand.

I had a situation in which the student was nearly completed with a first draft but had not finished. He and his family had set a late summer moving date. The house was packed and the movers had loaded the truck. They were leaving their apartment in two days. He had a contract at his new university that provided a substantial bonus for completion by January 1. But it also provided a serious penalty if he did not complete within the year. And I 'knew' that if he left without a completed first draft, the likelihood of meeting either deadline was slim.

I struggled with what to do. Our mutual investment in his work was great and I felt it was at risk. So I took an uncharacteristically heavy handed approach and told the candidate and his wife that he could not leave until a draft was in hand. His wife was unhappy but they agreed. The family took up temporary residence in a hotel for a week and he finished the draft.

He defended his thesis three months later and met the terms of the bonus and contract. Using present value of annuity calculations it amounted to hundreds of thousands in career income for his family, because it increased his base salary for the life of his career. We have spoken often of this point in our relationship and he has thanked me for helping him choose to stay and finish the draft. But without this strong personal relationship, and my knowledge of his new job setting, I could not have intervened so directly.

- *Finding a position.* Encourage students who desire an academic position to determine the three or four universities that seem most appropriate for their interests and abilities. Use your own network of contacts to make personal calls to introduce the student, and suggest universities that best fit the student's needs and profile. Then, advise that the student call each contact and ask relevant questions: How many open positions do you have now? What qualifications are you seeking? What support is available? A face-to-face meeting with the Chair of the academic unit might be appropriate, as well as with former doctoral students who might now be members of the faculty at that university.

- *Following up after leaving.* As doctoral students graduate and become faculty members at this or other institutions, they are often left to fend for themselves amid the turmoil of professional and personal change: new courses to teach, unknown department politics, conflicting demands on one's time, an unfamiliar living environment. A good supervisor should help former students focus on their goals and understand the expectations and criteria for promotion at the new institution. Be sure that they understand timetables and deadlines, what is required for tenure, and exactly how new faculty are evaluated.

4.5 Conclusion

This chapter has explored the supervision relationship mainly from the supervisor's perspective while paying special attention to the emotional dimension. Supervision is an evolving process that is cumulative and expansive. Even though there is no single formula for good supervision, this chapter has described some key aspects that are useful throughout the process, including keeping in touch, setting regular deliverable deadlines, building networks, being a role model, and being approachable and available. Other aspects are useful, depending on the specific activity of the process. During the initiation of the doctoral program and proposal, key aspects of good supervision include assessing the student's potential, and accepting advisees, as well as helping the student assess the decision to pursue a doctoral program, conduct a research project, teach careful planning and use of time, and choose the right adviser. During the research and development activity, a good supervisor can help the student in choosing a research topic, choosing a committee, teaching careful planning to increase productivity, and facilitating professional growth, and mapping academic goals and course work. During the finalizing stage, the supervisor can help by making the student aware of the evolving relationship as the student grows to become a peer, and as the student moves on after completing the doctoral thesis. Key aspects of good supervision include helping the student in setting career expectations, establishing market credentials, introducing to the academic institutional environment, finding a position, and following up after leaving.

5

Focus on the Student

Duane Truex, Ramiro Montealegre,
David Avison and Cherie Long

5.1 Introduction

In Chapter 3 we look at the supervisor–student relationship and in Chapter 4 focus was placed on the supervisor. In this present chapter, we focus on the PhD student. It examines some of the main activities faced by students, paying particular attention to times when 'dangers' might be heightened and thus warrant careful consideration on the part of the supervisor. The role of the institution also plays an important part, and this is also discussed early in this chapter.

The PhD is a highly individualized and customized degree program, and there are various structures and models of assessment (see Part V). It is, therefore, not surprising that there are many models of interaction between the supervisor and doctoral candidate as well. They range from the very hands-on relationship of an apprentice and a craftsman, to one in which the student largely fends for him or herself. This has been explored in Chapter 3. The supervisor is a key figure in the candidate's academic life, no matter which end of this spectrum. But what are other aspects of the PhD candidate's experience? One of the factors contributing to thesis completion is the candidate's *emotional* health and maturity in the context of a set of pressures. These were also discussed in the context of the supervisor in Chapter 4.

Figure 4.1 (see page 78) also provides a graphic framework for this chapter's discussion. It suggests that the process of completing a PhD is embedded in a host of contexts, each of which is important in the student's individual journey. These contexts can be broken roughly into two types. The first we identify as generic pressures on the degree-granting institution and pressures on faculty supervisors. The second are those contextual characteristics, pressures, and motivations more specific to the individual student.

> The task of completing a PhD has been likened to a race in which the student is running a marathon rather than a sprint. It is a process requiring concerted effort over time and one requiring singular dedication. To run the marathon one needs a general race plan, but the student must also possess the ability to change the plan according to changing conditions. He or she also needs the support of more experienced guides as well as family and friends. Ultimately, however, it is the student who must dig deep into personal intellectual and emotional resources to finish the race. For this reason it has also been said of the PhD that it is an exercise in emotional as well as in intellectual stamina and maturity.

The structure of this chapter is as follows. We first identify some competing forces that play on many doctoral degree-granting institutions, on the supervisors and thereby impacting on the student's PhD experience. We also examine some of the environmental pressures on the student and suggest why it is important to monitor the student's emotional state during the PhD process. We then identify stereotypic points and events in the path to a PhD where these many stresses converge and may signal 'danger times' of which both student and supervisor should be aware. Finally, we provide recommendations to supervisors for dealing with these times and for maintaining an emotional balance in the process of PhD supervision, a process we call *holistic supervision.*

5.2 Balancing competing forces on institution, faculty and students

It would be easy and perhaps attractive to limit the discussions in this book to those dealing with the student's intellectual growth. After all, the honing of intellectual maturity, confidence, and capacity is certainly a critical factor in the successful completion of a PhD. All parties agree to this requirement of the PhD experience. But all parties – the degree granting institution itself, the faculty supervisor, and the student – exist in a complex setting in which competing demands and forces can either enhance or threaten the likelihood that a student will finish the PhD journey.

Institutional pressures

There are, of course, forces on PhD-granting institutions that may be culturally determined. However, a number of demands are so common as to warrant discussion. These include: the budgetary demands and the competition for resources; the rankings, reputation, and periodic re-evaluation of the institution; the competition for top talent; and the need to staff research centers, teach courses, and provide senior professors with research assistants. These issues are discussed below.

- ***Budgetary demands and the competition for resources.*** Rarely do we find a university that is not engaged in the perpetual hunt for funding. This process is institutionalized in some disciplines, notably the sciences and engineering, where it is expected that much research will be 'funded research.' The competition for these government and privately supported funds is intense. Success or failure can help to determine the fate of a research institute, a faculty member's tenure, an the individual doctoral student (see also Chapter 7).
- ***Institutional reputation and re-evaluation.*** Most degree-granting institutions now go through rigorous and competitive re-evaluation of some sort on a periodic basis. The outcome of these evaluations determines whether the institution will continue to be accredited or whether it will receive higher rankings of accreditation. In the United Kingdom, for instance, the research assessment exercise (RAE) leads to a ranking of programs and academic units, and is significant in determining how research monies are awarded (see Chapter 13). In the United States and elsewhere, business schools vie for *Association to Advance Collegiate Schools of Business (AACSB)* accreditation; this designation translates to competitive advantage in attracting top-flight students and members of faculty. In these institutional evaluations, careful attention is paid to the research productivity of members of faculty (for example, funding successes and publications), the quality of the PhD program, the attrition and completion rate of students in the PhD programs, the ultimate placement of completed PhD students, and

measures of success of these students in their own research programs. This all translates to institutional pressure on the PhD supervisors, and students.

- ***Staffing of research centers and courses.*** The funded and non-funded research activities of faculty require numbers of trained, low-cost, junior researchers. These junior colleagues are taught to collect and analyze data, prepare briefing reports and research drafts, conduct literature reviews and provide support for more senior and experienced faculty scholars. Like the guilds and artist studios of the Renaissance, the process of journeyman training is continued in PhD programs worldwide. PhD programs can provide such labor pools. Universities also need personnel to teach large sections of undergraduate level courses. Therefore, PhD students are qualified and low-cost alternative instructors. Cultural norms, institutional history or the requirements of accreditation may also determine who may be allowed to instruct students. Because PhD students are engaged in the process of research, are reading and current in developments in a given field and are working closely with more senior teacher scholars, they present an attractive instructional labor force (see also Chapter 6).

- ***Competition for research scholars.*** Given the budgetary constraints and the demands to produce published research, research-oriented universities are under pressure to attract and retain productive research faculty. PhD programs that provide research assistants and provide a source of staff for funded research programs are essential in this faculty recruitment and retention process.

Pressures on supervisors
Similar to those demands faced by the employing institution, members of faculty confront a host of pressures that impact the development of PhD programs. Most research faculty contend with the 'publish or perish dilemma.' Evaluations, tenure, promotion and, increasingly in the United States at least, post-tenure review, all weigh heavily in a faculty member's research output. In many settings, success in attracting grants and fellowships is deemed important as well. Faculty also face competing demands on their time for teaching; student advising; and service to departments, colleges, universities, and larger research communities. Access to competent PhD student support, provided by an active and robust PhD program, greatly aids faculty in managing these conflicting demands on time.

Conversely, serving as a PhD supervisor also makes a substantial claim on a member of faculty's time. It is essential, therefore, to arrive at a proper balance in the relationship and nature of the benefits to both the student and member of faculty. This subject was covered in Chapter 4.

Pressures on the students

Given the extraordinary demands on faculty resources, it is possible to forget the kinds of intellectual, social, economic and emotional pressures the PhD student faces as well. The pursuit of the PhD is an expensive proposition financially and emotionally for the student. There are the direct costs of tuition and living expenses which, in some parts of the world, may be substantial. There is also the opportunity cost of lost income as many students leave positions in industry to return to university. For those who have been engaged in successful careers elsewhere, there are the psychological costs of leaving rank and position behind as they return to the role of 'mere' student.

- *Financial pressures.* Given the budgetary pressures faced by universities, an increasing number of educational institutions may charge the student full fees. The student also has to cover living expenses. It is not unusual for a graduating PhD to be encumbered with large student loans. Even in those programs where the student is supported with tuition and fee reductions and living stipends, these grants rarely cover all costs. In any case, the opportunity costs associated with getting a PhD are substantial. Furthermore, these costs are usually higher the longer the student has been in the workforce. Thus, the PhD program often represents a substantial change in life-style and standard of living that, in turn, adds to other pressures.

- *Social pressures.* The role of members of faculty is generally misunderstood by the general public. The latter often assume, for example, that members of faculty work only the few hours spent in front of the class. But the role of the PhD student is even more misunderstood. Rarely do spouses, children, friends, and extended family have much idea what the PhD student is facing intellectually and emotionally. Indeed, it is likely that the student him or herself cannot anticipate the challenges ahead. The PhD is unlike any other degree. If friends and family judge the PhD student's intellectual journey by their own pursuit of lower degrees, then they misjudge the life of the PhD family member.

The incidence of marital and relationship break-up is high in the PhD student population. It is estimated that one-third of all close personal living relationships do not survive the completion to the degree. It is impossible to know how many people drop out of PhD programs to save or resurrect their relationship. But it is clear that such a program places many strains on relationships. This requires vigilance by both the student and his supervisor.

- *Existential crises.* The general societal lack of understanding of the experience faced by the student, coupled with increasing research demands on time and attention, become intense and at times for some students, unbearable. Many students are of mature age. They bring with them the experience of roles in industry where they have enjoyed some measure of prestige. The transition to being a 'lowly' doctoral student can be an extraordinary blow to the ego amid a seemingly unending set of challenges to the student's value system and self-esteem. Without social support systems, the student faces a very difficult time. When coupled with the epistemological and ontological challenges that the student must weather, it is typical to find the student facing one or more existential challenges in the course of the degree.

5.3 The student's emotional health and growth

The aforementioned pressures on faculty and programs are well recognized. The pressures on the student, however, are often overlooked by institutions and advisors when designing and running PhD programs. It is therefore important to give greater consideration to the emotional health and emotional maturity of the student. As suggested above, the PhD often represents a period of extreme change in a person's life, including changes in values, thought processes, world view, self-esteem, and personal preferences. Furthermore, our own experiences indicate that the critical emotional dimension of the PhD journey is not sufficiently recognized nor addressed.

What do we mean by 'emotional maturity' and why do we believe this to be the case? We will define emotional maturity as the capacity, at any given time, to tolerate and adjust to the demands and pressures placed on the student from his or her environment. Emotional health is defined as the matching of appropriate and balanced responses to the mixture of demands and challenges at the time. These are somewhat focused and ephemeral definitions. After all, there can be little precision in anticipating the limitless range of life's pressures set before a student from family, economic conditions, teaching, and research. However, there is a universally shared experience in the process of acquiring a PhD and this is the transformative nature of the process. People come out of the process different than when they started the degree. The degree of transformation varies of course, but values, beliefs, and relationships are challenged in the process. Some social or familial systems mature and grow as a result, while others cannot take this constant stress and subsequently fail.

The PhD experience is characterized by a great deal of personal change. Some candidates do not weather these changes well. Divorce rates are high and degree completion rates are very low in many settings. This is partially explained by the degree of emotional support required and not provided to many candidates.

> A PhD candidate at the University of California, Berkeley, after 11 years of research for a PhD, was failed, took a ballpeen hammer to the head of his advisor and killed him. After eight years in prison he was offered parole. But a requirement of that offer was that he should recant his act. Parole was denied when he replied that in the same circumstances he would do the same thing all over again!
>
> In Canada a disaffected candidate entered the dean's office, shotgun in hand, and killed a number of administrative staff and students.
>
> More recently in Cleveland, an ex-student shot several staff, killing one. The 'trigger event' was the erasure of research files from the server.

In moments of despair, some students in mid program have taken their own lives, leaving families in great difficulty. Faculty and friends in contact with the student often had some idea that the student might be in crisis. But without a kind of 'early warning system,' the signs were missed until it was too late.

We are concerned that the supervision process is not taking into account the extreme pressures placed on our students. There may be warning signs and discernable stages in which these pressures build and can be dealt with. These signs, however, may not be seen or may be ignored by those charged with shepherding the students through the PhD experience.

Next, we describe several stages that are common to many PhD students and contribute to the emotional and intellectual stresses that challenge the student. Finally, we identify stereotypic points and events at which these stresses converge, perhaps signaling 'danger times' of which the advisor should be aware.

5.4 Emotional stages of the PhD journey

Figure 5.1 identifies stages of emotional events that we have seen in our collective supervision experience. While the figure suggests a linear series of emotional states, it may be somewhat misleading, for though many students seem to experience a pattern similar to that shown in the figure, some of these states may appear at different times in a student's program. The figure represents an approximation; not all students are certain to experience the full range. However, the set of events is sufficiently robust that it is generally representative. More importantly, we think the figure has some diagnostic benefit in reminding supervisors of certain delicate and critical points, such that the supervisor may be especially attentive to the student's emotional health at these times.

We will briefly describe each of the stages and point out those we consider most 'dangerous.' Those states that concern us the most are those when the student is at a psychological low, while at the same time milestone

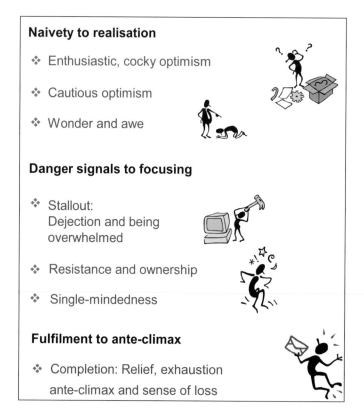

Figure 5.1 *Emotional stages in the PhD process*

events in the PhD experience are occurring. This combination, on top of personal life challenges, could bring the student to a 'danger point.' It is at these moments that the supervisor needs to be particularly vigilant and may at times need to intervene in the student's life. These stages and possible supervisor roles are described below.

- *Enthusiastic cocky optimism.* In this stage the student has entered the program fresh with enthusiasm and self-assuredness born of past success in academe and industry. The idea that led him or her to decide to begin this journey is fresh in his or her mind and there is excitement in the new endeavor. This is often when the student sees the prospect of academic life to be particularly intriguing and may feel it to be a 'calling.' Although the motivations for beginning a PhD are complex and varied in our experience, students approach the degree with the expectation that they will succeed.
- *Cautious optimism.* During this stage the realities of a return to the role of student and the demands of the intellectual and conceptual work load begin to impact on the student. As the requirements of the journey begin to be laid out in more explicit terms, such as mastery of the literature, additional courses to take and deadlines and milestones to complete, the student often begins to encounter or formulate more questions than he or she can answer. Thus the unabashed enthusiasm of stage one becomes tempered with caution and, perhaps, self-doubt. When this occurs it is often necessary to have a frank and open discussion with the student to air these concerns and assure the student that they are concerns that are common to many.
- *Wonder and awe.* At this stage the initial shock of the transition has been replaced with a growing awareness of how much the student does not know. There may be growing awareness of the magnitude of the challenges to follow. This is a time when supervisors are probably still held in high esteem.

    The search for a thesis topic may have begun by this time, or the student may still be completing coursework (if required), and it is not atypical to find students re-evaluating their initial decision at this stage. The realization often hits home that the PhD experience is really quite unlike previous degree programs that the student may have experienced. Some programs allow for a graceful exit strategy at this time. For instance many US programs, by virtue of year one and year two qualifying exams, encourage this self-examination phase. Performance may be judged as good or as not up to standard by the evaluating body and by the student alike. Some students set standards for themselves that are unrealistic. Thus an encounter with the types of intellectual evaluation typical of the PhD program is a shock to them. Poor performance in any of these evaluation milestones may cause a crisis for the student. Many students are accustomed to prior academic or business success and may have a difficult time accepting the kind of evaluation and criticism that accompanies these milestone tests. This is one of the stages when the astute PhD supervisor keeps a close eye on the student and tries to measure the student's emotional health as well as intellectual progress.

In one institution where the information systems department had trained PhD candidates for more than twenty-five years, the program had adopted a two-stage process for evaluating the progress of the PhD students before allowing them to proceed to the formal proposal development process. The first evaluation occurs at the end of the first full year in the program and involves interviews with the members of faculty working with the student and appraisal of progress to date. The second stage of evaluation includes formal written and oral examinations designed to test the student's mastery of the discipline and of various formal research methods. There are three outcomes of each stage in the evaluation process: fail, pass or conditional pass upon completion of remedial work and re-examination. The student is, however, allowed only one conditional pass. There is no provision for a third try. The system is designed to focus student's attention and to expedite the process so that students do not languish in a kind of PhD purgatory for years. But it also has the effect of putting considerable pressure on the students.

I recall one instance when four students were experiencing the second of the two evaluations. All students were approaching the evaluation for the first time. At the end of the exams two were passed to the next stage, one was counseled out of the program, and a third was given a conditional pass with instructions for remedial work and a deadline by which to retake the exam.

The program had about 20 active PhD students, many of whom had become good friends. The failure of one colleague was quite distressing to the PhD cohort. And the person receiving the conditional pass took the failure of his friend and his own failure to pass unconditionally very badly. This student had been a professional engineer manager with two previous degrees in hand before entering our program. He had been very successful academically and professionally. He was not, in short, used to being adjudged, as he put it, inadequate. He felt humiliated and as a result was on the verge of withdrawing from the PhD program. Only active intervention by key faculty and PhD student friends convinced him that a conditional pass was not a failure, rather that it was a kind of weather gauge allowing him to adjust and help guarantee reaching the desired destination, even though it might now take a bit longer than planned.

- ***Stall out.*** This is a phase of dejection and a feeling of being overwhelmed. There comes a point when the student may find it 'all too much', when the intellectual isolation is bearing down excessively. In our experience this often occurs after the thesis topic has been identified, and in US schools at least, defended. At this stage the student's role begins to change from that of trainee to that of an independent scholar. Knowledge creation is a demanding challenge, and the dissertation research stage is typically the first time the student has had to face these challenges independently.

At some point things may not go well: there is an insufficient sample size, research subjects are uncooperative, the study site shuts down, a supervisor or colleague leaves the school, political climates change in the field site, the experiments go awry, technology won't cooperate. This often follows a period of hard work and, perhaps, social isolation, perhaps with personal tension at home. The student may be working against self imposed or institutionally imposed deadlines including the termination of funding. Hence it is a stage when there are many pressures.

This is perhaps the most critical point in the whole of the PhD. It is a time that the astute supervisor needs to anticipate and must be extremely attentive to the student's emotional health. If the student does not make it past this stage, the dissertation may go unfinished, producing simply another ABD (all but dissertation) outcome. In more extreme cases when the pressures from several fronts peak at once, it may end in more drastic consequences. Far too many student suicides have occurred to warrant this cautionary note. It is wise for supervisors to have systems in place to monitor students during key and critical phases of the research activity. Some larger programs have formal 'buddy' systems. In other instances supervisors make it a point to inquire about the student's life in regularly scheduled meetings. But this is a delicate matter, with issues of privacy and confidentiality important.

- *Resistance and ownership.* There is another key event during the preparation of the dissertation, perhaps best described as the point where the student has taken ownership of the topic, and becomes the expert. He or she is the person on top of the literature and is the only person truly versed in the subtleties and particulars of this aspect of knowledge creation. At this point roles may shift; with the student becoming more independent and more focused.

The supervisor's role remains critical however. Even though the student is better versed in the research area, it is the supervisor's role to keep the scope of the thesis to reasonable and manageable levels. The supervisor's role may also be to remind the student that despite his or her narrowing focus, other aspects of life need to be attended to as well. The astute supervisor may help by ensuring that the student sees the necessity of maintaining a healthy balance in work life and social relationships.

- ***Single mindedness.*** At some point the student comes to the conclusion that the thesis is done. It is a remarkable transition where the student has become junior colleague. He or she is convinced that the process has run its course, the research is sufficient and that the thesis needs to be read and evaluated as completed work. Most supervisors know this experience and await it with proud anticipation. But it too presents challenges to the student and to the supervisor. There are occasions when the student's assessment of 'sufficient completion for a defense' and the supervisor's assessment differ. In settings where a dissertation proposal defense has yielded a formal document describing what will be sufficient for the dissertation research, the candidate or advisor may be able to use this document as an arbiter of differences. Occasionally a supervisor may have difficulty in 'letting go' and in seeing that enough is indeed enough. Here it is helpful to have others to help arbitrate differences. Most students understand, however, that to complete the final hurdle it is essential to have the agreement of the supervisor. The advisor is obligated to be reasonably certain that the document presented for dissertation defense is very likely to pass, either wholly or with revisions. Thus, the student and supervisor must work out differences before the defense proceeds.

- ***Completion.*** This stage is frequently marked by exhilaration followed by relief, exhaustion, anti-climax and a sense of loss. A successful defense is truly an exciting and celebratory experience. It is often one accompanied by *bona fide* celebrations. But there is a downside born of exhaustion and a long, concentrated push to this end goal. It can be an anti-climax, where some of the meaning has left the new PhD's life. Thus, even after a successful dissertation defense, there remains a role for the supervisor. This role may involve helping the new colleague refocus by completing thesis revisions and write papers related to the dissertation. In other words, the supervisor's role is to help the new PhD's transition into a successful post-doctoral life.

5.5 Holistic supervising

Because of the concerns expressed above, we recommend 'holistic supervising'; that is, tending to the needs of the whole person, and we again refer the reader to Figure 4.1. Holistic advising can be defined as:

monitoring and considering the student's emotional and intellectual state, in addition to being aware of and appraising the student's motivations, capabilities, and scholarly achievements, such that the advisor and institution are able to access and interact with the student in the most appropriate way befitting the circumstances.

In this chapter we have concentrated on the PhD student part of the supervisor–student relationship. However, we also looked at pressures on the institution: budgetary demands and competition for resources, institutional reputation and evaluation, staffing issues, and competition for research scholars. We discussed the many pressures on the PhD student including financial, social and existential pressures. We looked at an archetypical 'life history' of a PhD as the progression is made from naivety to realization (enthusiastic and cocky optimism, cautious optimism and wonder and awe), danger signals to focusing (stallout, dejection and being overwhelmed, resistance and ownership, and single-mindedness) through to fulfillment and anti-climax (completion and relief and exhaustion through to anti-climax and sense of loss). Of course not all students will pass through each of these stages and not all in this sequence. Indeed, there may be several iterations as many students make more 'jumpy' progress. However, this life history describing the emotional stages of the PhD process does have some truth based on the experiences of our students.

Part III:
Social and Practical Issues

This third part focuses on a number of important social and practical issues. Almost all students will have some other major commitment apart from research. In Chapter 6 Björn Lundell, Jan Pries-Heje and Cathy Urquhart discuss the issues relating to students doing a PhD and something else, whether it is teaching, working in industry or looking after a family. Chapter 7 by Frantz Rowe and Jan Pries-Heje covers funding. Although not normally an academic concern, financial issues often seem important throughout the process, and sometimes they are an overarching concern. Most of the issues discussed in Part III are concerned to a greater or lesser extent with ethical values and in Chapter 8 Robert Davison introduces this sensitive but important topic. Chapter 9 of Anita Greenhill and Lynette Kvasny looks at gender issues 'one of the most important unspoken aspects of forging a relationship between supervisor and student.' Chapter 10 by David Wilson on sexual orientation looks in particular at gay students and supervisors. In Chapter 11, David Avison, Muhammadou Kah, Jainaba Kah and Abimbola Soriyan discuss various diverse cultures existing in a supervisor–student relationship, when undertaking a PhD in a different country, language and cultural differences, racial issues, and the particular problems of students studying in developing countries.

If you are a supervisor: do you have part-time students? If you do, how do they cope with pressure from the research and other demands? Are you supporting them? Use chapter 6 as a checklist to avoid ignoring important issues in relation to your part-timers. Can you help resolve conflicts for those students doing their research in practice, as these will inevitably occur? Consider carrying out a stakeholder analysis together with your PhD student.

Take a look at Chapter 7. What funding sources for PhD students do you have available? Does your university have a central resource to give support on funding issues? What influence do you have on who gets what? Have you considered industry and government as well as university sources? Are you aware that too much funding from teaching (and associated load) may inhibit research?

Reflect on the ethical issues concerning joint publications with students that Robert Davison raises in Chapter 8. Where do you stand? How involved do you get with your students' personal issues that impinge on research? Does it involve some risk element?

Regarding gender issues, do you treat male and female students differently? Think about the requirements of a supervisor as depicted in Section 9.2. Do you follow these suggestions? Are you sympathetic to students who need to juggle the demands of children and research and therefore can only see you or attend courses at certain times? How would you react to your student's 'coming out'? Do you follow the advice to supervisors given as Section 10.2? How do you and your university support students from other countries or who are minorities in some way? Read Chapter 11 and put yourself in the place of these students. What would it be like to have a PhD student from a developing country? Do you celebrate diversity, as it enriches the supervisory experience?

If you are a PhD student: Chapter 6 provides support to help you cope with pressures from all your commitments. Do you compartmentalize your time well? Do you involve your supervisor in your personal life in any way?

If you are a potential PhD student then scan Chapter 7 to consider possible sources of funding. Have you harvested them all? Industry, government and university are possible sources. What particular funds are available in your country? Are you aware of the dangers of too much teaching, even if it does mean financial support?

Have you published with your supervisor or do you expect to? Do you resent publishing with your supervisor? Chapter 8 discusses some of the issues. Use the chapter to decide on what is reasonable.

How well do you and your supervisor follow the advice at the end of the concluding section of Chapter 9 on gender differences? Do you feel that you are not being treated equally because of your gender? Are you getting 'gender sensitive supervision'? Gay or lesbian: does it matter for a PhD? What if your supervisor is different from you? Does it have an influence? How do you cope with it? Chapter 10 may be an inspiration for this discussion. Read Chapter 11. What efforts do *you* make to put your other minority colleagues at ease?

6

Serving Two Masters

Björn Lundell, Cathy Urquhart and Jan Pries-Heje

6.1 Introduction

This chapter is dedicated to the problems that may arise when PhD research has to share priority with other things in the student's life. We have called the chapter *serving two masters*. One master is the research itself, but there will be other pressures demanding of the student's time. The other master may well be practice, either as the study object or, alternatively, as a source of income or funding. But the other master might be teaching or family, and the second part of the chapter discusses issues related to being a part-time PhD student. The first part of the chapter discusses tensions between academia and practice.

6.2 Interaction between academia and practice

Many PhD students engage in field research involving practice. This might consist of interactions with representatives from external organizations. Funding for the project may come wholly or partly from an external organization. Therefore it is important both as a PhD supervisor and as a PhD student to consider the relationship between research and practice, because the involvement of practice, especially if the relationship involves financing, rarely comes without expectations. Practitioners are likely to be looking for pragmatic goals, whereas the PhD student is hoping to achieve some research goals thereby building the foundation for an academic career. There is therefore a built-in tension between the academic environment and practice.

As the discipline of information systems is a highly applied one, it is common for PhD students to engage in field research involving external organizations. The most frequent interaction between research and practice is the study of practice in one or several organizations to identify problems or best practice. The data may be used to develop theory and models. Another frequent interaction concerns the testing of models and theory. This can be done as quantitative positivist research (discussed in Chapter 14) focusing on quantitative validation in some form. Alternatively, it may be qualitative research (discussed in Chapter 15), for example, where practice is studied as a case study or where theory is tested and refined using action research.

Another interaction is a more indirect one. Research often results in publications. Papers in international journals and presentations at international conferences are attractive outcomes for a PhD student, but the readership of most of these outlets is mainly academic (the *Communications of the ACM* and professional society journals are exceptions). Therefore the interaction with practice in this case is often indirect. On the other hand, a book on an IS topic might be read by non-academics, and course books may impact on practice, particularly via practitioner-oriented courses such as an MBA.

Since 1985 undergraduate students at the Copenhagen Business School have been trained in the Multiview methodology (Avison & Wood-Harper, 1990) for the development of information systems. In 2000, Karlheinz Kautz and Jan Pries-Heje undertook a study of its impact on practice. Questionnaires were sent out to 572 graduates. 16% answered that they use or have used the Multiview methodology. The remainder was non-adopters. Several reasons for non-adoption were given:
1   The methodology was not relevant due to the fact that the respondents were not working within systems development.

> 2   It was perceived as not fitting the kind of systems the respondents were developing.
> 3   It was perceived as too academic, long-winded, complicated and time-consuming.
> However, one crucial thing was adopted broadly, namely the philosophy embedded into the basic principles of the methodology – the 'Weltanschauung' as it was named in the Multiview methodology. It seems that students are influenced, at least a little, by research frameworks discussed in class when they are in practice.

In Figure 6.1 we have tried to picture the research processes where IS practice most often becomes involved. The person top centre of Figure 6.1 symbolizes the PhD student. One important consideration in relation to practice is whether to develop normative models and theory or do more descriptive research. Often normative models and theory are immediately useful to practice when compared to descriptive models and theory. Nevertheless, it is possible to formulate the research question in ways that increases relevance (see, for example, Robey and Markus, 1998).

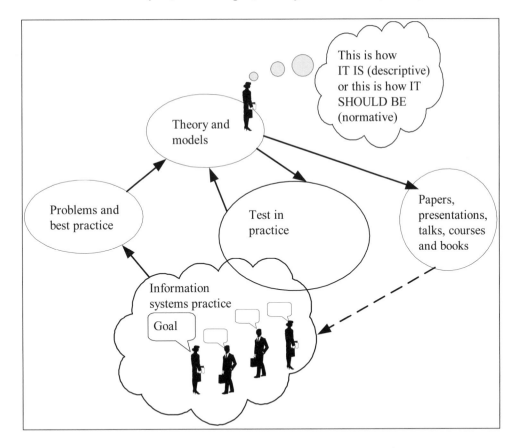

Figure 6.1 *Research processes where practice becomes involved*

6.3 Differences in goals

When PhD students engage or cooperate with practice, or receive funding from external practice-related sources, there are inherent tensions built into that arrangement. These tensions are exacerbated if the PhD student is doing research part-time or in his or her own working environment. This is often the case for industrial PhD students (see later in the chapter). It is important for a PhD student to consider potential tensions which may occur between different goals in a PhD project as they may have a significant influence on progress and likelihood of success. Figure 6.2 shows these potential tensions. The figure is used as a basis for discussion in the following sub-sections. The figure also shows that there are at least two potential tensions between the different goals (the company's goal, the goal of the project and the student's research goals). These tensions need to be acknowledged and controlled during the progress of the three related processes.

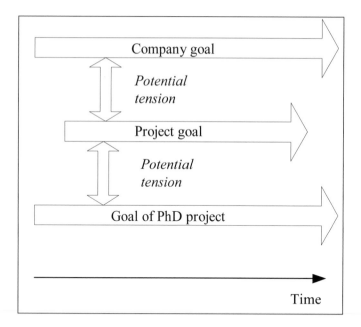

Figure 6.2 *Potential tensions between different goals in PhD projects involving practice*

6.4 Different goals

When a PhD student conducts research in an organization, the student needs to distinguish clearly between the goals of his or her own PhD project, and the goals of others involved. For some PhD projects, a significant part of the student's time will be spent in the field (perhaps in a single organization), whereas in others, the student may only conduct a small study in the field, perhaps undertaking a few interviews with practitioners. However, irrespective of the extent of engagement in the field, it is important that the student clearly distinguishes between the goals of his or her own PhD project, and the motivations and goals of the other stakeholders (and organizations) involved.

Initially this PhD project started off without very precise goals, and the whole process was subject to some 'drift' in scope and focus. However, in reporting from the PhD project the goal had evolved into a much more focused thesis statement:

In this thesis we:

1   *Identify problems with current techniques for CASE-tool evaluation, and in particular establish a lack of method support for certain aspects of an evaluation activity. Specifically, there are strategic weaknesses in available method support for aspects of initiating and structuring a CASE-tool evaluation activity. We recognize the importance of context-dependency when addressing CASE-tool evaluation within a specific IS development organization.*

2   *Present and analyze a method which addresses all of the above within the specific context of CASE tool evaluation within a given IS development organization.*

The first part was addressed through a literature analysis and there was no field-based research involved here. The second part was addressed by means of field studies. As the goal of this research involved an 'analysis' of the method presented, and as that analysis was to be carried out in an 'organization,' it naturally led the PhD student into practice. Consequently, in conducting this field-based research, the method was developed, analyzed and refined using field studies, which were conducted in IS development organizations. In this process, the ideas embodied in Figure 6.2 were found to be very useful for stimulating an open discussion concerning goals with all stakeholders involved.

In order that the student can control his or her project, he or she needs to be fully aware of potential tensions between all the different goals of all stakeholders involved. Without such an understanding, there may be complications throughout the project since different actors will act according to their own goals, which may be very different from the PhD student's goals in the project. It is therefore important, quite early in a PhD project, to resolve any such differences, and thereby have a chance of resolving any potential problem that may be caused by misunderstandings and differences in perceptions about goals.

Nikolaj was hired as a PhD researcher in a large 4.5 million Euro project. About 25 people were actively involved in the project aimed at developing a model for 'improving the ability to improve' a software developing organization. As a basis for this model, it was decided that each of four participating companies should find two successful and two failing projects. Nikolaj organized four to five interviews in each of 16 projects provided. He then started an analysis using grounded theory techniques. This analysis was time consuming. However, before the analysis really had taken off, some of the participating companies grew impatient. They insisted that a prototype of the final model was built and tested. At this point the rigorous analysis of the data gathered could have stopped *due to opposing goals* of the project. However, the supervisor stepped in and reorganized the work in the project so that Nikolaj could continue his data analysis while the companies got their pilot test of a model at the same time.

Avison et al. (2001) discuss the issue of control in action research. However, the framework they develop is also useful in uncovering possible tensions for a PhD student in an industrial setting. Their control framework has three dimensions:

1   Procedures for initiating an action research project
2   Procedures for determining authority within the project
3   Degree of formalization.

Academic-industry cooperation can be initiated from either side or together. The 'classic genesis of action research' is when someone in industry has a problem they cannot solve and turns towards academia to solve it. This classic approach will of course come with a lot of expectations, typically having the problem solved. Tension can then arise if the researcher does not find the concrete problem sufficiently interesting or research oriented. If the researcher, on the other hand, initiates the cooperation then problems might arise if too many promises have been made during the initiation. As a supervisor it may be of importance to join the PhD student in visiting the industrial partner and making sure that expectations are instilled correctly.

Authority is about 'who is really in charge of the research project.' For example, this person will make decisions about changing the problem scope. If a model or theory is developed, it is this person who will decide how to test it or make it operational. If the PhD student or supervisor has no decision authority, it may ruin the research. On the other hand people in industry are often reluctant to hand over authority about how to run things. So the issue of authority is another source of tension.

The degree of formalization relates to how much is written down and formalized about the cooperation. This ranges from an informal oral agreement to a long legally binding contract. As a PhD student it is recommend to have 'something in writing,' for example on what and how you can publish results. It does not have to be in the form of a legal contract; indeed if you have to involve lawyers and legal negotiations then the PhD research is likely to be difficult.

> In a large research project involving several companies and more than one PhD student tensions arose when the issue of publishing came up for discussion. The companies wanted to be able to veto what could be published. This was of course not satisfactory for the PhD students. Imagine that they had studied and followed something for 6-8 months in a company and then having the company vetoing their publications.
>
> After lengthy negotiations a compromise was reached. The PhD students had the right to publish their findings. However, the companies had the right to see the analysis and findings before they were published, and they could veto or 'correct' lines or paragraphs that were 'incorrect' from their perspective. Furthermore it was decided that the companies could ask to be anonymous. It was also agreed that the companies should have papers at the same time they were submitted for blind review at a conference or for a journal. This ensured that no 'incorrect' information was ever made public.

Avison et al. (2001) recommends that in action research, researchers and their industry counterparts actively and collaboratively determine the three types of control structures in the early stages of a research project. This also applies in other research between academia and industry.

The issue of potential impacts and influences implied from external funding agencies will not be explicitly discussed here, even though it is an important background factor, as it is covered elsewhere (Chapter 7). But the problem of potential tensions may be exasperated by funding issues. Ultimately, this background factor of funding may also be regarded as a 'constraint' on what kinds of goals a PhD student may address in a PhD project.

6.5 Stakeholder analysis – A tool for handling differences in goals

Stakeholder analysis is often recommended as a technique for information systems project managers. However, it can also be a valuable tool for coping with the tensions of a PhD project. This section presents a model that can be used for identifying and handling opposing goals and other potential conflicts.

A stakeholder is a person, group or organization which has an interest in the PhD project. To get an overview of the stakeholders in your research project, stakeholder analysis should be carried out. The top row of Table 6.1 shows the basic questions to answer in this stakeholder analysis. In Table 6.1 only three stakeholders are mentioned. There may well be many others. For example, there can be more than one industrial partner. In some cases a PhD can also have more than one supervisor. So the first activity in using Table 6.1 is to identify stakeholders, evaluate their importance, and decide on how to handle the most important ones.

In deciding how to handle the stakeholders, the four questions given horizontally in Table 6.1 are valuable:

1   Consider what outcome they each expect
2   Consider what and how each stakeholder can contribute (providing a positive angle)
3   What, formally, is their goal?
4   What will really make them happy?

As an example of the difference between questions 3 and 4, Table 6.1 shows how the stakeholder analysis could look for a large 4.5 million Euro research project aimed at developing a model for 'improving the ability to improve' that might be used in a software developing organization.

Table 6.1 *A stakeholder analysis identifying potential tensions*

	What is the expected outcome?	What can they contribute?	What do they say is their goal?	What will make the stakeholder happy?
PhD supervisor	Interesting research plus the honor of supervising a PhD	Experience and management of industrial partner	Building a model of the ability to improve	That papers on the model can be published in top journals
PhD student	The award of PhD	Time and dedicated work	To write a thesis within the allocated 3 years	If the thesis is good, then it can be a 'ticket' to a research career
Industrial partner	A model that can be used to improve the ability to improve	Practice	Actually to improve the ability	Fast improvement – the faster the better

6.6 Tensions between goals

As a basis for discussing the complexity of goals and tensions in a PhD project, we have found Table 6.1 to be useful, illustrating as it does the tension between student goals and the project goal, and also the tension between the organization and the project goal. It is obviously useful as a basis for discussions between a supervisor and a PhD student when initiating the PhD research project, but it can also be used as a basis for discussions with representatives from practice.

There may be different kinds of tension in a project, indeed without them the potential of a project with practice is likely to be greatly reduced because:

- If there is no tension between the project's goal and the company's commercial goal, we have a situation which typically faces a consultant. There is limited scope for doing a PhD project where the project conforms entirely to the commercial goal of the company.
- If there is no tension between the project's goal and the goal of the PhD process, we have a situation where the PhD student has total control over the goal of the project, a situation which typically faces a PhD student undertaking an internally funded PhD project. However, for work with a company, it would be much more difficult for a student to uphold a genuine interest from organizations and practitioners.

Consequently, for an applied field such as information systems, it may be very difficult to pursue a good applied project if there are no tensions, as genuine interest and engagement in the project from companies can be expected to be very limited. Therefore, in this case the issue is not so much one of eliminating the tensions, but rather keeping them under control. From our own experience, we would observe that it is important for both students and company representatives to be aware of these tensions, and have ongoing discussions throughout the project in order to minimize the risk for the project.

It is also important to recognize that it is likely that different people will have very different motivations for engaging in the project, since they all have their own individual goals. This is not surprising since a PhD project is to a large extent an individual endeavor, whereas a bigger research project is usually undertaken by a team. Such a project will often involve several PhD students and other non-academic stakeholders, where a student has his or her own goal. For the PhD student, a project like this may be seen as a *means* for conducting empirical work and thereby a necessary prerequisite for the fulfillment of the goal of the PhD project. Conversely, for a company representative, the project may be seen as a *means* for conducting empirical work (with academia), which contributes to the fulfillment of a company goal.

6.7 On the complexity of managing tensions

Sometimes a PhD project is supervised by more than one person and this adds further complexity. This may be particularly complex in situations where there may be several PhD students involved in a field-based project. Several other researchers and other stakeholders may be involved, and it may be that the project is led by a different researcher to that of the supervisor. Sometimes the supervisor of a specific PhD project is not even involved in the field-based project, which consequently increases the likelihood of further tensions. In such situations, it is even more important to actively consider what can be done to minimize tensions that may impinge negatively on the progress of both the field-based project and the PhD project.

Another aspect which adds to this complexity relates to the time dimension for the project. As expectations and interests amongst people involved will change over time; so will the extent of each tension in the project. In all projects, as stakeholders learn and reflect on their experiences, they will develop new ideas which may change their view on the goals. Where these new ideas go in different directions, it can be particularly difficult. It is therefore important to consider goal perceptions actively throughout the whole process of a project, and not only at its initiation. Otherwise, there is a risk that increasing tensions will 'creep up,' affecting involved stakeholders negatively in the long run.

Furthermore, various demands from an external party (whether explicitly or implicitly expressed), may also impinge negatively on a student's research process, perhaps by imposing 'constraints' on what can and cannot be done in (and published from) the process. This may be especially significant for students with a research question that naturally leads to a qualitative research method, as the process in such situations typically cannot be pre-planned, or at least not in any detail.

In the following, we look at some examples from some situations that illustrate the different tensions and perceptions on goals.

This example stems from an organizational project where a method (here referred to as 'method X') was to be applied in an organizational setting, to study its use in practice. Thus the PhD was driven by the company goal of applying method X. A basic idea of the project was to evaluate if method X could be used in a scenario for which it had not been originally designed. The (primary) aim and its two related objectives in this project eventually became:

Evaluate an application of method X in a post-usage scenario, including issues of transfer.
Objective 1: How to use method X in a post-usage scenario.

Objective 2: How to transfer the method to the organization where the application is evaluated.

Even before this project started, a researcher and company representatives discussed ideas which led to this project. All participants felt that Figure 6.2 and Table 6.1 facilitated an open discussion about different goals and underlying motivations for initiating a joint project. In particular, this strategy was well received by management in the company, and by talking explicitly about different goals and potential tensions it was seen as a good way to 'test' whether there was scope for a joint project.

The overall project goal is clearly a synthesis between different interests. It embodies elements from both the student's and the company's goals, and hence there is scope for tension. From the student's perspective, the initial motivation was a desire to learn about method X and to see if it could be applied in a company, under the given organizational conditions. In that sense, the student saw a method application in the field as an obvious activity right from the start of the project. From the company's perspective, there was an interest at the early stage of this project to learn more about the method, and by means of a joint project it was seen as a good way to explore its potential. This interest was eventually formulated as 'objective 1' by the student, and it was addressed by means of an application of the method within the company. It should be noted that the formulation of the first objective colored the researcher's desire to test a specific method's applicability in new circumstances, but that this was secondary to the company. What the company wanted to explore was its potential (regardless of its origin).

The second objective involved various activities to do with the 'transfer' of the method. As there was a genuine interest from stakeholders within the company to explore the method and its potential for use within their own company, it necessitated that such aspects became part of the study.

In retrospect, it might appear that without a focus on the second objective, the student would have had a much easier task. However, without that, the company might not have been interested in the study at all. Since the first objective is heavily field-based and necessitated access to stakeholders in an organization, such broadening of goals was seen to be highly appropriate by all stakeholders involved. As the different goals and potential tensions were discussed throughout the project, the overall feasibility of the student's task was more easily envisaged beforehand to avoid unpleasant surprises later in the project.

6.8 The part-time experience

The second part of the chapter is dedicated to exploring the particular concerns of part-time PhD students, who may include those working in industry in the above arrangement. Part-time students generally are very common in the field of information systems, particularly outside the United States. An acute shortage of IS doctorates in the US (Freeman et al., 2000) may well increase the numbers of part-time students in that part of the world as well.

The main driver of the part-time PhD seems to be the high salaries offered to graduates in IT and the high demand for teaching in this area, which make it less likely that students will go straight into postgraduate study on a full-time basis. Thus, the typical PhD student in IS, and not atypical as might have been assumed, is a mature entrant to the program; who has an external income; from a company or university; and carries out the PhD part-time. Other research students opt for part-time study because of family commitments.

Quite often the PhD students are academic colleagues of ours. For instance, in a survey conducted in Australia in 1998 there were 99 part-time IS PhD enrolments in the 23 Australian universities (Keen, 1999). A total of 58, or 59% of these, were part-time PhD students in IS who were also employed as academic staff.

Taking a PhD part-time creates particular challenges for students and supervisors alike, and we describe the experience and suggest strategies for both students and supervisors. Little beyond anecdotal information is known about the experiences of part-time PhD students. An Australia-wide Internet survey of part-time PhD students (Urquhart, 1999) yielded 20 detailed and rich responses about the part-time PhD experience for IS academics. We are using responses from this survey to support the arguments made in this section. Respondents were asked the questions given in Figure 6.3. Three major issues were revealed: support, conflict and isolation. Although these issues are intertwined, we will look at them separately.

---

1 Do you (did you) find your department/school supportive of part-time PhDs?
2 Do you (did you) get any special time release arrangements for your PhD, other than the normal time allocation for research also given to those with PhDs?
3 What strategies do you (did you) find helpful in getting time to do the PhD?
4 What personal support do you (did you) have in doing your PhD?
5 How do you think the situation for those doing part-time PhDs could be improved?
6 Do you have any comments on how part-time PhDs can best be supervised?

Figure 6.3 *Internet survey of part-time PhD students*

Conflict (between obligations)

Conflicting priorities are a source of stress and the PhD researcher can suffer greatly under this stress. There are many conflicts that become apparent in part time research. Two of the most critical are those between research and teaching and research and family.

Ryan (1999) talks about the high degree of role conflict between the need to do well in a PhD program and the graduate teaching assistant role. Teaching concerns are more immediate. This could be the first time that the researcher gives a course and he or she may not be a very experienced teacher, so the pressures and the work are necessary compounded.

As a junior colleague points out: 'I have to teach two courses to survive financially. Reading needs to be done, content needs to be decided and slides have to be produced before the class, and students need to be tutored and marking needs to be done afterwards. The next class is this week and the PhD needs to be handed in much later in the year. It is obvious which gets the priority.'

One respondent said that 'Essentially you are forced to make sacrifices. The emotional issues associated with this are the problem. To an extent, your teaching suffers and thus your students suffer' and another respondent said that 'It is the teaching, marking ... [long list of activities] ... that constantly interrupt your PhD. You are frowned on if you miss these activities; you are also frowned on if you don't keep up with your PhD. Which do you choose?'

At the IT University in Copenhagen PhD students are given a reasonably good salary for three years. However, as part of the 3 years they have to do 'mandatory work' for 6 months. This workload can be aggregated in a short time period or distributed. Mandatory work will typically consist of teaching a course or advising master students in 4, 12 or 16 week projects.

    As supervisor to PhD students, I try to help them minimize the mandatory workload. I can do that in several ways. I try to let them teach courses that are introductory, because advanced courses usually require more preparation. I try to let the PhD students teach courses or parts of courses that are as close as possible to their research area. For courses that I have taught before I often hand over my slides, my teaching plan, my exams etc., to make it as easy to take over as possible. Finally, I try to ensure that the last year is kept free of teaching responsibilities. This means a higher workload in the first 2 years, but with the other measures in place it should be feasible.

The supervisor should put the issue of teaching duties on the agenda for meetings with PhD students. Discuss how much teaching is needed. Discuss how the teaching can be directed in a way that it is synergetic with the research leading to the PhD, and finally discuss whether you can be helpful in organizing the teaching in a way that is the least problematic to your student.

One of my PhD students did not make any real progress for a long period of time. I asked what the problem was and she answered that teaching took all her energy. Furthermore students came to her office and disturbed her regularly and she was not good at saying 'no'. She wanted to be helpful and friendly. When I put the issue on the agenda for one of our meetings I also found out that she used a disproportionate part of her time for preparing slides, exercises and so on. Three hours of teaching had turned into 40 hours of work, leaving no time for research.

    My suggestion was to set aside 1 or 2 days for teaching. The teaching was on Monday so I suggested that Thursday and Friday each week could be dedicated for teaching. This would leave Tuesday and Wednesday for research. I strongly emphasized that a 'research

> day' should be used only for research. She should make it clear to students that 'office hours' were on Thursday and Friday only. I also suggested that she should work at home for the rest of the week. I am happy to say that following this meeting, research moved forward again.

The other main source of conflict is that between research and family demands. Partners, children and parents may well get less time and attention than they are used to. These particular conflicts can also be seen as a conflict between one's own ambitions (to gain a PhD) and the needs of others.

> My partner uses emotional blackmail to make me spend more time with him because he feels neglected. I feel that the kids are suffering from a lack of attention. The main feeling I have about doing my PhD is that of guilt. Am I only doing it for my selfish satisfaction? I may give up.

A number of women who participated in the study characterized this conflict as an emotional one. Many women feel they are somehow being selfish in pursuing a goal so strongly identified with them. Thus, supervisors need to be aware of this emotional dimension to the PhD experience, particularly with regard to women candidates. More discussion on the gendered nature of the PhD experience can be found in Chapter 9.

Another issue that can create conflicts is when PhD students change marital status or become parents while doing their studies.

> In Northern Europe a PhD scholarship has the same status as a job in the public sector which means that you have a right to take maternity leave with pay. In Denmark and Sweden, for example, maternity leave can create a pause in the research from 6 to 12 months.

> Two years ago a very bright student applied for a PhD position in a research project that I was heading. I was very happy that he got the job. Soon after he started he told me that his wife was pregnant. He asked whether it was OK to take 3 months parental leave over the summer. I agreed and eagerly awaited the return of the student. The research project did not progress in the meantime. Unfortunately, when he returned, he told me he had been offered a job as consultant which he preferred. So he quit. We ended up paying him for 8 months of which nearly 50% of the time ended up being parental leave pay. I am still annoyed because I feel he was misusing the system.

Support

As we have seen, doing a PhD part time can lead to many conflicts. This can be increased or decreased, depending on the level of support from family, friends, peers, academic institution and the academic community in general.

Thus enrolling support from all stakeholders in the PhD is critical in helping to reduce conflicted feelings.

PhD students might well expect good support from the university. This includes supervisor time, work space and equipment. Teaching obligations should be reasonable, a maximum of 3 to 6 hours class contact per week might be deemed reasonable with lenient obligations regarding administration. Yet what is promised is not always what is delivered.

> I was promised a light teaching load, no administration, a room of my own and every other support needed. But a teaching colleague in my area left, a visiting lecturer shares my office and I was asked to take on personal tutees. I am sure these promises were made in good faith and in any case I haven't got the power to say no. But this has not turned out in the way I expected.

It is certainly important to involve your family, or you might not have one as a consequence of that lack of involvement. Married female PhD candidates, at least, have a much higher chance of divorce *before* the completion of the PhD than the average (Boufis, 1999). Thus, good communications with family members are essential and an agreement about scheduling should be a family decision with these times and commitments being respected by all, including the part-time PhD student.

The most outstanding aspect of the responses (see Figure 6.3) was the degree of emotion attached to the issue of support. For these respondents, the issue of support (or lack of support) for their part-time PhD loomed large in their working (and home) life. Most felt conflict between their obligations at home, work and to the PhD. The demands of work and family life were not well balanced with the less immediate but very important PhD.

Isolation

For some students the situation might be one of adequate or good intellectual and physical resources but little personal support. Those students that do not receive personal support might find the whole part time experience a negative and isolating one. In the survey, isolation was prevalent amongst the respondents.

As we have seen, the intellectual experience itself might isolate research students from family and friends. But in an area like information systems, it can be personal, in that you may be isolated from others undergoing the same experience. Not many universities have a large number of PhD students undertaking IS and few have large groups working on one major project. Other PhD students doing related work may be very geographically dispersed. Indeed, the part-time researcher may work a lot at home, for family or other reasons, and therefore face-to-face meetings with supervisors and other students may be difficult and comparatively rare.

Thus from the point of view of supervision, efforts should be made to reduce that intellectual and social isolation, and to assist the student to enlist many different sources of support. The academic department should find funding, at least in these cases, for researchers to attend PhD consortia, conferences, research meetings and the like. In Chapter 7 you can find a number of different models for financing the PhD.

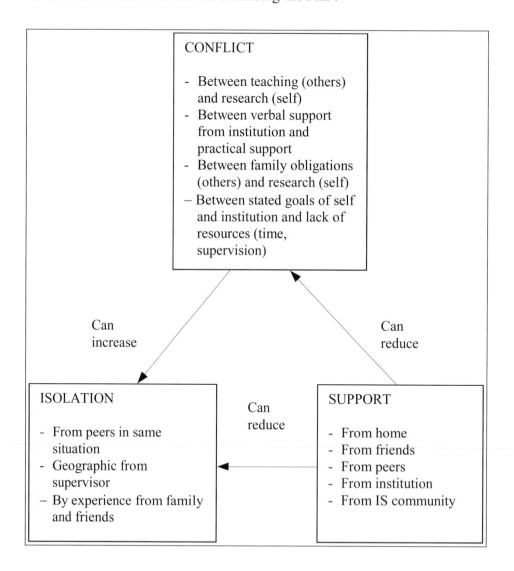

Figure 6.4 *Themes of conflict, isolation and support (Urquhart, 1999)*

Luckily in many countries these things are included in the 'PhD package.' In Denmark, for example, the cost of a PhD is estimated at €200.000 of which 40% is set aside for supervision, conferences, books, etc.

Institutions as well as supervisors may need to be reminded, therefore, that doing a PhD is not an entirely personal exercise. The acquisition of a PhD has flow-on benefits to institutions and to the supervisor; indeed, there are many stakeholders in a PhD. These stakeholders should be aware of the issues of potential isolation and conflicts, and provide the support necessary. They also have a lot to gain from the success of the part-time PhD student. The issues of support, conflict and isolation are summarized in Figure 6.4.

6.9 Strategies for supervisors suggested by students

At a follow-up workshop at the Australasian Conference in Information Systems in 1998 (see Urquhart, 1999), attended by twenty-four students, it was suggested that supervisors need to be aware of the following issues for part-time students:

- The student–supervisor relationship needs to be defined clearly, in terms of responsibilities on both sides.
- A standard of regular meetings and agreed turnaround times for feedback on written work should be set and agreed. This could be seen as equivalent to a 'service level agreement' where expectations are clarified on both sides.
- Supervisors need to be sensitive to cross-cultural issues.
- Milestones need to be set and the process towards them actively managed.
- Supervisors need to be sensitive to the circumstances of part time PhD students and expectation for them need not necessarily be the same as for full-time students. Part-timers are frequently 'juggling' many responsibilities as 'real life' intrudes from time to time and affects progress.
- Supervisors need to assist part-time students to find 'blocks of time' at critical periods; for instance, at the writing up stage.

Most importantly, although codes of conduct for supervision do exist in universities, there is a need to supplement this with an *individual* agreement between the student and the supervisor. The student-supervisor relationship for a part-time PhD student very often encompasses many years, and therefore a good understanding on both sides is extremely important.

Potential strategies are suggested in Table 6.2. Some of these involve the supervisor or require his or her support and lobbying.

Table 6.2 *Strategies for managing time and gaining support (modified from Urquhart, 1999)*

Issue 1: Managing Time
Efficiency – teach the same course several times, working smarter not harder.
Scope – saying 'no' to extra tasks such as committee work.
Meeting management – ask if you have to be present for the whole meeting, and schedule meetings and appointments in blocks.
Blocking time – clearly delineate time between research and other tasks. Allocate one day or half a day a week off campus and fix a 'do not disturb' sign on the door if forced to work on campus. Find another place to work if neither home nor campus is an option. In busy times, use the 'salami technique' – half an hour a day, just maintain momentum and connection to the research.
Relate teaching content to the PhD – teach courses and supervise students in a similar area to your own, use your students as subjects.
Project planning – the PhD is a large project, so apply standard project management strategies such as milestones, Gantt charts, resource allocation and the critical path analysis
Tools and software – Use software to manage time and for data analysis, plus packages like Endnote, which all increase efficiency.
Distinguish between the urgent and not important; and important but less urgent (like the PhD)
Issue 2: Gaining personal support
From your partner - Be clear about what time and support you require from your partner. Involve your partner in the PhD and make it a joint concern. Ensure you allocate some quality time to be together - maybe scheduling a 'date' with your partner (even if you do live together) to go to the cinema, lunch or have a special dinner at home.
From your children - Children need to understand *why* they have less of your time. Schedule time for them alone. Be prepared to work in the evenings after the children have gone to bed.
From colleagues, friends and fellow PhD students - Have regular meetings (real or virtual) with colleagues and friends to enlist advice and support. Build networks with those in other institutions in the same position, to share concerns, worries, breakthroughs and successes.
Support from yourself - Do not abandon recreational activities, these are energizing and supply much needed balance. Find time to nurture health and well being to maintain productive capacity. Celebrate successes along the way. Find other activities ('getting a life') while waiting for the PhD to be examined.
Personal support universities could provide - A PhD support counselor should be available for non-academic issues; child support needs to be provided for PhD students/single parents; and a facilitator for informal PhD student chat groups.

6.10 Strategies suggested by supervisors

Supervisors who participated in the Internet survey suggested a number of generic strategies that could be applied to part-time PhDs:

- It is essential to think in terms of getting some uninterrupted blocks of time for the student, for writing up or doing all or a portion of the fieldwork. There were many ingenious solutions, for example, people teaching all their courses in one semester, getting grants to buy out teaching, using vacation time, etc.
- The relationship with part-time students should be actively managed, with expectations about feedback, frequency of meetings and deliverables clearly outlined.
  * Supervisors should take a more holistic view of the candidate, and appreciate that the relationship is likely to be different from that with a full-time candidate.
  * The part-time student is likely to be older, and to have responsibilities that will compete for their attention. There is also likely to be much less of a power differential between mature students, who have developed a career of their own, and the supervisor.
  * If the student is also a colleague, there are issues of reconciling one's demands of the person as a PhD student with any work related demands.
  * The relationship may extend for 6 to 8 years, so supervising a part time PhD is a considerable commitment in terms of a working relationship.
- The topic chosen has to have some longevity to fit in with the longer timescale of a part-time PhD. Thus, topics tied to fast moving information technologies are risky. It is much better, from the point of view of part-time students, to concentrate on new approaches to perennial issues in information systems.

6.11 Conclusion

It is apparent that expectations and influences from external parties impose an 'extra dimension' of complexity on the preparation and fulfillment of the student's process. We have discussed important aspects that need to be actively considered and controlled in any PhD project that is not purely academic.

The key recommendation of this chapter is that the conflict, isolation and lack of support that is involved in serving two masters need specific supervisory strategies to overcome those negative aspects. The strategies can sometimes be the same as recommended for students; for instance, actively managing the expectations among stakeholders or in the supervisory relationship, with regard to feedback, frequency of meetings and deliverables is of huge benefit to both supervisor and supervised.

Where PhDs involve a collaborative relationship with industry, it is recommended that the PhD student, the supervisor and the industrial partners meet very early to discuss in an active and collaborative fashion how the control structures of the research should be set up.

Supervisors and students are encouraged to give potential tensions between different goals due consideration to avoid unnecessary frustration later in the process. Supervisors should try to give the PhD student's goal highest priority, which may cause problems with respect to consistency between goals over the project as the student's goal evolves from an initially rather open goal to a more precise goal later in the process.

A part-time student may well be the same age, or older, than his or her supervisor, and this can create some interesting power differentials, especially when one is supervising a colleague doing a PhD. Again, actively managing expectations about the relationship is a key to avoiding difficulties.

I was heartened to read that a local resident has just completed his third PhD at Brunel at the age of 93. He is very unusual, but there are others of around my age, wishing to pursue another interest following retirement. But there can be problems: we need to adapt, and learn a new culture and jargon. But we also have advantages: our experience, our capacity for hard work and our commitment.

Supervisors should not underestimate the isolation that can occur for a part-time candidate, and should actively find ways to combat that isolation by ensuring that the student meets other students and attends conferences and PhD consortia. The conflicts that many older PhD students feel should not surprise us, they are the product of living a full and balanced life, and supervisors should be able to help their students navigate these conflicts by having a holistic understanding of their students' circumstances. In other words, we should treat our candidates as we would like to be treated ourselves when we have conflicting priorities to manage. One of the most valuable and practical things a supervisor can do for a part time candidate is to 'find' them some time. There are many ingenious ways of doing this, for example, study leave, extended leave, outside funding and teaching relief.

Short blocks of time can be put together with other types of leave to give time to write up.

The part-time student can be regarded as a nuisance by some supervisors. They are liable to be older, have more challenges, complete the work more slowly and generally be more difficult to manage. They are also likely to be more passionate about their PhD work, more able to manage that work, and bring to their intellectual endeavors some very real insights from their practice. For these reasons, the part-time PhD student can also be a joy to supervise.

7

Finance

Frantz M. Rowe and Jan Pries-Heje

7.1 Introduction

Research is an intellectual exercise, but we need money to support the years of study necessary to gain a PhD. The issue of financing the PhD is a very important one for the student and often for the supervisor as well. This chapter will help you answer the key questions on financing such as:

- What are the sources of funding available?
- What is the appropriate funding amount?
- What is the appropriate time span for funding?

This chapter also provides a starting point for discussions between a supervisor and PhD student on the advantages and disadvantages of the various funding alternatives.

7.2 Sources of funding available

The sources for financing PhD students are highly diverse, and yet financing is one of the most critical elements of the infrastructure for PhD studies. The nature of these sources can vary according to academic discipline as well as geographic region. Within information systems there are three main sources of funding for a PhD:

1   Universities
2   Government
3   Industry.

Many universities have a number of PhD grants that one can apply for. However, it is rare to find that the funding is generous. In the United States, for example, the grant may only be for a few thousand dollars per year; in the UK it may only cover the university fees; whereas in Scandinavia PhD grants are comparable to the salary levels of a 'normal' job – here, PhD grants offered by universities tend to be highly competitive.

At the IT University of Copenhagen four or five PhD grants are given out every year. In 2003 there were close to 100 applicants that were qualified – that is, they had an MSc or equivalent, with very good or excellent grades, and they had written a 3-4 page research proposal.

Government is the other major source of funding. In France, for example, the Ministry of Education has a number of PhD grants every year. These are given to a candidate coming from the French speaking world or Europe, younger than 30, who has obtained the best grades in the prerequisite masters in research degree. This is a course aimed at training potential researchers in the discipline. Following this, the PhD program will usually be of 3 years duration with very few formal courses.

In many countries discussions on 'hot' issues, such as the information society and the future of industry, have led to the establishment of special funds that can be applied for by researchers who wish to look at IT related issues. In the UK, 'technology transfer' and 'technology foresight' were two such initiatives. Government agencies may have funds for research and a student applying for this type of funding will have to phrase his or her research question within the scope of the agency and initiative.

In some countries it can be hard to see the difference between university and government funding, mainly because universities can be close to 100% publicly funded and admission is therefore mainly paid for by taxes. In other countries universities are private corporations and students might have to pay high tuition fees. However, they may well have different goals. Whereas governments might be interested in increased welfare and value for money for their citizens, universities often have the goal of increasing knowledge at an international level.

The third source of funding is industry. In many countries this source is of growing importance because government money is under pressure from many sides. There are quite a number of models. The most industry-oriented occurs when an employee in a company is admitted into a PhD program as an industrial PhD student.

> The *Information Systems Research In Scandinavia (IRIS)* conference is one of the oldest academic conferences dedicated to IS. At the 2004 conference there was a special workshop for industrial PhD students. About 35 people showed up and discussed common difficulties. As a result, I-IRIS was established to give industrial PhD students a forum to discuss their special problems and needs.

A variant of this is when government supports industrial PhD students. In France, this is mostly done through the *Convention Industrielle pour la Formation par la Recherche en Entreprise (CIFRE)* contract. Here, the PhD student is hired by a French company, which in turn receives funding from the *Agence Nationale pour la Recherche Technologique*. The latter is a governmental agency for technological research. Funding will only be granted if the company has a corresponding research contract with the university laboratory where the PhD supervisor is employed.

> Mohamed had a 3 year grant from Tunisia. He passed his Master of Research in Paris under my supervision and he enrolled in the PhD program at Nantes. While here and with two other colleagues, myself and Pierre, he participated in a research contract between *La Poste* and the *Maison des Sciences de l'Homme de Nantes,* which is a joint venture for research in social sciences between the *Université de Nantes* and other companies and institutions including *La Poste.* He did all his data collection based on a questionnaire we had designed together for that contract. It took him 5 years to complete his PhD. His case is fairly standard since he combined two financing modes.
>
> Pierre has had experience of at least three modes. Most of the time he taught courses at a number of schools, He taught marketing, management and accounting, but rarely information systems. He participated in the same contract as Mohamed with *La Poste,* but he was also part of a large team working at call centers in response to the Ministry of Work

> and Employment demands that followed a year later. Then he spent one year as a teaching assistant at *Ecole Polytechnique de l'Université de Nantes,* before getting his degree in 2003, after six years.

Another variant occurs when industry cooperates with a university for a period of time. In Denmark there is a requirement that industry should pay 50% or more of the cost in such a scheme. A similar scheme exists in the UK.

> As a supervisor I twice negotiated a research center contract with industry. I had difficulties with the negotiations especially concerning the time that should be available for the PhD student's research. This was because the PhD student wanted a regular employee contract including a comparatively high salary. As a result, the company became very demanding of the student's time. Furthermore, the company tended to forget about the requirement that the student needs to work at the research center and also he or she needs time to write up the thesis.

Table 7.1 *Financing sources: Availability and implications for supervisor*

Source of funding	Availability	Supervisor involvement
University grant or fellowship	Few. Highly competitive. Often requires a very good research idea and an excellent description	Low, at least before the grant is awarded
University teaching with admission into PhD program	In some countries many	High, especially ensuring that teaching does not take all the time
Government grant	Few but can be more frequent in focus areas defined by government	High, especially ensuring that the PhD research question is within scope
Research project with government agency	Variable. Can be very narrowly defined	Low, at least before PhD study is initiated
Industrial PhD	Depends on country and company. In Scandinavia there are plenty	High, especially ensuring industrial work can be used as a case study or a basis for action research
Industrial cooperation	Variable. Often research assistants with connections to the cooperating university will have the best chance of early involvement	Very high. It often requires much effort to negotiate and agree on research projects with industry

Of course one can also find examples where industry sponsors a PhD at a university. At the Copenhagen Business School and the IT University of Copenhagen several companies have sponsored research and at the same time had their company name attached to a room, a laboratory or an auditorium in a sponsorship arrangement.

For a supervisor, negotiating contracts with different parties (companies, governmental agencies and students) is very time-consuming and a demanding task. The PhD supervisor might have to accept additional controls and requirements, such as making presentations in the company and providing other deliverables. On the other hand a contract generates new opportunities, not only in terms of financial resources, but ideas and ways of working that may bring more benefits than constraints to the supervisor.

Finally, there are also students who have no financing at all apart from that coming from their own savings, loans or private income gained from an unrelated job.

In Table 7.1 we have given an overview of the sources of funding, as presented above, together with our evaluation of availability and the need for supervisor involvement.

7.3 Appropriate funding amount

There are really three things that may need to be funded. The first is the income for the PhD student; the second concerns payment relating to the contribution of the supervisor; and the third covers the cost of the office, books, library access, traveling, etc. of the PhD student.

The financing resources for PhD studies may be quite varied even in the same country. In the United States there are three major approaches:

1 *Admission with little financing.* This is the norm for part-time programs such as those in education where students take on full-time work in the summer. It is also used by programs that admit students who have employment outside. The completion rate tends to be low, perhaps only one-third of those who begin graduate studies.

2 *Admission with financing based on grants.* This is usually associated with projects run by the supervisor. This method is very common in the physical sciences. A large percentage of students take non-academic positions. It is also common for research-oriented graduates who take up a post-doctoral research appointment before taking a permanent position.

3 *Admission of a small number of students with financing for the normal period of a doctorate.* In this scheme, the students do some teaching, some research with faculty and research for the PhD in parallel. Financing is linked to the time taken to do a doctorate, which has been increasing significantly. In the past 20 or 30 years, the average

time to complete in the US has increased by 1 to 2 years. In Europe it also seems that the average duration of the PhD is closer to 4 years than the official 3 years in most countries.

> At the Carlson School of Management, they follow the third method. They try to identify students who are likely to become world class scholars. The completion rate is about 65%. Almost all of their students who get the PhD take academic positions.

At many universities major parts of the PhD funding may come from teaching. At one extreme the PhD student may have 100% of his or her income from teaching and be 'allowed' admission into a PhD study in addition to his or her heavy teaching load. Financing is often attached to the type of post, whether it is an assistantship, teaching assistantship or part-time research fellowship:

- *Assistantships* will often embody a tuition waiver and a small stipend. Usually the tuition waiver is the most valuable aspect, and the stipend is rarely enough to cover living expenses. Students with laboratory or research assistantships are usually assigned to work with a faculty member on the faculty member's research projects. Depending on the roles assumed, a fortunate student may be assigned to work for his or her supervisor, who in turn may defer the workload to the student's own thesis project. In such a circumstance, students essentially use the assistantship to fund their own research.
- *Teaching assistantships* will also carry tuition waivers and a small stipend. These assistantships vary in responsibility. In some cases the student will assist a faculty member in teaching responsibilities, for example, by marking student work, invigilating exams, or delivering some lectures. In other cases, the student will take complete responsibility as the instructor-of-record for a study topic or course.
- *Research fellowships* can be full-time or part-time appointments that will often pay salaries, better benefits, but also involve a larger time commitment away from the student's own thesis topic.

An issue that should concern the supervisor is the amount of time that the student is allocating for teaching and research that is outside of the thesis topic area. In search of more stipend support, better pay or better benefits, the student will lose time to devote to the thesis. This decision can extend the time required to complete the PhD study. We also discuss this issue in Chapter 6.

In Sweden, most PhD students are employed by their universities for a period of 5 years with a guarantee to spend 80% of their time on research (including course work). The remaining 20% is devoted to other commitments such as teaching and/or administration. It is also common for staff members in Sweden to undertake a part time PhD with a 50/50 relationship between research and other commitments. In a recent Swedish national evaluation of the IS subject (HSV, 2004), it is reported that PhD students with an 80/20 relationship between research and other commitments are often seen more as colleagues than students amongst full-time staff. However, it is also reported that PhD students in this scheme sometimes become too committed to departmental activities during their 20% (of non-research time) thereby affecting their research progress negatively. It is therefore important to carefully plan and monitor the PhD student's activities, in order to fulfil both research and departmental expectations throughout the process.

So the answer to the question about how much funding the potential PhD student should be looking for, is really a question related to whether he or she has alternative sources of income, in particular, a job as teacher or one in industry and costs; for example, whether he or she has to pay for an office and how much is needed to pay for supervision.

7.4 The role of the supervisor in relation to finance

The role of the PhD supervisor can vary greatly across countries, and the financing sources and modes can be quite varied, even in the same country. For instance, in the United States and Scandinavia, once a PhD candidate is selected for a doctoral program based on intellectual abilities, the PhD supervisor does not need to be involved in the financing issue. On the other hand, in the United Kingdom and France, the supervisor feels responsible for finding and adjusting the financial support as the research progresses.

Supervisors and students need to be aware of this diversity and the impact that these different financial resources can have on the PhD study program. It is important to know about this diversity even if PhD supervisors do not get much involved in the financing process, as supervisors may be required to point to alternative financing modes; for example, one better suited to part-time work or where research is carried out in a company.

In contrast to the US model, in the UK and in France the supervisor often becomes responsible for finding financial resources to support the PhD studies, at least at the beginning and possibly later during the studies if the financial support is in need of adjustment. In these contexts, it is very important for supervisors to be familiar with, and agile at obtaining, various modes of financing.

In France, we can identify six types of PhD financing, all used for PhDs in information systems:

1. *Ministry of Education grants or a grant from a foreign ministry* for a PhD in France. Within these grants teaching may be possible but is limited to 64 hours per year. The idea is to allow the PhD student to obtain some teaching experience and at the same time receive some extra financing – without having the PhD work suffer too much.
2. *Research and development employment in a company – A CIFRE contract.* Here the PhD supervisor must negotiate the amount of time and the mission of the candidate in the company.
3. *Teaching position* in a business school, an engineering school or a university.
4. *Teaching hours* in a business school, an engineering school or a university (if less than 28 years old).
5. *Teaching and research assistant.* This is a 1 year appointment, with 1 year renewal possible. Eligibility is for the last 2 years of the PhD study only.
6. *Research center contracts.* Here the PhD student must spend at least half of the time in the research center in order to make sure of academic and sustained intellectual learning, as well as time available for writing the dissertation itself.

In Canada, we find a very similar system, with national councils *(Conseil de la recherche en sciences humaines (CRSH)* or *Conseil de la recherche en sciences naturelles et en génie (CRSNG)* and in Québec in particular*, le Fonds québécois de recherche sur la société et la culture (FQRSC))* deciding on a competitive basis grants of an annual amount of 15 000 dollars for 3 years. The main difference is probably the French specificity of the CIFRE type of financing.

There are other ways to get financing related to teaching or research. However, those do not cover all living expenses for the 3 year period of the research to PhD.

In France some very motivated PhD students take the risk, generally after several discussions with their supervisor and others, of undertaking a PhD with no financing for the first year. During this year the candidate formulates the research question and the supervisor gets to know the PhD student better, especially his or her teaching ability for different kinds of student populations and his or her capability of participating in existing or potential research contracts linked to the research topic.

7.5 Impacts of financing on PhD success

The source and amount of funding will greatly influence the PhD. It is therefore important to discuss the merits of different types of financing and their impacts on:

- Getting the PhD degree, publishing and securing a job
- Developing the competencies of the student
- Developing the potential of the candidate as an academic.

While obtaining the degree and publishing is certainly what constitutes the objective success of a PhD, the development of some competencies and their role in developing the profile of a university member of faculty is important too, and is related to the ability to succeed in performing research tasks and establishing good relationships.

Impact on degree completion, publications and securing a position

Success is always very difficult to measure. But for candidates who have committed to a PhD program, getting the degree and therefore passing their dissertation is certainly an indication of success. Once the person has been granted the title, he or she can contemplate looking for a job in or out of academia, and in our field there are outstanding opportunities on the labor market.

In France the rate of success for the PhD is very high (in our survey of leading IS professors, it was almost 95%) and for all types of financing. We may conclude that financing does not make a difference, at least, in France. However, in circumstances where candidates have no financing at all from some research or teaching activity, completion rates decrease to a much lower level. So pay-it-yourself would seem to be the least preferable financing mode.

However, the French data, as well as those from the United States, show that full financing for 3 years leads to:

- Shorter time to get the PhD, although, even here it generally takes 3 years and 4 months before passing and 4 years before getting an assistant professor position;
- More publications, which again favors future employment and career.

Impact on the PhD process, resources and competencies

It is clear that the impact of financing on the PhD is multifold and not always direct. Whether the PhD is completed whilst working in a company, working at home or in a university, they are three completely different situations that have socio-cognitive impacts on the student. The more students spend time with members of faculty and other research students, the more they socialize with them and learn both tacit and explicit academic knowledge and competencies. Office space and access to computer, printing and on-line resources are also important. But, even more important, is the possibility of presenting one's research to the supervisor(s), and to the research center as a seminar and in doctoral consortia or conferences. Many remote students do not have (or think that they do not have) these possibilities, because of their isolation from academia.

In Table 7.2 we qualify, what we believe makes a difference, the various financing modes according to socialization and interactions, including publishing, with the research and teaching world it supports. We also emphasize the kind of competencies in doing rigorous and/or relevant research (see Chapter 15 on qualitative research for a description of this distinction) that PhD candidates develop partly according to their financing mode.

Table 7.2 *Impact of types of financing on competencies, socialization and publications*

	Academic socialization	Publication record	Research rigor	Research relevance	Teaching skills
Research income, e.g. university grant	++	++		–	–
Teaching as main source of income	+				+
Industrial job as main source of income	–	–	–	+	–
Industry or government source	–			++	
University source	+	+			+
Short term funding			–	–	–
Long term funding	+	+	++		

For socialization, independent of the personality of the student, the financing mode has a clear impact due to infrastructure constraints. However, the impact on competencies is more difficult to describe. The competencies of the new incumbent in a PhD program may also have an impact on the choice of financing mode made by the PhD supervisor, as well as other considerations such as age, rank of student, opportunities and the knowledge about financing possibilities and desired commitment of the PhD supervisor.

Some modes have very positive (or high) impact on the outcomes (competencies, socialization and publications). Others have a rather negative impact because they do not allow development of one of these beneficial outcomes at a sufficient level. Typically, with the main source of income coming from industry, even if the doctoral student is exceptionally bright and hard working, he or she will have much less time to develop an understanding of academic attitudes and behaviors. Such students may gain their PhD, and yet have problems finding posts in academia as they have not taught and are not familiar with the university system. They may also have problems publishing. To a lesser extent, those who make their living giving courses (teaching as main source of income), but without having a recognized position also tend to socialize less with researchers.

Table 7.2 suggests modes which are positive or negative in this regard. A plus means a potential positive impact and two plusses an almost certain positive impact. A minus suggests a potential negative impact. If the field is empty then the impact from the funding mode is fairly neutral. In many cases, however, much depends on the particular PhD student and supervisor and there is no strong evidence that the financing mode offers an advantage or raises a serious problem.

Time availability for research is strongly linked to the mastery of research methodologies, and greater time availability leads to higher levels of publication. Therefore, not surprisingly, full grants and fellowships, as well as research contracts when linked directly to the PhD research, offer the best perspectives in developing that kind of competency. But, in order to get an employment position in universities, at least in Europe, the ability to communicate by teaching is very important and therefore teaching experience is also crucial.

Impact on the future of the candidate as a member of faculty
These impacts are also important, not only because they concern the kind of knowledge and know-how that the PhD candidate can develop, but because of the kind of learning they then tend to reproduce when they are recruited as members of faculty. Of course there is much room for evolution, and young members of faculty are more or less conscious of their strengths and weaknesses. As an academic community, we would like to recruit colleagues with both the capability for publishing research, with rigorous and original methodologies, and the ability to communicate with students in

a knowledgeable way about IS. The financing modes available do not favor such a balanced profile. It is therefore necessary to favor a type of financing that is consistent with the policy of the institution or better, and try to maintain this diversity by recruiting people with different backgrounds, not only in terms of specialization, but also in terms of experience. This should maintain the faculty diversity that is linked to financial diversity.

7.6 Conclusion

The main conclusions are that financing:

- Is a major concern for supervisors, as well as students, in many countries, and raising finance often requires significant effort on the part of the supervisor on behalf of their PhD students.
- Does not normally have a major impact on getting the PhD degree.
- Does reduce the chances of getting a PhD in cases where there is no financing at all linked to teaching or research. Students who are self financing therefore have a reduced chance of success.
- Is also a major concern to students, because it influences the time required for completion and therefore impacts on stress levels. It also indirectly influences the kind of knowledge and abilities that students develop, and thus plays a role in the kind of faculty we tend to (re)-produce.

8

Ethical Issues

Robert M. Davison

8.1 Introduction

Ethics is a sensitive topic. We all hear about it, we probably all know more or less what it is. We know that there are codes of ethical practice or conduct that are designed to regulate our professional behavior. Yet few of us have received any formal ethical training. As with so many things, we learn by experience and develop our own ethical principles as we go along. So why is ethics so important and why should supervisors and their students read this chapter? The short answer is that by reading about and reflecting on the beliefs and practices of others, so one's own ethical principles can be informed and, ideally, strengthened. It can also be used as a starting point for a debate with your student and supervisor colleagues.

Much of this chapter is written in a fairly formal, even strict, style. This is deliberate, not because there is only one ethically correct way of doing things, but because in this way I hope to stimulate and provoke you, the readers. You may disagree with what I write, or you may feel that I underplay or overplay the issues. My objective is to encourage you to think and reflect on your own ethical values and principles in this context, and debate these with others.

I should remark at the outset that any chapter on ethics is inevitably going to be somewhat personal. I cannot fairly represent the myriad views of all IS academics worldwide. I cannot present umpteen different cultural or philosophical perspectives on how supervisors or students should behave in different situations. Nevertheless, I have consulted with a number of colleagues from a variety of cultures (American, Australian, Chinese, Dutch, English, Latvian, Tunisian), as to the identity of key issues or ethical dilemmas.

Ethics involves the systematic application of moral rules, standards, or principles to specific, concrete problems. Ethics creeps into many aspects of our professional lives as academics. There are ethical issues associated with teaching, conducting research (including the use of students as subjects), managing academics, applying for grants, writing up research (including issues associated with plagiarism), and so forth.

The focus of this chapter concerns the ethical issues associated with the relationship that exists between research students and their supervisors. My intention here is to identify and discuss a number of salient issues which students and their supervisors are likely to encounter.

There are a number of areas in the supervisor–student relationship where there is a likelihood that ethical dilemmas may emerge. For the purpose of this chapter, the following three areas are discussed:

- Building and maintaining a relationship
- Supervising and being supervised
- Writing and publishing research papers (and the research thesis).

These three broad areas cover much of the interaction in the supervisor–student relationship and indeed are designed to be roughly sequential, in that the research process starts with relationship building, continues with doing the research and culminates with a thesis and further publications. Of course, there is much iteration and interaction between these three areas as well. It should be noted that the discussion here will not focus on how to do the various activities in these categories (this is discussed elsewhere in the book), but rather will identify ethical issues associated with them.

In addition to these three areas, a number of themes permeate this chapter informing much of the analysis. These themes involve the tensions inherent in supervisor–student relationships, particularly those associated with power, politics, conflicts of interest, culture, status and personality.

It is not the intention of this chapter to engage in an extensive discussion of every possible ethical permutation. Rather, a fairly concise and pithy approach is taken that is designed to stimulate further reflection and discussion on the nature of ethical dilemmas in the supervisor–student relationship.

8.2 Building and maintaining a relationship

It seems to me that it is fundamental that the supervisor–student relationship be developed out of a mutually acceptable framework of parameters that define both the roles played and the responsibilities incumbent upon the supervisor and the student. Such a framework can help forestall the subsequent development of ethical dilemmas. Establishing this framework is not as straightforward as it might seem, given that supervisors commonly have a number of roles and associated responsibilities including, but not limited to, supervisor, gatekeeper, teacher, academic, assessor and colleague. Indeed, students may also function in more than the student role if, for instance, they are studying part-time and teaching full-time. PhD students, of course, should also be considered as future or emerging academics.

The precise nature of the supervisor–student relationship will be structured according to the infinite variety of individual students and supervisors. In this sense, it may be helpful to recognize that every supervisor–student relationship can be characterized as an idiosyncratic dyad, that is, a unique two-person team. Thus, direct comparisons with other dyads and their relationships (successful or otherwise) may not be helpful as a basis for suggesting how the supervisor–student relationship should develop.

However, let me interject my own experience of the supervision process following the British model. My first (of four) supervisors was an Australian, a professor of software engineering, who knew little about my topic of interest. He was supported by another Australian (at that time studying for his own PhD) who identified this research topic and encouraged me to pursue it. After a year or so, the Australian professor died of a heart attack. By this time the second Australian had completed his PhD, so he became my supervisor for about 18 months, whereupon he returned to Australia. The third supervisor was an Egyptian, who had recently moved to Hong Kong. As an engineer, he was relatively unfamiliar with my research topic and entirely unfamiliar with my chosen research method, action research. A year later he too emigrated, never to be seen again. The fourth supervisor, an American, who is mercifully still alive, was my supervisor to completion.

Over the course of 5 years, I thus had to develop four separate supervisor–student relationships, each of them quite different from the others. But I don't see this necessarily as a fatal problem. It provided the opportunity to learn from four very different people and, at the same time, to develop a certain tenacity and perseverance, essential characteristics of researchers I believe.

Considering the roles of the supervisors and students, differences in power and status immediately become apparent, with the supervisor almost invariably having more of both (at least in the academic context). This should not, *per se,* be a problem, but student awareness of and respect for power and status differences may ease the relationship building process. One can foresee that tensions might arise in situations where there is a lack of cultural congruence between the values espoused by the student and those of the supervisor. Thus, to use Hofstedian terms, if a student from a low Power Distance culture has a supervisor from a high Power Distance culture (or vice-versa) then cultural conflicts may well emerge, given the individual's differing expectations about how the other should behave. Such cultural conflict does not constitute an ethical dilemma in and of itself, but it may lead to disagreements in the supervisor–student relationship that later on do indeed spiral out of control and take on an ethical hue.

My supervisor–student relationship with my Egyptian supervisor was the one that I found most difficult to handle, primarily because of cultural differences. A humble and modest man, he encouraged me to emulate his personal style. Humility is a virtue seldom present in research students (and academics in general)!

At the other extreme, such personality characteristics as arrogance, dominance, egocentrism and laziness can be significant causes of conflict in the supervisor–student relationship. Students in particular are advised to be aware of the potential that their supervisor will exhibit such characteristics, and need to learn how to manage the supervisor appropriately. Given power differences, these kinds of personal idiosyncrasies are likely to be much harder for a student to resolve than a supervisor.

Students may also experience problems with supervisors who are hard to find or who have little time for their research students. In some countries, it appears to be the norm that academics only come to the office to teach and attend pre-arranged meetings. Supervisors who adopt this work habit may be very hard to locate.

A student once complained to a colleague that she could never find her supervisor. Not only was he never in the office, but he ignored her voice mail and email. In desperation, she requested and received the supervisor's home (ex-directory) telephone number. The supervisor, far from being apologetic, was furious! In the end, the student, reluctantly, had to report the situation to her Head of Department. The frequency of occurrence of such unethical behavior on the part of the supervisors is hard to estimate, but the position of the student is unenviable: even if retribution is most unlikely, the student will still fear this, given the difference in power.

The quality of interaction time then becomes an important issue, as well as the quality of feedback received from the supervisor. The form of this feedback is likely to be culturally conditioned. I have seen some students receive very precise and detailed feedback that, in toto, is tantamount to specific instructions for the entire process from research initiation to research completion. Whether it is ethical to give such precise feedback is another matter, students may appreciate it if it makes their lives easier, but it may not help them develop their powers of investigation and analysis. Quality may thus be measured in terms of the extent to which students need to reflect on the feedback before taking action.

The last issue to be considered here concerns sexual, financial and emotional needs or offers. This is an area of the supervisor–student relationship that is as dangerous as it is important. Legal and cultural norms will vary around the world, but supervisors are strongly discouraged from engaging in any kind of sexual or financial relationship with their students, whether initiated by the supervisor or the student.

Sexual relationships in particular are likely to run foul of university regulations, quite apart from the ethical concerns associated with maintaining a relationship that involves both professional and personal elements. One would expect that it would be extraordinarily difficult for a supervisor to guarantee to the University that he or she will continue to provide impartial, balanced and critical advice to a student, and to reach decisions associated with the student's academic progress including recommendations for conferment of a degree or expulsion from the university, whilst at the same time engaging in an intimate relationship with that student.

Such complications do not mean that sexual relationships never occur and it may be particularly difficult for some individual supervisors to resist sexual temptations or offers made (for whatever reasons) by students. Nevertheless, supervisors are strongly discouraged from engaging in such behavior. In similar vein, supervisors are discouraged from actively or passively expressing any interest that might be construed as containing a sexual element in their students.

Such complications do not mean that sexual relationships never occur. In fact, by coincidence I read on the Guardian newspaper's website (dated 9 June, 2004, http://www.guardian.co.uk/italy/story/0,12576,1234658,00.html) that an Italian professor was acquitted of having allegedly promised exam passes in return for sex. Three of the professor's students were also acquitted on corruption charges, since they allegedly offered sex in return for good marks. After the acquittal, the professor boasted that all the women involved had had sex with him voluntarily. According to this newspaper report, Italian professors 'enjoy a god-like status and the power to make or break the careers of their students and assistants … There have been repeated claims of students being coerced into sex by the offer of good marks or the threat of bad ones.'

Financial relationships may not seem to be as serious an area as the sexual ones discussed above, yet situations of financial dependency between the student and supervisor may well distract attention from the academic side of the supervisor–student relationship. Financial relationships that involve the supervisor borrowing money from the student (an unlikely prospect it is admitted) would be particularly difficult to handle, as many questions would be raised as to the supervisor's integrity in academic decision-making contexts. Nevertheless, students may give their supervisors small gifts or trinkets of token value, perhaps on return from an overseas conference. This is very likely to be part and parcel of the normal student–supervisor relationship, but supervisors must distinguish between such token gifts and more substantial items (a Rolex watch for instance), that could run foul of anti-corruption/bribery legislation.

Where emotional issues are concerned, it is not unreasonable for a student to turn to a supervisor in times of emotional stress or difficulty. The role of supervisor includes a certain counseling component, and it is not always possible to distinguish between academic and personal issues.

My own inclination is to recommend that a relationship based on honesty, transparency and mutual respect – in so far as it is academically, administratively and personally possible, recognizing power and status differences – is likely to be a healthy one.

8.3 Research process

In the conduct of research, there is a serious risk that the supervisor (or the institution) will treat the student as a resource available in unlimited quantities for whatever purposes that are deemed most appropriate. These might be as trivial as locating a journal article on a library database, or as serious as creating a set of lecture slides and then delivering that material to a class. Such arrangements may even be quasi-institutionalized: my own university requires all research students to undertake up to 4 hours per week of in-class support, typically running tutorials and laboratory sessions or providing limited administrative support. This can easily be justified on the grounds that students are being prepared for their future working environment, but then so too could a supervisor's requirement that students prepare and deliver lectures.

Research students should really be engaged in investigating research topics that are germane to their own thesis area. This investigation should extend to readings about research methodology and epistemology as well as current debates in the literature. They should not be jumped from project to project at the supervisor's behest, nor should they be blinkered by the supervisor so as to consider only one epistemological stance or methodological perspective.

At the same time, students should not expect to 'free ride' on the work of their supervisor. They cannot take the supervisor's work as their own, nor indeed rely on the supervisor to control each and every aspect of the research process.

Although still students, they must mature through the process so that when they graduate they too will be academically qualified to lead research projects and supervise students. Students who are excessively spoiled with too frequent or detailed supervisor–student relationship contact, monitoring, checking and who are not given (or required to take) responsibility, are unlikely to reach academic maturity very quickly.

Supervisors have a key role to play as promulgators of academic values and judgments. As such they should be extremely careful when transmitting value-laden knowledge to students. Examples of situations here include questions about:

- How grant money should be used
- What tone should be adopted when reviewing a paper for a journal or conference
- What is data fabrication and why it is considered unethical
- The importance of keeping promises and deadlines
- The need to ensure that you do not plagiarize (intentionally or unintentionally) in your writing; and
- How one should make a useful contribution to the broader research community.

Students often know little about these important issues, and may receive no formal training, relying on the supervisor for guidance. The duty to provide this guidance in a professional manner should not be taken lightly.

In this context, supervisors should also ensure that students are familiar with professional norms, for instance those established by professional societies such as the *Association for Information Systems (AIS)* or the *Association of Computing Machinery (ACM)*. In addition, individual universities usually have codes for both students and staff. Funding bodies may also have codes. These are more or less developed according to the legal culture of the jurisdiction where the code operates, and perhaps the propensity for expensive litigation. The AIS has recently promulgated an extensive set of ethical guidelines relating to the research process, many of which directly apply to the student–supervisor relationship. These can be accessed from: http://www.aisnet.org/conduct/AIS_Code.htm. This code attempts to balance the different positions and cultural values practiced by IS researchers internationally. Thus, while it indicates that plagiarism and data fabrication must never be undertaken, other activities are recommended rather than being mandated. These include respect for the rights of data subjects, suggestions against the multiple parallel submissions of research papers, and acknowledging the contributions of all authors. The code also includes a number of pieces of 'good advice,' such as maintaining documentation about one's research publications.

> As a co-author of the *AIS* Code of Research Conduct, I clearly have a conflict of interest in critiquing it. However, I would like to say that as with any code, it is imperfect. It reflects, as best can be expressed at the current time, a set of values that is acceptable to the *AIS* Council that approved it and by proxy to the membership of the *AIS* that is expected to abide by it. The three co-authors (one American, one Canadian and myself, English but living in Hong Kong for the last 13 years) of the code had many frank discussions about precise wordings and interpretations, with a fair amount of respectful disagreement. It is certainly a valuable document and guide to ethical behavior that all students and supervisors are encouraged to read and reflect on.

A further ethical dilemma that supervisors may encounter from time to time concerns the student who is really not cut out for an academic career, does not fit into the research mould, has little or no interest in teaching, cannot think for him or herself, and so should really be encouraged/invited to withdraw from research studies. Issues of political acceptability may intrude here, as drop out rates may affect funding, as well as the supervisor's reputation. One could also argue that in times of funding cuts, the failing student who is not terminated is denying another, brighter, better motivated or otherwise more deserving student the opportunity to study for a research degree. Giving students the benefit of the doubt is reasonable to a point, but not *ad infinitum.*

It is also possible that students will encounter a situation not dissimilar to the above, where they perceive that their supervisor is incompetent to supervise, indeed to serve as an academic. Such a conclusion might be based on various sources of evidence, including laziness, poor quality or inaccurate feedback, lack of reliability and integrity, etc., even extending to plagiarism of the student's (or anyone else's) work or harassment, whether psychological, sexual or any other form, of the student (or anyone else). Power and status differences are likely to make such a situation extremely complex to resolve for a student who will quite naturally fear retribution, expulsion from the university, personal attack and/or humiliation. In general, I would counsel students in such cases to seek advice from a senior academic outside the immediate supervisory context of the department, such as the Dean or a Vice-President (Pro Vice Chancellor) responsible for education or research matters.

8.4 The publication process

In asking colleagues for ideas about what to cover in this chapter, the most frequently suggested item corresponds to the problem of authorship in publications. It seems to me that there are at least two key topics here:

- Who owns the work that has been done?
- How should the ownership and the level of work be reflected in the order of authors on any paper submitted for publication?

I suggest that the role of the supervisor (or advisor) is, very simply, to supervise (or advise) – i.e. to facilitate the student's progress through the research degree. In this context, I would argue that it is the research student who is (or should be) actually doing the vast majority of the work, and hence the student should be the owner of the intellectual property created. One exception to this may occur when the student uses in large part previously developed work such as an instrument or technique developed by someone else (possibly the supervisor) – but I imagine that this should be a fairly small component of the overall research if the student is to be awarded a research degree premised on individual and novel work.

Given that the work undertaken should be the student's, I would expect that the student should, at minimum, be the lead author on all papers that emerge from the research. Indeed, if there is no significant intellectual contribution from the supervisor, then the supervisor should not be listed as an author at all, but should be relegated to an acknowledgement in a footnote. This does not mean that supervisors cannot collaborate with their students – quite the opposite – but that they have an ethical obligation to ensure that they do make a significant intellectual contribution to any joint publication.

An extension of this argument concerns the too altruistic supervisor who humbly withdraws his or her name from the authorship of a paper in order to ensure that the student gains all the credit for the work with an apparently single-authored paper. The student might well appreciate such generosity, but it is also a form of intellectual dishonesty: all contributing authors should be acknowledged appropriately.

Ideally, all authors will agree on the extent of this intellectual contribution at the start of any paper write-up. Certainly I feel that free-riding is utterly unacceptable, whether by the student on supervisor work or by the supervisor on student work. This expectation of intellectual contribution is roughly in line with the code of research ethics developed and promulgated by the *Association of Information Systems.*

I have encountered a situation where a recently graduated PhD student added the names of three non-contributing senior colleagues to his conference paper submission, presumably in order to increase the chance of acceptance. I regard this as an instance of unethical behavior for the same reasons as those identified above; that is, if there is no intellectual contribution, then there should be no authorship credit. You may imagine the reaction of these three scholars when they received a rejection letter for a paper that they were not aware they had submitted!

8.5 Conclusion

Ethical issues are an intimate part of IS research, whether we like it or not. It is thus critical that all research students and supervisors are aware of the ethical dimensions of the activities in which they engage, including the supervisor–student relationship itself. It is important to distinguish discussions of appropriate ethical behavior from legal requirements: ethics is very much a personal matter. Each individual student or supervisor must be able to defend his or her actions in any situation by means of ethical principles and reasoning. The material discussed in this chapter is thus not intended to set out universal principles. Rather, it is designed to stimulate individual readers (students and supervisors) to reflect on the ethical issues that are salient to their research. Ideally, they will in consequence be able to develop a stronger set of ethical principles that will assist them in decision-making.

9

Gender

Anita Greenhill and Lynette Kvasny

9.1 Introduction

Considering gender within PhD supervision, is arguably one of the most important unspoken aspects of forging a relationship between supervisor and student. An appropriate working relationship between these roles throughout the PhD process is essential to its overall success and completion. In this chapter, we focus on the way gender shapes the supervisor–student relationship.

Gender itself is a complex socio-cultural arrangement and this further adds complexity to the establishment and maintenance of a successful PhD supervisory relationship. In thinking about gender relations in PhD supervision, it is important to be alert to potential points of tension and contradiction in this relationship as they are cues to future potential changes in individual PhD programs as they evolve over time.

In negotiating the supervision role within the PhD process it is important to acknowledge the role of gender in creating dilemmas (some insolvable), provide resources (or restrict them) and suggest solutions (some of which won't work). These are issues to which the supervisor and student must respond collectively. Importantly, the practices followed by a supervisor for this particular parameter of human relations must be seen as creative responses to situations that are influenced by still wider social forces.

The negotiation of gender relationships creates particular challenges for students and supervisors alike and this chapter is devoted to describing the experience as well as to suggesting creative and dynamic strategies for both students and supervisors. We focus specifically on the issues of negotiating gender roles, how to approach and manage gendered authority, and finally make some practical and strategic supervision suggestions based on the PhD supervisors' own experiences.

9.2 Negotiating gender roles

We begin with a practical suggestion that two foundational steps are taken at the beginning of the supervision process and then regularly returned to throughout the project to negotiate individual gender roles:

1   The supervisor enters his or her role with a clear understanding and assessment regarding his or her ability to work and interact with women and/or men. Specific consideration must be taken, for example, of existing gender-biased attitudes regarding the intellectual, social and personal capacities that they hold. This consideration should not imply any specific overtones and should be conducted without the preconceptions of one's own sexual preferences and gender identification. To achieve this objective the supervisor should examine his or her own academic and work-related success, and realistically consider whether there has been more success and greater fulfillment when he or she has worked with men or women.

2   The supervisor should determine and clarify the form and style of the supervision strategy he or she will utilize. Will supervision be conducted at a purely professional level with minimal personal and social interaction? Alternatively, will supervision occur within the context of an established friendship or is this a new relationship? Is the existing (or potential) friendship based on an association that is distinct from the PhD topic itself?

Once these decisions are made, the supervisor needs to establish an understanding with the student about the distinctions between 'everyday' issues that directly relate to the PhD research project such as administration, write up and completion (discussed in other chapters in this book) and to clarify to what extent the supervisor is willing to discuss those issues that are not involved in the PhD process and more likely to be personal and pastoral in nature.

9.3 Clarifying the complexity of the supervisor–student relationship

Clarifying these positions early in the project minimizes any possible source of confusion between the supervisor and student about the form and nature of their interactions. It cannot be ignored that in many situations the supervisor and student will establish a variety of relationships, both friendly and antagonistic. The full breadth of supervisory styles can be bridged with the application of clarity and openness about individual expectations and the boundaries within which each part is working.

> This female student discussed her experience with her male supervisor and the confusions that can arise: Supervisors, let me tell you about one of the supervisors I had. It has taken me a long time to find a supervisor. My first [supervisor] was good but sent many mixed messages about how I was to engage with him. He was casual and open when we spoke face to face, he liked me to drop in to see him even sometimes without an appointment time. But often he got very worked up in email correspondences; he, on one occasion, went mad at me for not addressing him in the appropriate formality required by a supervisor from a student. He never clarified this so I never knew how to appropriately talk to him or if he was only referring to the emails? Luckily he changed post and I didn't have to deal with him any more.

The above example highlights the ways in which confusion can and does arise. Significantly, this example also highlights the propensity for confusion to occur between men and women interacting with one another.

> This male PhD student illustrates an alternative perspective from a male point of view: I had three principal supervisors during my candidature – two women and a man. In general I felt it was more difficult to interact with the female supervisors. However, I don't entirely identify this as a gender issue as I had known my last (male) supervisor for at least 10 years, had worked as a teaching assistant with him and share a number of interests. I also felt that neither of my first two supervisors were particularly excited about my project and resorted to a very mechanical and process-oriented form of supervision. I wouldn't dismiss it as a tick box approach but I did become quite frustrated many times with both these supervisors.

Issues relating to personal communication and interaction are more complex when they occur between males and females. Cultural cues, social norms and appropriate behaviors all intertwine to aid in the social construction of gender. An individual's own gender is developed via those experiences that are shared and understood, therefore misinterpretation and misunderstanding often occur when no common social reference point exists.

The particular needs of doctoral students with children may be overlooked by PhD supervisors who do not themselves provide primary care for children. Students with children experience special difficulty managing multiple competing demands for time and emotional energy. Not only must they cope with demands made by insensitive colleagues, they can be systematically disadvantaged by institutional traditions such as early morning classes and evening or weekend social events. Often, demands such as caring for an ill child occur unexpectedly at the most inopportune times. Challenges such as these are illustrated by a female colleague who recounted her experience.

> The first two years of the PhD requires attendance and participation in seminars, classes and meetings, many scheduled in the mornings or late evening. As a practical matter, children cannot be dropped off at child care or school before 8 am and must be picked up after school at 3 pm or extend-a-care at 5 pm. Yet there is little understanding about the scheduling of seminars that begin early or do not end until 6 pm or later. In my case this problem was compounded when, to pursue the PhD, I moved to an unfamiliar city in which I had no support system from family or friends. In this city all the child care options started at 8 am and ended at 5 pm. In the first year of the program classes began at 8:00 and did not end till 6:00. I was in a terrible bind. To make matters worse the culture was such that women simply could not complain or ask for help.

9.4 Issues of gendered authority

All gendered interactions are fraught. This is a result of established social norms, expectations and hierarchies. Successful social interaction demands appropriate responses between individuals. A substantial component of these social expectations and role formation for the supervisor and student operating in a PhD program is the impact of power and, in particular, the negotiation of the location of specific forms of authority. The full scope of authority power relations cannot be encompassed in this discussion. Nevertheless, it is important that the supervisor acknowledges or at least is aware that academia is an educational system that perpetuates wider social patterns of separation and association between males and females. Compounding this situation is the fact that a teacher's authority is constructed in isolation, through the supervisor's own resources and as an extension of his or her own experiences.

The extent that a student resists challenges or subverts his or her authority can be perceived as a personal threat to the supervisor. Consideration to the negotiation of authority and power by the supervisor can be practically addressed by applying the earlier suggestion of this chapter: that the supervisor needs to establish an understanding with the student about the distinctions between the 'everyday' issues that directly relate to the PhD research project, and to clarify to what extent the supervisor is willing to discuss those issues that are not directly involved in the PhD process and are more likely to be personal in nature.

The following example provides a personal account of the negotiation of power and authority from a student's perspective: My interactions with my first supervisor often felt like I was being pigeonholed into the PhD she wanted to see rather than exploring and developing my own agenda. This supervisor's own research interests were very close to my original research topic – in an area that is often positioned as an extension of feminist human geography. This seemed to influence our interactions. My own naivety of the research process in the early stages of my candidature also had a bearing on my attitude. At the time I felt that my frustrations were at least partly the result of a negotiated gendered relationship and in hindsight this does have some truth but it was also the relationship of an experienced researcher and a new research student overly confident of their own abilities and ideas.

I would also stress that in at least some of the interactions with my last (male) supervisor I was also conscious of an authority relationship but it was an authority exerted with a more clearly understood (for me) purpose. My last supervisor would tell me I 'had' to do 'x' or 'y' in order to finish the thesis.

Social cues play a major part in negotiating the supervisor–student relationship. Dominant social cues enable both parties to interact and engage in an appropriate manner. The complexity of social cues such as gender and hierarchical authority can lead to misinterpretation regarding the appropriate ways in which to socially engage and progress in the PhD process.

The following example is a personal account of what happens when a student is unsure of the social cues the supervisor offers: Not being able to have a flowing conversation was clearly an issue – to the point that some meetings were simply frustrating and possibly even detrimental to the establishment of a positive supervision relationship. This went so far as finding it difficult to simply communicate 'in the corridor.'

The complexities of authority and power cannot be reduced to individual rules and regulations or to considerations of curriculum and course development as suggested by Robertson et al. (2001). Instead we advocate that the supervisor and the supervisors' own strategies must be seen as creative responses to their current situation and wider socio-cultural environment. As a guideline, consideration to past supervision experience and existing gender-biased attitudes regarding intellectual, social and personal capacities can ultimately guide the supervisor about what they should do individually. The additional consideration to the complexity of gendered authority can further exasperate the supervisory process.

When males manage female PhD candidates

Information systems has significantly less women than men in all areas of the industry including academia (Robertson et al., 2001; Ward, 2001; Wajcman, 1991; Webster, 1996). For this reason it is highly likely that many men will have to supervise female candidates through their PhD. This gender imbalance makes these suggestions all the more important for the production of successful PhDs and lasting professional relationships (Wilson, 2002; Webster, 1996: 5). Successful relations between female PhD candidates and advisors do in fact occur when all parties acknowledge and work through their respective roles and expectations. It is important to note that supervisors will have different styles, and these styles may be exaggerated or diminished by gender disparities.

One female faculty member reflected upon her experience of working with two male co-chairs on her dissertation: I actually didn't think about gender when I chose a supervisor. There were so few women faculty that I just took for granted that I would have a male advisor. Plus, working in the IT industry for 10 years before working on my PhD, I was quite comfortable with male colleagues. My main concern was finding someone who would value my research topic as it was not considered 'mainstream' IS research. My initial advisor made it quite clear that I would be in charge of managing this relationship. I was to schedule the meetings and the agenda. I was to provide drafts, and he would comment. This was fine with me. I don't like to be micro managed, and I am quite self-directed. My advisor never questioned my ability or commitment, and issues such as work-family balance never came up in conversation. I suspect that this is because I worked hard to keep my personal relationships to myself. However, shortly after I started my research, my advisor assumed the role of department chair. He suggested that another committee member assume the role of co-chair of my PhD. I was quite concerned about this (how do you ever complete a thesis if you have to please two supervisors), but the co-chair made it clear that he would defer to my initial advisor. He remained true to his word, so I never had to deal with battling advisors. I also found that the new co-chair had quite a different style. We had weekly meetings, and each meeting started with me sharing my personal well-being. It was extremely hard for me to share my personal struggles, but over time, I began to open up. Gender became important in this relationship since we often talked about the stresses of the PhD process on marital and parental arrangements. We also talked about my pressing need to finish my dissertation rather quickly. Whereas my initial advisor kept me focused and on task, my second advisor let me wander and explore. This worked to my advantage because I read broadly and at the same time, I didn't fall into the trap of wandering aimlessly. Although my PhD research used theories and research methods that were somewhat unfamiliar to both advisors, they trusted me enough to let me find my way. I included faculty from other departments to provide the requisite expertise, and took a faculty position before I actually finished the thesis. My co-chairs supported me as best they could, and for that, I am grateful. I was able to complete my thesis during the first semester of my faculty position, and maintain a close collegial relationship with both advisors.

When female faculty manage male PhD candidates

When female candidates complete their PhDs and take on faculty positions there is the very strong possibility that they will find themselves in the position of supervising male PhD students.

A female professor reflected upon the difficulties and tensions that surface within this relationship: I was just 1 year out of my PhD program when I took on my first PhD student. The student had just finished his Master's thesis, and had research interests quite similar to mine. We got along great, and initially had much success with our research. However, we faced many challenges. For one thing, we were the same age and were often mistaken for husband and wife. At other times, people assumed that he was the professor and that I was the student. I also found it hard to direct a 6-foot tall, male student who had formerly served in the military. He was having a very difficult time settling down on a research topic for his PhD, and I wasn't having much success directing him. In addition, the student had made some major political mis-steps and some faculty felt like this student didn't want to follow the rules. When I asked senior faculty to help, my colleagues perceived that I was either not intellectually up to the challenge (she's not smart enough to supervise a PhD student) or that I was not being treated fairly because of gender (no one would ever step in the middle of a supervisory relationship if you were a male professor). For these reasons, I had senior faculty encouraging me not to work any longer with this student. I was funding this student out of a major research grant and I was not tenured. I was really quite stressed about the whole situation, and eventually I decided to share my predicament with the student. We jointly decided that it was best that I remain as a co-chair on his PhD committee, and that he find a more senior member of faculty who could help with the political aspects of the research. We remain good colleagues, often using email and phone calls to keep in touch socially. Luckily, I was dealing with a mature student who understood that the situation was larger than either one of us.

This example highlights the power dimensions that complicate the supervisory position for female faculty. Even when the individual supervisor and student manage to cultivate a relationship of mutual trust and respect, broader institutional forces can strain these relationships. If a female supervisor asks for help, for instance, is it seen by colleagues as a sign of weakness? If a male offers assistance, will this be perceived negatively? Since relatively fewer females have achieved senior faculty status, female supervisors tend to be less experienced. Well-meaning colleagues may in fact stymie opportunities for gaining further supervisory experience with students that they perceive as hard to manage while providing genuinely supportive opportunities for gaining this type of experience with those students that they see as more malleable and manageable. In this situation, the female faculty negotiates the subtlety of being assertive about the students that she chooses to work with, and at the same time gaining the respect of more senior colleagues.

In a similar manner, gender relations and the early establishment of a supervisor's own research agenda can be problematic if not clearly communicated with the student being supervised: This did seem to be a problem particularly with my second supervisor where the combination of ethnicity, gender difference and my supervisor's own pressures to establish herself (as she was a new staff member who adopted me after my first supervisor left the university). My second supervisor was also very insistent that I should consult with her during her 'normal' student contact hours. These were always the same times and during the entire time she was my supervisor I was teaching a three semester program which always involved lecturing at this time. This was doubly frustrating because of what I saw as a lack of flexibility on her behalf and the lack of consideration she gave to my own attempts to establish a career in the same field.

Similarly, uncertainty about appropriate social responses can lead to tense and uncertain moments: It is a fairly long time ago now but I do recollect some strangely tense moments. I am probably most conscious of our seeming inability to have a flowing conversation. I am conscious of how men often speak over women and know that I do this myself. In our supervision meetings I feel that I often overcompensated.

This section presented a brief overview of the complexities associated with the gendered authority and power relations that exist in the supervisor–student relationship. Although this is not an exhaustive list of 'all' forms of negotiated supervision, we have attempted to illustrate that regardless of the complexity of the role formation, social cues or the life situation of supervisor or student, the best approach for the supervisor is to follow a clear and realistic assessment of their supervisory abilities and then utilize further consultation between the supervisor and student in order to minimize misunderstandings brought through attitudes of resistance, challenges and daily changes in events associated with the social life.

9.5 Gender and the PhD assessment process

Supervisors, or at least most supervisors, most of the time, find ways of surviving from day to day rather than once and for all. Relationships are constantly being negotiated in the flux of daily academic life, and this is so much a matter of how supervisors and PhD students get on with each other as people. The students' relationships with the curriculum and PhD administrative process are contained within the structure of practices that they construct. It can be very disappointing for a student if no clear direction or understanding of where they are in the progress of their PhD is conveyed by the supervisor.

> One student explains their experience: I felt that with my second supervisor she was never clear of the point in the process where I was currently situated. I feel I picked up 'learning the process' of crafting a PhD largely from observation of other students around me and learning from their (and my) experiences.

These experiences which may extend over years and years, precipitate the attitudes and traits that are the 'PhD life'. Because these attitudes and qualities are the result of complex practices they are hard to strategically plan. We, therefore, suggest a periodic yet continuing collective reassessment to be carried out by both the supervisor and the student about the current status of their relationship.

9.6 Conclusion

The key recommendation of this chapter is that communication and realistic self-assessment of supervision skills and ability is core to overcoming those negative aspects associated with the complexities of managing the personal elements of a supervisory role. These strategies should also mirror those recommended for students. For example, specific consideration must be made of existing gender-biased attitudes regarding intellectual, social and personal capacities that the supervisor possesses (see Figure 9.1).

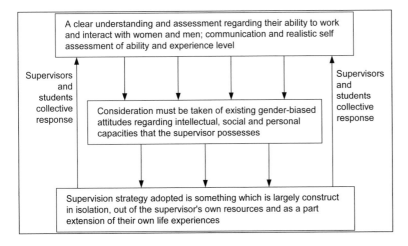

Figure 9.1 *Developing gender sensitive supervision*

In conclusion, we suggest the following bases for developing gender sensitive supervision:

- The supervisor enters their role with a clear understanding and assessment regarding their ability to work and interact with women and men.
- Consideration must be given to the existing gender-biased attitudes regarding intellectual, social and personal capacities that the supervisor holds:
  * Such consideration should be conducted without the preconceptions shaped by their own sexual preferences.
  * Supervisor should examine their academic-related and work-related success and realistically consider whether there has been greater success when they have worked with men or women.
  * Establish clear demarcation between 'everyday' issues that directly relate to the PhD research project, administration, write up and completion.
  * Clarify to what extent the supervisor is willing to discuss those issues that are not involved in the PhD process and more likely to be personal in nature.
  * Clarify these positions early in the project to minimize any confusion between supervisor and student about the form and nature of their interactions.

10

Sexual Orientation

David W. Wilson

10.1 Introduction

Archbishop Njongonkulu Ndungane has criticized his African colleagues and said that the church's attention should be focused on more pressing concerns such as AIDS and poverty.

This quotation from the BBC News Website on 3rd November 2003, relates reaction to the controversy following the installation of the Reverend Gene Robinson (an openly gay man) as Bishop in New Hampshire, USA. It may seem an odd way to open a chapter in a book advising on PhD supervision in the information systems domain, but it was chosen because it illustrates aspects of the dilemmas that may be faced in supervising students of a minority sexual orientation. The best thing about the quote is that it puts the 'problem' into perspective. If a candidate is coming to you for supervision for a PhD, the most pressing problems are likely to be relating to getting the PhD, not issues surrounding his or her sexual orientation. A relieved supervisor might inwardly say, 'Ah, that's fine then, let's forget about it and sweep it under the carpet.' This highlights the second problem revealed in the quotation, that is, the tendency not to talk about or ignore issues surrounding sexuality. In the majority of circumstances that will be fine and this may be the way the PhD student would like the issue handled as well. Here, it is not an issue for the student either. However, there may be times when it may be an issue.

Condemning some people's natural sexual orientation as sinful cannot be other than homophobic and it is undeniable that there is homophobia in the world. So, whilst it is well understood that those readers who have not skipped to the next chapter already are unlikely to be homophobic themselves, they are required to acknowledge that other people might be homophobic and can act in homophobic ways. They may also seek advice on supervising students with different sexual orientations than themselves. So what advice is useful to PhD supervisors in IS?

10.2 Advice to supervisors

The supervisor should never assume heterosexuality. Sexual orientation is rarely obvious, most of all to those who are not of a minority sexual orientation, even in accepting and enlightened societies.

> A student of the large course for mature students in work that I direct, on returning from the gay games, recently told me that of his cohort 33% are gay. I think he is fantasizing and exaggerating. His orientation hadn't crossed my mind till he asked for time off to go to the games and I can't for the life of me think who the others might be.

In fact, various societies react to minority orientations in different ways. Some positive changes have taken place comparatively recently in Europe, North America and elsewhere, concerning attitudes and legislation about gay males. In some other societies, there are long traditions of tolerance. In Thailand, for instance, transsexual and transgendered people, known locally as *katoey* have long enjoyed tolerance. In the last twenty years, with the international acclaim troubadour troupes have enjoyed, they seem to have reached high levels of acceptance and respect. Yet Bangkok gays bemoan the fact that whilst they don't feel particularly persecuted, they do wish that the general public didn't think that all gays are *katoey*. They feel reluctant to come out to family and friends for fear of being thought something they are not.

Thus those people with minority sexual orientation are not the same. Although there is an alliance of lesbians, gays, bisexual and transgendered

(LGBT) people who come together to lobby for changes in the law and to assert pride in and celebrate their differences, it needs to be recognized that differences between people of minority orientations run deep and they are not happy to be all lumped together and labeled *queer.*

> A colleague who openly proselytized his own religious background replaced my line manager when I was preparing to register for a PhD. This was a background from which there was a great deal of homophobic 'noise' emanating. The person in question couldn't look me in the eye, yet at the same time attempted to pressurize me to divert my research in the same direction as his own. I decided not to have him as supervisor.
>
> My future PhD supervisor had strongly espoused the emancipation of women. It was this that convinced me that he was to be morally trusted. My thesis had nothing to do with sexual orientation, but this trust was very important to me. I had confidence from the ethos displayed on other matters that he was likely to be sympathetic with regard to my 'difference.'

So what is the relevance of this to prospective and actual PhD supervisors? We have already suggested that the supervisor should never assume heterosexuality. But the supervisor should also be open and aware. The two stories above show the potential impact of this issue in respect to choosing a supervisor. The story below shows the impact of a supervisor appearing closed. It also shows the necessity for academic departments to reflect the world outside in terms of a balance of all groups, including gays.

> Whilst doing my doctorate, my partner was diagnosed HIV positive and I was left wondering whether I was infected (I am not). However, as my partner lived in Scotland, I had no one to turn to (except the charity Terry Higgins Trust, for counseling). I am not 'out' and I assumed that my own supervisor would be horrified and also question my ability to finish. When things became too much I approached not my supervisor but an academic colleague of his who was kind and approachable and who did indeed help me. The help I did receive was also thanks to an openly gay colleague who was able to recommend the academic I did talk to.

Of course there is a broader concern here. The student's inability to approach his supervisor on this issue suggests that students generally may not feel the supervisor can be approached to discuss any difficult issue. Supervisors need to appear open and sympathetic so that students feel as if they can discuss academic and non-academic concerns that can impact on their research (and not just the concern of this chapter).

Supervisors may give negative signals because they are simply ignorant of the issues. There are training programs available relating to how to deal with students' sexuality, gender, race and so on. These are popular (indeed, sometimes mandatory) amongst school and further education teachers in the

UK, but rarely taken up by university academics. The university should give all supervisors anti-discriminatory guidelines and have a counseling service available. Generally, it should be recognized that people with minority sexual orientations are likely to be discriminated against at least as much as other minorities.

> My university was anxious that I underwent the anti-discriminatory training that was provided, as I was to be involved in appointment panels. However, there was nothing in the program about discrimination against gays. It concentrated on sexism and racism in the workplace.

To provide an example of the complexity and subtlety of these issues, we discuss one issue concerning the gay community in the next section.

10.3 One issue – coming out

The great awkwardness concerning gays is often how 'out' they are, in other words, the extent to which the people that they deal with know and acknowledge their sexual orientation. We will use this concern as exemplar showing the complexity of such issues and the potential support that the supervisor may give.

> I have worked with gay colleagues who took great pains to ensure that everyone that they worked with was aware of their orientation. Sometimes it seems a bit 'in your face' and my own position is that I prefer people to get to know me and my work before my sexual orientation.

Gay PhD candidates will come in all shades of 'outness' from some people who are in self denial, that is, not even out to themselves, to the person who is out to everyone. Most people who come out (and many never do) come out to a friend first, followed by other close friends, followed by siblings, colleagues and perhaps lastly, to parents. Of course many people only go some way in this process and the sequence may be different for many, but that sequence is common.

> One student colleague was in self-denial. Although in his mid-twenties, he had not fully accepted he was gay. He believed the gay world was second rate and he did not wish to be part of it. He had been brought up in the world where 'gay' was a synonym for 'bad'. This world of locker room jokes had made him apprehensive. To others, including his supervisor, he seemed introvert and very mixed up, in short, a 'difficult' student.

A related matter concerns how the gay student perceives himself, as the history above illustrates. Some gay people think they are in some way inferior because the world seems to be dominated by heterosexual people. Such worries may have a negative impact on research. But then the impact on the research of a straight person who has just split from his or her partner can be equally detrimental. However, to a straight supervisor, the latter concern may be one that he feels able to support, within his understanding and maybe experience, whereas he may feel out of his depth with the former. The supervisor, at the very least, needs to be aware of potential sources of help for his student, for example, the university student counselor or advice center.

Ideally, the supervisor should try to position himself as a reliable colleague, maybe friend. But the groundwork for this has to have been done beforehand, as an 'unapproachable' supervisor cannot become 'approachable' at a stroke.

Some gays have brought up families before they accepted their real sexual orientation. This can turn out well, with families mutually accepting the situation. In other examples it has left bitterness and resentment and this can play on the thoughts of people throughout their working life (including their life as a research student) as well.

It is not recommended that the issue is raised by the supervisor first as the student may not want it to be raised and may not even have outed himself. Unless it affects their work, it is simply a factor in their personal life that will work itself out in time. It could surface as bouts of depression or self-doubt, but it is unlikely to be explicitly brought to the attention of the supervisor. The supervisor needs to be paying a more general confidence building role, concentrating on the potential or actual value of the research work. This may help the student in many ways, but it is surely not the role of the supervisor to intercede in a gay student's personal questioning, unless asked.

People who do come out will begin to accept themselves and perhaps meet others they view as being like them, having had the same or similar journeys. This period can be both troublesome and euphoric. Some may 'get obsessed' with their new-found circles and spend much time in the commercial gay scene. Others may still have moments of doubt. If this coming out period starts in the middle of a PhD, his supervisor is very likely to notice, through a change in demeanor or new demands on the student's time.

Students at universities situated in a large metropolis are likely to have available a vibrant scene; students at universities situated in country areas or small towns may only see a highly regulated and oppressive culture, and spend time looking for different social settings. Either way, there is potential for the research to suffer, and the supervisor needs to monitor the situation carefully. Again, the supervisor finds himself in a delicate and difficult situation. It will obviously be easier if the supervisor has a good open relationship with the student already and the student feels it beneficial to discuss the issue with the supervisor.

Even if people do eventually come out to themselves, some never come out to others. With some justification, they may feel that their sexual being is intensely personal and no business to anyone other but themselves. Alternatively, they may feel it is inappropriate to 'thrust' their sexuality on someone else. Some continue to feel it is a homophobic world and coming out further invites discrimination.

Others do come out further. They may start with a few close friends and then parents. This may come as a response following incessant inquiries as to when they are getting married, sometimes used as veiled enquiries regarding their offspring's sexual orientation. Although coming out to families can be a smooth and joyful process, for others it can be traumatic.

10.4 When the supervisor is gay

Most gays do not seek gay supervisors, although a few do avoid gays as supervisors 'for fear of complications.' It should not make any difference and most students, gay and straight, choose supervisors on the basis of their knowledge and interest in the project. Clearly, most students expect their sexual orientation to be insignificant to the supervision process.

Gay supervisors may, however, feel that being a person of non-majority orientation, they need to be 'above suspicion' and, for example, arrange their room so that there is always clear space between the supervised and the supervisor. Accusations of inappropriate behavior can come from straight and gay students and although straight supervisors need to take similar precautions, minorities are more at risk from unwarranted accusations.

> I remember having to be very careful with a gay student who I suspected of plagiarism. Checking the student records, my colleagues seem to have had the same suspicions ('his contribution in class is small and unimpressive but his essays show very much greater resourcefulness'). When it came to an interview with him, I made sure that the office door was open, that we were visible from the corridor, and that a colleague was sitting in their office opposite, door also open, keeping an eye on us. This is a normal precaution for me, as a gay supervisor I have to be especially careful.

10.5 Conclusion

Some readers may think that the concentration on coming out has been over-emphasized. However, it is a useful exemplar of concerns and situations that might impact on the research student during the time of PhD research. Many gay people do come out at the ages when they are likely to be doing the PhD research, and therefore will impact at this time. It is also an issue where it is not always obvious to the (even) enlightened supervisor how to react in the student's best interests. We do not argue that it is best for the supervisor to raise the issue first. The supervisor needs to have already put in place the measures that make him sympathetic and open so that the student himself raises the issue if he wants to and it is relevant in some way at that time to his PhD research.

In summary, discrimination on any grounds other than the veracity of the research will lead people to assume that they may be discriminated against. Discrimination is not always overt and mechanical; it is often subtle and not even understood by the discriminators. Creating 'a locker room atmosphere' may look like team building to 'the boys.' It looks like exclusion to women, gays, bisexual, the transgendered and others. Advocacy of non-discrimination needs to be part of the university's culture and this will help others believe they will not be discriminated against. An awareness of the issues needs to be one of the important bases for all supervisors.

One final story concerns this chapter itself. For some time, unlike every other chapter in the book, there were communication difficulties between the author and the editors. It turned out that the ESSEC web mail filtering system, or 'spyware', deleted all these incoming emails automatically because of its content, without notifying the receiver or sender.

11

Diverse Cultures

David Avison, Muhammadou Kah, Jainaba Kah and Abimbola Soriyan

11.1 Introduction

Much of Part IV is about diversity. We have already looked at part-time PhDs when the majority in IS are full-time; women PhD students when the majority in IS are men; and LGTB students when the majority in IS are straight. This chapter looks at other forms of diversity, in particular, studying abroad or belonging to a minority race in the country of study.

If we look at this diversity together, it is readily apparent that most PhD students are atypical, in that they do not belong to the category of white, male, straight, full-time, or home students. Thus, the aware supervisor will expect that the majority of his or her students do not conform to any perceived 'norm' in some way. But the aware supervisor will also think of this in positive terms. It is important to embrace diversity for the enriching experience it provides. It would be a great loss to us individually (and the discipline as a whole) if supervisors avoid diversity because they are unsure of themselves in different situations and unsure about what might happen. This chapter, therefore, provides some further support for supervisors contemplating minority students as supervisees and also provides some insight into the potential problems and concerns of their students.

In this chapter we look at some other ways in which students may find themselves in the minority. We focus on 'international' students who are taking their research degrees in institutions away from their home country; students who are taking their research degrees in developing countries; and students who belong to a minority race in the country where they are doing the degree (whether home or international students). In so doing, we raise a number of issues, including those relating to problems of language, cultural differences and sensitivity to race. Many of the issues are described through personal histories.

11.2 International students

We will consider first international students, that is, those students who are taking their PhD in a different country to their own. Many of these students will have taken their earlier courses at home, so they may be unfamiliar with everything – the host country, food, language, culture, education system and the rest. What the supervisor may not realize is that the student may have already had a traumatic experience before they meet on the first occasion. The first experience in the country where the student is studying may be negative, but out of the control of the university, department or supervisor.

> I arrived in January, when the temperature was below 10°C. It was 33°C at home. My first worry was the thought that I will not survive the climate, never mind the PhD. We went through immigration and the officer asked some absurd questions such as 'How much money do you have?' and 'Are you going back to your country after you have completed your studies?'. The impression we got was that we are not welcome here and we still feel it to this day.

Other early experiences may also be negative, including finding somewhere to live, in which the university should have been able to help. Students with families may find this particularly difficult.

> My first 'trauma' was to find suitable accommodation for a family with three children. Many landlords turned us down because we had children. Once we lost our deposit money

to an agent when the landlord did not allow us to move in. We felt as if the system in this country was all against us. I felt like taking a drastic decision to quit the idea of doing a PhD. We eventually found accommodation after 3 tearful weeks with the help of a colleague from the department. We have to make do with a small space. Although it is a three-bedroom house, it is small compared to what we are used to back home.

For others, they are alone for the first time without their family. Leaving a partner and children at home can be an extremely difficult and lonely experience. It is therefore particularly important that the first experience of the university, department and supervisor is positive. This is not always the case, and even the welcoming party may not be successful for some, despite good intentions. Supervisors should ensure, for example, that all tastes are catered for, including those who do not drink alcohol or do not eat certain foods.

I attended the department's welcoming party and was expecting some exciting food, but was only served sandwiches. There was a lot of alcohol about, which I have never touched. I felt awkward and I was still hungry when I left.

A research student can feel isolated, lonely and vulnerable. Being in another country can intensify these feelings of alienation. Having basic facilities for each of the research students on the first day is very important. It gives them an academic home with belongings and access to the outside world, through the internet and telephone.

Two of my sisters are also doing their PhD in the UK. One does not have a desk or a room where she can work and meet other PhD students in her research area. She is an outsider, a visitor. Another does have a research room but there are only hot desks there and she never uses them. She feels very uncomfortable. She also feels that she does not belong there. I was very lucky. I was given a desk in a room, filled with other PhD students. I did not have to go through the PhD experience alone. My desk, the room and friends gave me a sense of belonging.

When I started my PhD study I expected that someone would tell me what and how to do things. But nobody did. You have to explore things yourself. Planning travel, booking a hotel and getting a computer are examples of things I had to do myself. These are not easy things in unfamiliar surroundings.

Students may see themselves and their qualifications as undervalued. This may be a break from a successful career with status back home.

There is a mistaken assumption here that Eastern European education is not of high quality. Several of my friends from Russia have told me that employers were greatly surprised about the skills they had mastered from their studies. They simply didn't believe that a Russian qualification could be as good as a Danish one.

I am a senior lecturer and head of department back home and came here to get a PhD, necessary for a full professorship. I am back to being a student and am treated very differently. Now I am treated like a high-school student. I cannot teach. I cannot supervise. It is a bit humiliating. It is a great challenge for me.

The welcome party does give the supervisor an opportunity to socialize with the new research students and trying to establish a rapport. However, despite the supervisor's best intensions, this may be difficult as well, due to language problems or cultural differences. Supervisors need to empathize with students having these difficulties and we look at this next.

11.3 Language and culture

Many international students may have a good academic background in the host language (we will assume this is English in this chapter), but much poorer knowledge of English language in practice. This is complicated by local accents and dialects, but also by cultural references, with which the student may not be aware. It will take time for students to acclimatize to the pace of conversation and to understanding messages that are being communicated without words: facial expressions and the like.

At the beginning, students may be concerned about saying the wrong thing, and may prefer to say little or nothing. Supervisors who themselves lack good communication skills or be generally unsympathetic may well assume the worst of their students and they may accuse them of everything from poor English language skills to having little personality to being very rude. Supervisors who appear unsympathetic early in the student–supervisor relationship may find the relationship never recovers from this bad start. Let us look at a few examples coming from students.

It is true I have a 'foreign' accent, mispronounce words frequently, misuse words and make grammatical errors. I feel self conscious and these problems get in the way of discussing research topics with my supervisor. There are times when I have had to repeat the same word a few times as my supervisor could not understand me. This makes me say less, but then I am seen as someone with no thoughts and no character. I know I have to talk more so that my supervisor can guide me properly. Frequently, I don't understand what he says. I have to make a judgment, 'should I ask or not?' when I do not understand a word or expression. Usually I say nothing, because I am worried that I am seen as incompetent and my supervisor is impatient with me. It is all very frustrating.

> I was very quiet in the beginning. You go into observation mode. I do not know whether it is personal or female. You think about things like: Can you ask questions here? What kind of questions? There are many tacit rules and it takes time to discover and understand them.

> It is quite difficult to converse in English after spending all my previous life speaking my native language. However, frequent use of English in formal and informal occasions and regular attendances in a number of English classes have helped to improve my English in many ways. I try to converse in English as much as I can to gain confidence.

> English is a second language for me, but people tell me that I speak it reasonably well. However, an English friend of mine has told me that my facial expression sometimes mismatches with what is expected. I am sometimes seen as impolite and ungrateful and I don't understand why. It is not easy to know all the social protocols. It is all very tiring as a lot of thinking is involved.

Experienced supervisors may well understand these issues and be supportive. However, they may not realize that the lack of confidence such problems engender may have deeper repercussions on the research, affecting, for example, the research approach used, where it will be used and the research itself.

> I am going to avoid any method that involves a high level of communication and interpretation unless I can do the data collection in my own country. I would just not feel confident enough.

Supervisors may assume that some misunderstandings are due to weaknesses or naivety about research, but they may actually be more to do with cultural differences. The following example relates to plagiarism, and reveals much about the attitude of the supervisor (who tells the story) as well as the student.

> I took on a mature Japanese student who had good Japanese qualifications and had worked as an IS Project Manager in American and Swiss Banks in Japan and Europe. He seemed a very good prospect but is 'very Japanese' in that he bows, hisses and uses a particular Japanese thinking word a lot during discourse. The second time I saw him he explained his proposed research methods. He was reading from a computer print-out. I saw that what he was reading from was the output of a Japanese translation program. On closer inspection it turned out to be a document from the research methods area of *ISWorld* and underneath each paragraph there was the Japanese translation. I tried to explain that this was plagiarism and that it was not acceptable simply putting it into his own words without acknowledgment. I gave him a written warning that any repetition would endanger his registration.
> Last week I reviewed his proposal. I began to get suspicious about some of the language used. On putting it into Google, up sprang the sources. He admitted he'd pasted

> in text but he didn't have better words than the ones used. As I have learnt from my own reading, citing 'the masters' is common practice in the Far East and that people from that region have great difficulty in knowing when they are plagiarizing. Nevertheless I got him to sign a document that gave me permission to submit any document that he presented to me to the *Joint Information Systems Committee (JISC)* database of previously submitted work which detects plagiarism.

Perhaps this student and this supervisor will learn together, sometimes time is all that is required.

> Being in a different country and a different culture is difficult, but it also enriches our learning experience. At the first meeting with my supervisor, I realized that I needed to be in charge of my own learning. It was not me who should ask 'What should I do?' but my supervisor to ask 'What do you want to do?' I was not used to deciding for myself when there is a teacher in front of me. I felt lost, like leaving me in a forest and asking me to find my own way back. I would ask 'But where should I go?' and 'what path should I choose?' He refused to answer those questions. It has been two years and only now do I begin to understand why he did not answer my questions. I am learning to be a true researcher.

A further temptation is for people to cluster in their natural language and cultural groups. They might do this for reassurance, to discuss issues that are common to them, or just to avoid having to make all that effort to speak in a foreign language. These groups need also to ensure that they are welcoming of outsiders, even those from the majority!

> There was a large percentage of international students in my program. A big challenge was the language barrier. Many of these students studied in their own language outside of classes. Consequently, studying with them was initially a challenge. However, eventually it was no longer a problem as we got to know each other more, so that we could exchange research ideas and discuss research topics.

But it is vital that research students are provided with the facilities and encouragement so that they can make these changes themselves, and supervisors will then be rewarded with enthusiastic and highly motivated students.

> The quality of the university, department, faculty members and facilities provided to us, including access to references and development programs, is excellent … It is amazing to learn that scholars are willing to share their knowledge and assist students without hesitation, despite their status and busy schedules.

Another important topic concerns racial issues. Again, an understanding, awareness and better management of these issues by supervisors can help the quality of research and completion rate of minority students and better prepare them to succeed. We look at this next.

11.4 Racial issues

This section is in the main about pursuing and completing a PhD in IS by minorities. Examples might include African-American and Hispanic students in the US, North African students in France, Indian students in the UK, Maori students in New Zealand and Chinese students in Australia. They may have come from abroad to do their studies or they may be citizens of that country, with their family living there for generations.

In spite of demonstrated capabilities to conduct research in mainstream areas, the type of topics chosen by minority students can gravitate around issues confronted by their respective communities. Other students may be perceived as more capable of doing mainstream topics due to commonality in heritage, race, culture and values. It can be more difficult to find supervisors willing to get involved in these topics, the research itself might be more difficult and publication opportunities may be reduced.

> Going to Africa to collect data from my research was quite expensive. It was also tough to get people to be interviewed or even filling out a questionnaire for some research that they cannot see direct benefit for themselves. Another problem was the dearth of good quality literature in my field of research.

On the topic of racism, although some racist attitudes are clearly evident sometimes, most of the issues are more subtle and often very difficult for members of faculty and supervisors to discuss. Mainstream students (and some supervisors) may perceive minority students as less qualified, as not 'belonging here' and only 'here' because they are rich or to fill some actual or hidden quota.

> A challenge that continually occurs even to this day is proving that I belong in the program because of my intelligence, qualifications and professional experience. I am continually asked how I obtained the knowledge and the educational background I currently have.

This can impact negatively on student relationships and the building of social networks. Under-represented students might withdraw from the 'other' students after having had some unpleasant encounter and thereby miss out on having a much more complete PhD experience. As a result, they tend to cluster together, which also has detrimental effects on language skills (if that is an issue).

These clusters tend to consist of one minority group as minority groups themselves may also not mix well.

I'm an African-American woman, married with kids, with considerable industry experience. For the most part, my relationship with PhD students from other races is fine. At my school, most of the other PhD students are foreign students of Asian descent, in their 20s, unmarried, and without much industry experience. We just don't have much in common, and there is a language barrier. The Chinese women hang together and talk in their native tongue.

Members of faculty should not make assumptions about people based upon their cultural background, but cultural issues can affect social relationships with supervisors as well as fellow PhD students. Indeed, in many cultures, but certainly not all, the academic has very high status.

As a doctoral student, I can count the number of times I went to my professors' offices. I was never comfortable to drop by my professors' office to chat, which is important in nurturing relationships. Many years later, after completing my doctorate, I learnt from my colleagues the kind of relationships they had built with their supervisors – even spending time in their supervisors' homes whilst writing their dissertation or having a drink at a bar or coffee at a café. I never had such a relationship. I was even scared to call my supervisor; I just never built that kind of relationship.

Other students appear (I stress appear) to have a closer relationship with their supervisor. They go to lunch on a regular basis and they are much more sociable than I am with my supervisor. This may have just as much to do with my professional background as it has to do with race. In my training, subordinates and supervisors did not socialize much. It's a challenge to overcome this barrier.

Wonderfully enough, the faculty in my program treats me as a human being like everyone else. Occasionally I am asked to provide answers to questions about my race and there are occasions of discomfort when certain subject areas are brought into conversation. Although these do occur from time to time, it has not occurred enough for me to feel any ill will to others or bad feelings towards me.

Members of faculty need to be sensitive; for example, they should not gossip about students, and the failings of students should be kept confidential. Many students will not like details of their life, even private successes, to be known by others.

Fortunately we are also seeing more minority students, albeit slowly, becoming supervisors themselves, supervising majority and minority students. The students from these previously under-represented groups may now be able to work with supervisors with similar backgrounds and are therefore relieved from previously challenging issues such as language and cultural barriers still confronted by the rest of the minority student population.

> I did my undergraduate, masters and PhD in IS and Management. We did not have one black faculty member in my entire school. There is a need for minorities to become academics, proving that the IS profession is a field in which we can excel. I am now one of those numbers.

Some minorities, such as Indians and Chinese, have already established themselves in the IS profession in critical numbers. Therefore, many IS programs may even have faculty members from these countries. When students from these parts of the world come into IS programs, therefore, they may already have a support network to tap into.

Finally, we look at another situation, students from developing countries studying in their home country but doing a PhD remotely from a university in a developed country.

11.5 Students studying in developing countries

Developing countries differ a great deal. Looking at the African context, for example, the situation in Nigeria differs from that in Zimbabwe or Mozambique, and in any one country there are likely to be differences between universities. Such countries might be able to sponsor some candidates to do their research in developed countries, but many governments cannot sustain such expenditure. They may be able to hire lecturers with PhDs from abroad to introduce postgraduate programs into the universities, but this also requires that facilities, equipment and other resources are available.

PhD candidates in general face similar challenges, but these challenges can be emphasized and exacerbated in developing countries. Four major issues that are of particular concern are:

1 Selecting a topic
2 Selecting supervisors
3 Following correct PhD procedures
4 Finding resources.

Of these, funding seems to be an over-riding concern. We look at this issue separately in Chapter 7, but we look at it later in this section as well because of its importance in this context.

Selecting a supervisor can also be a major concern here, partly because there can be so few qualified academics in the area chosen for research. Sometimes topics are chosen to fit in with the interests of the only potential supervisors available.

I had no idea about the problems involved in selecting a supervisor. In the PhD application form, there was a need to indicate who the supervisor would be, and also a statement to be written by the proposed supervisor that they will supervise the work. In this case, a senior lecturer that had undergone a PhD program was the only qualified individual in the local university. It was him or nobody. I had hoped for an external supervisor, but I was informed that the tradition of external supervisors had been discontinued, as the university could no longer fund the traveling expenses.

Getting through the administrative system can be difficult. It seems universities in developed countries can be so concerned about not having lower standards than elsewhere, that they over-compensate.

There were a series of forms to be completed and submitted. The research title, objectives, methodology and expected outcome need to be detailed. It is as if any course work has had to have been completed and the research commenced before permission is given to start the course work and the research!

Another issue is the standard of the expected work itself. External examiners will frequently be based in developed countries and there tends to be great concern about what they will require. Internal supervisors may be viewed (rightly or wrongly) as having a mindset very different to external examiners and this might also lead to over-compensation.

Funding does not only concern supervision as literature, databases and the Internet, for example, may not be easily accessed. This is a major problem in most developing countries, even in universities with Internet facilities.

Funding any external examiner's traveling expenses is also a major issue. It is normally mandatory that at least one of the supervisors is present at the oral examination. During examination, comments from absentee panel members might be read for the candidate's response. The candidate normally will have to correct the thesis based on the panel of examination recommendations and within the stipulated time as recommended by the panel members.

In this short section we have discussed some of the special considerations related to students taking their PhD in a developing country. It is hoped that these insights will, if nothing else, ensure that potential external examiners are aware of the problems of students in that context and the achievements of those who have come to the stage of submitting their thesis.

11.6 Conclusion

In this chapter we have looked at some other reasons for diversity amongst PhD students, in particular those students studying overseas in developed countries, those who are of a minority race in the country of study and those taking their PhDs in developing countries. It is important for members of faculty to be aware of the difficulties and challenges for them and their students, but the aware supervisor will also think of this in positive terms and embrace diversity for the enriching experience it provides.

PhD candidates in general face similar challenges, but these challenges can be emphasized and exacerbated in these circumstances because of language difficulties, cultural differences and other sensitivities. Some problems may occur in realms, such as immigration authorities, which are impossible for the university, supervisor and student to control. Many are not academic but are areas where the supervisor can help, not least, by making the student feel welcome and at home, and providing an infrastructure, such as computing equipment and space to put it. Opportunities also need to be provided for students to mix with others. Many are academic issues, but as we saw in the plagiarism example, due to cultural differences rather than genuine academic failings. Supervisors need to empathize with their students and more than anything give their time and patience to them.

Part IV:
Academic Issues

Part IV focuses on important academic issues. In Chapter 12 Steve Elliot and David Avison discuss IS as a discipline and give an overview of the history of the field and key academic issues. Chapter 13 by Jan Pries-Heje and David Avison targets two issues of key importance in any PhD, namely quality and originality, and give you a number of ready-to-use tools to foster and ensure quality. Chapter 14 by Detmar Straub, David Gefen and Marie-Claude Boudreau, and Chapter 15 by David Avison and Michael Myers, look at quantitative and qualitative research methods, respectively.

If you are a supervisor: reflect on what makes your own research 'information systems' research. Try to use Figures 12.1 and 12.2 to place your research on the two dimensions: fundamental-applied and soft-hard. Does your research use any of the other disciplines that IS is 'close' to? Does it contribute to any other disciplines?

Use the questions from Chapter 13 when evaluating a PhD research proposal. Plan and carry out a review with your PhD students. Use the appropriate lists from Chapter 13.

Take a look at Chapters 14 and 15. Can you supervise only one specific type of research, using a single research method, and therefore only one specific type of research question? Do you know who amongst your colleagues are expert at research approaches with which you are not familiar?

If you are a PhD student: consider why your research is 'information systems' research. Use Chapter 12 as inspiration. Reflect on what reference disciplines you are going to use or use already. Check out Figures 12.1 and 12.2 to inspire your reflection. How is your research question related to the IS top management issues (see the tables in Chapter 12)? Are you studying a dying fad? Will your answer to your research question also be important in 3 to 5 years?

Check out the list of top journals in Chapter 13. Do you know them? Do you read them? Could you publish some of your research in one of them? If you send your work to other outlets than these journals, how do you then ensure that your research is of high quality? Will your PhD be sufficiently original? Have you made a quality review together with your supervisor? If not, then see Chapter 13.

Look at Chapters 14 and 15. Are you only doing one type of research, be it quantitative or qualitative? Why? Consider which research method fits best with your research question. Have you chosen your research method only because of your supervisor's experience? Do you need to consult an expert in another type of research approach? Look into what courses at the PhD level are offered on research methods. Have you trained yourself so you can use both quantitative and qualitative research methods, and combine them if needed? How will you ensure validity and generalizability in your research?

12

Discipline of Information Systems

Steve Elliot and David Avison

12.1 Introduction

This chapter is about the academic discipline of information systems. By 'discipline' we mean 'a branch of instruction or learning' though we do not wish to imply agreement on a limited field of study nor total 'control,' 'obedience' nor too much 'order' about what we research. This would give ground for concern, for as we shall see, information systems is a pluralistic field, founded on knowledge from other, more established, source disciplines.

Information Systems (IS) is an exciting area for researchers. Since the 1990s, applications of Information Technology (IT) have been fundamentally changing the way organizations conduct business. These changes create opportunities for researchers to make significant contributions to knowledge while they assist organizations to manage this change better. The *Organization for Economic Cooperation and Development (OECD)* acknowledges the structural impact of these technology-enabled innovations:

> *The Internet and related advances in information and communication technology (ICT) are transforming economic activity, much as the steam engine, railways and electricity did in the past* (OECD, 2001).

This chapter provides an overview of the foundations of the IS discipline. It defines and to some extent scopes the discipline; considers its foundations, boundaries and focus through examination of major research categories and key IS research concepts from the perspective of education and industry; identifies seminal and other essential works; and looks at resources available for IS researchers. Most importantly it introduces the reader to some of the debates that feature in this young and exciting discipline.

12.2 Evolving definitions of IS

IS is a relatively new discipline. We consider the start of the discipline to be the widespread use of computers to process data in the 1950s. Of course there were data processing systems well before the advent of computers. There can today be IS without computers. The grapevine is a powerful information system. Further, if technology is used, it does not have to be sophisticated. But in practice, information systems are now almost invariably computerized. The rejoinder is simply that people will be involved as much as computers, and that not all parts of the information system will be automated.

IS as a field of study developed in response to the increasing necessity of organizations to improve their capabilities to process and to manage data. Reflecting this origin, an information system was initially seen to be an application of computers to help organizations process their data so they could improve their management of information.

While the types of computer technologies developed and potential areas of their application increased, so too did the role of an information system and the scope of the discipline. IT and IS are now ubiquitous in industrialized nations and widespread in much of the rest of the world. Their impact extends from business to government, the community and into many private homes. We will distinguish between IS and IT later in this chapter.

Information systems incorporate:

The effective design, delivery, use and impact of information technologies in organizations and society (Avison and Fitzgerald, 2003, p xi).

Recognizing that successful applications of IT require broader attention than just on the technology, the IS discipline steadily developed from its initial 'techno-centric' focus to a more integrated technology, management, organizational and social focus. This is reflected further in the following definition suggested by the UK Academy for Information Systems:

The study of information systems and their development is a multi-disciplinary subject and addresses the range of strategic, managerial and operational activities involved in the gathering, processing, storing, distributing and use of information, and its associated technologies, in society and organizations.

From a researcher's perspective, major landmarks in the development of the IS discipline were the publication of the first research-oriented IS journal, *Management Information Systems Quarterly (MISQ),* published in 1977 and the first *International Conference of Information Systems (ICIS)* held in 1980. It is interesting that, at that first conference, Dickson et al. (1980) suggest that IS has an image problem due to an identity crisis, definitional uncertainty, moving target, communication and integration, practitioners vs. academics, research quality and fragmentation, and being the new kid on the block. As we shall see in this chapter, some of these are still concerns, although much has been achieved since that time.

More recently, the *Association of Information Systems (AIS)* was formed in 1994 as the international organization for IS academics, to add to the many national organizations already existing. These landmark events were intended to support development of IS research and theory.

We will discuss later how much the editorial policy of the *MISQ* has changed over the years. Although the *MISQ* is generally recognized as the leading research journal, *Communications of the ACM* probably has the most impact, having a large circulation list (83 000), the majority of the subscribers being practitioners.

Today, the IS discipline is seen to be located within, and providing leadership, to a broad domain defined by the development, use and application of IS by individuals, organizations and society as a whole. The IS discipline is distinct in that it:

> *examines more than just the technological system, or just the social system, or even the two side by side; in addition it investigates the phenomena that emerge when the two interact. This embodies both a research perspective and a subject matter that differentiate the academic field of information systems from other disciplines.* (Lee, 2001, p iii)

12.3 The potential contribution of IS research

At its simplest, IS research is an attempt to explain observations or to predict likely outcomes of actions. The hypotheses tested may be a distillation of experience from organizations sourced directly from observations of organizational practice, indirectly from experimentation or by other means. Theory development arises from attempts to improve business practice based on the distilled experience of prior and current practice.

The process of distilling experience to enable its utilization in other contexts is 'generalization' (Lee and Baskerville, 2003). As seen in Chapters 14 and 15 on research methods, generalization from the results of research may be based on quantitative or qualitative analysis. Statistical generalization develops inferences about a larger population based on the collection of quantitative data from a smaller sample. Analytic generalization utilizes previously developed theory as a template for analysis of collected qualitative data (Yin, 1994, pp 30–32). The proposed dynamic capabilities theory, the net-enabled business innovation cycle, illustrates many of the issues to be considered in theory development (Wheeler, 2002).

Theory revision occurs where current theory is compared with, or tested against, dynamically developing practice and, to the extent necessary, the theory is reviewed, redefined or revised to reflect current practice more closely. A classic example of theory testing is Markus' paper on IS implementation in organizations. Markus (1983) compared three rival theories on resistance to IS with current practice and showed that one of the theories was supported by the case study data.

However, the word 'theory' can take on a much bigger dimension than this, as shown in the following citation from Kerlinger (1973):

A theory is a set of interrelated constructs (concepts), definitions, and propositions that presents a systematic view of phenomena by specifying relations and variables, with the purpose of explaining and predicting the phenomena.

As we shall see, some theories are fundamental to academic disciplines: systems theory, information theory and structuration theory are three theories developed in other disciplines which have been used to attempt to explain IS phenomena. However, as Gregor (2003) argues, we have been notably poor at developing such grand theories of our own. We also discuss this aspect later in this chapter.

12.4 Differentiating IS from related disciplines

Among computing-related or IT disciplines, IS is differentiated by its focus. In a controversial article in the Harvard Business Review of May 2003, Nicholas Carr argues that IT doesn't matter. He compares IT to the electricity or telephone infrastructure: the early mover advantage has gone, everyone has it and organizations cannot gain competitive advantage because of it (Carr, 2003). In some respects this is similar to the OECD perspective given at the beginning of the chapter.

But IS is different from IT. As illustrated graphically in Figure 12.1, compared with two other IT-related disciplines, computer science and computer systems engineering, IS emphasizes the applications of technology rather than a focus on fundamental technologies and theories. It focuses more on interactions between people and organizations (the 'soft' issues) and technology rather than on the technologies (the 'hard' issues) themselves. Over time, as the IS discipline matures; it is highly likely that more emphasis will be given to the development of theory that is fundamental to IS. This would result in the IS discipline increasing its depth of focus, as suggested in Figures 12.1 and 12.2 by the dotted lines. It should be noted that the figures represent the focus of the different disciplines, not the quantum of work conducted in or contributed by any of the disciplines.

This emphasis on soft, or human and organizational, issues may suggest that IS should be seen more as a social science discipline rather than science or engineering. But as shown in Figure 12.2, sociology, psychology, anthropology and other social sciences do not share our emphasis on the applications of technology to organizations and society.

Like computer science, they can be seen as both related disciplines and foundation disciplines of IS.

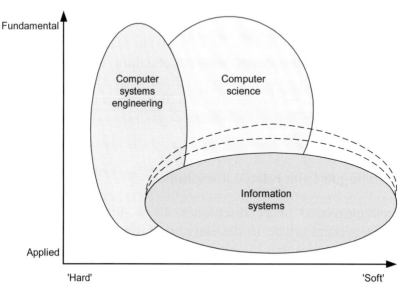

Figure 12.1 *Differentiating IS from other IT-related disciplines* (adapted from ACS, 1992)

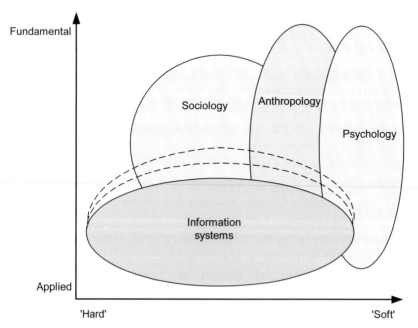

Figure 12.2 *Differentiating IS from other social science disciplines*

Thus, while there may be considerable overlap of the disciplines at the boundaries, the disciplines are still differentiated by the focus and orientation of their activities.

12.5 The theoretical foundations of IS

Notwithstanding a strong design component, the IS discipline in essence is an applied social science pertaining to the use and impact of technology. As researchers were drawn to the new discipline, they applied the theories, methods and research practices from their original disciplines, primarily computer science on the one side and social sciences and management on the other. A diversity of theory from reference disciplines, including economics, mathematics, linguistics, semiotics, ethics, political science, psychology, sociology and statistics, along with computer science, was applied.

Within these disciplines, different theories exist and these may be mutually inconsistent. The theories include systems theory, information theory, the theory of science and scientific method. It is true that many disciplines (including medicine, management and geography) also do not have a simple and single disciplinary status and can further be described as a collection of social practices. However, such a discipline can be seen by other academics as confused and lacking in coherence and academic rigor: in short, the discipline of information systems could lack credibility because it does not have theoretical clarity. Although it may be unrealistic to expect an agreed and consistent theory to emerge, it is important that more researchers work in areas that may establish the theoretical underpinnings of information systems.

The interdisciplinary nature of the subject is no excuse for a lack of rigor. However, IS researchers have been aware of the dangers and as Baskerville and Myers (2002), amongst others, have shown, there has been much progress over the past few years.

One of the problems with the use of concepts from another discipline is that they may be used uncritically. Avison and Myers (1995) give an example of the uncritical use of a concept within information systems with the use of the term 'culture'. Researchers in information systems may be unaware of their historical development within the source discipline, and may gloss over the fact that there may be a range of perspectives that operate concurrently. As Orlikowski and Baroudi (1991) argue, the social sciences *are marked by a plethora of 'schools of thought,' each with its own metatheoretic assumptions, research methodologies, and adherents.*

The way that IS seems to take on board major theoretical underpinnings of other disciplines has been lax at times. In attacking the once-prevalent view that systems theory can be used to underpin IS, Checkland (1999) argues that this should be dispelled as 'naïve optimism': *there is no simple link between systems theory and information systems.* Similarly, information theory (Shannon and Weaver, 1949) is a very technical, indeed mathematical, way to perceive communication between humans and organizations that is the essence of IS. It is not mathematical complexity that underpins IS. Stamper (1997) argues the case for the related theory of semiotics (and also linguistics) to be fundamental to IS. This is also argued by Mingers and Stowell (1997), which contains a number of articles relevant to this chapter. The unifying work of Simon (1981) continues to be influential in branches of economics, sociology, psychology, computer science and elsewhere, as well as IS. The theory of communicative action (Habermas, 1979), structuration theory (Giddens, 1987), and actor-network theory (Latour, 1987) have also become popular in some IS academic circles. As an emerging discipline, IS has also been influenced by writers giving a sociological perspective from within and outside the discipline (for example, the socio-technical theory expressed in Mumford, 1995, and also by Kling, 1996).

Currently, there is ongoing discussion within the discipline about the extent to which IS should continue to utilize theory from reference disciplines instead of developing a more IS-centric theory coming from within the discipline. Arguably, the constant review and application of IS theory strengthens its applicability.

Even well-established concepts in IS research such as 'users' have been found simplistic and unrepresentative of the multitude of roles undertaken by users in their interactions with a diversity of applications and people within varying social contexts (Lamb and Kling, 2003). The authors consider earlier research approaches based on the concept of an individualistic user to be limited, leading to an inadequate understanding of information selection, manipulation, communication and exchange in a variety of social contexts.

New insights into the strategic role of IT have also been sought, for example by Sambamurthy et al. (2003), by drawing on recent thinking in strategy, entrepreneurship and IT management. Stressing the critical impact on organizational performance related to its capabilities (agility, digital options and entrepreneurial alertness) and strategic processes (capability-building, entrepreneurial action and co-evolutionary adaptation) these authors consider their antecedents to be research into IT investments and capabilities.

12.6 Unity and diversity

Since the range of IT is rapidly developing, applications of IT are also developing rapidly. In consequence, IS research is characterized by diversity, flexibility and dynamic development. These characteristics may be seen to provide the discipline with both strengths and weaknesses.

The IS discipline's strength lies in its ability to support research into applications of IT that are structurally transforming traditional business practice. The weakness is that the discipline may focus on such a diversity of phenomena that it may appear to lack a central core. This potential weakness is examined in Benbasat and Zmud's (2003) paper where the authors express concern that the IS research community is contributing to an identity crisis by under-investigating what they call core issues in IS and over-investigating non-core issues. They define the IS field narrowly and, while acknowledging its multi-disciplinary principles, seek to limit multi-disciplinary practice in IS research. The authors also challenge the current approach of borrowing and adapting theories from other disciplines to explain IS phenomena better and suggest that focus would be applied more beneficially to original contributions to the IS field. On the other hand, this view has been challenged widely by the IS community.

The narrowness of their proposed re-definition of IS appears to be too restrictive. It excludes the 'information' in information systems and the rich tradition of diversity in IS. Instead it promotes a narrow focus in research approaches (there is a strongly positivist flavor in their research examples). It omits the major role played by IS in the transformation of organizations, industries and the community as a result of e-business applications; and much of the excitement and the energy that is associated with assisting to address major issues confronting organizations and the community.

Ironically, in the same *MISQ* issue that Benbasat and Zmud propose limiting the application of reference disciplines to IS theory, two essential concepts of IS theory (both mentioned previously), 'users' and the 'role of IT in firm performance' have been reviewed and substantially revised through exactly this process (Lamb and Kling, 2003; Sambamurthy et al., 2003).

While Benbasat and Zmud (2003) raises many contentious issues, it does serve as a timely reminder to IS researchers that while a plethora of research opportunities constantly confront us, we need to ensure our research focus remains distinctly IS in order to develop our discipline.

A contrary view to that frequently held, that IS serves as a reference for emerging disciplines in a discourse with other reference disciplines, has also been promoted. Baskerville and Myers (2002) note the development of new fields of study that refer to IS theory for explanations; for example, biotechnology. They also note the increasing influence of IS on disciplines, including accounting, banking and marketing, experiencing structural transformation resulting from application of IT. As illustrated in Figure 12.3, they present an argument that no single discipline is able to completely address today's multi-faceted research issues so well as IS. A more viable reference model is a network of disciplines in continuous dialogue and exchange, with IS at the center of the network.

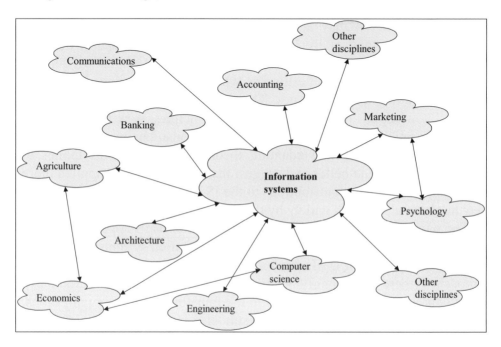

Figure 12.3 *IS as a reference discipline in discourse with other reference disciplines* (adapted from Baskerville and Myers, 2002)

These diverse perspectives on the focus of IS theory development, with compelling arguments on all sides, should be recognized as being complementary. The discussion is beneficial to the discipline. The dynamic IS domain requires both excitement and enthusiasm in its research as well as reflective consideration on how dynamically developing research may contribute to, and be consistent with, the discipline's overall development. The diversity of perspectives means that IS is vibrant both as a discipline and as an area of research.

12.7 Major categories in IS research

IS research students and their supervisors may wonder how to select a topic of sustained interest to the IS community. This section and those following consider IS research classifications. They incorporate the views of both IS educators and industry regarding those IS issues that are considered most important. These reviews will help identify critical areas of IS research.

In June 1988, *MISQ* published a classification scheme of IS keywords *to provide a description of the discipline, introduce a common language, and enable research of the field's development*. This scheme was updated in 1993 with an additional 175 keywords bringing the total to nearly 1300 *to incorporate the new research topics and methods, hence reflecting better the evolution of the IS discipline* (Barki et al., 1993). Table 12.1 shows the scheme with nine major categories.

Table 12.1 *Major categories in IS research* (Barki et al., 1993)

A	Reference disciplines, including behavioral science, computer science, decision theory, information theory, organizational theory, social science, management science, economic theory, ergonomics, political science and psychology.
B	External environment: economic, legal, political and social.
C	IT, computer systems and software.
D	Organizational environment, including characteristics, functions and tasks.
E	IS management, including hardware, software, personnel, projects, planning, evaluation, security and other management issues.
F	IS development and operations, life cycles, IS development, implementation and operations.
G	IS usage, by organizations and users, and their support, access and processing.
H	IS types, application areas, components and characteristics.
I	IS education and research.

In a dynamically developing technology and business environment, individual keywords may become out of date and emerging research areas may not receive specific mention. The categories do, however, help to identify the focus of research within the IS discipline. Even where a new phenomenon is not identified explicitly as a keyword, analysis of the categories can provide a framework for its research. For example, although e-business is not included as a keyword in the classification scheme, e-business research could be located within several different categories depending on the particular topic. These categories include: B, for external drivers and inhibitors of Internet purchasing; C, for specific e-business technologies; D, for organizational aspects of e-business adoption; E, for planning, evaluation and security of e-business applications; F, for development of e-business applications; G, for usage of e-business by organizations; H, for characteristics of e-business systems; and I, for research into the levels of education and research activity in the e-business area.

Indeed, we could complete all the categories if we consider the reference disciplines influencing e-business, thereby adding A. If the research was, for example, concerned with website design characteristics to facilitate online consumer purchasing, then theory from other disciplines including decision theory, ergonomics and psychology may also be considered applicable. The research could be located in category A which is the category relating to reference disciplines (for example, AC sub-discipline decision theory; and AP sub-discipline psychology) and, potentially, categories F (for example, FC development methods and tools) and H (for example, HD IS characteristics).

The research would be classified as IS research not because it could be allocated totally to an IS category, but because the primary focus of the research was within the IS classification categories. If the primary focus of the research was, for example, within a reference discipline such as psychology or ergonomics, rather than in its application to the IS discipline, then the research may be more properly classified and conducted within the other discipline. Indeed, with IS research now impacting on other disciplines, this may well be the case. This categorization of website design also shows how essential IS research issues are sustainable. The particular phenomenon being examined may change, but the underlying IS research issues remain.

12.8 Key concepts in IS – educational perspective

As this chapter is attempting to acknowledge the broad scope of IS, it may be useful to examine the perspective of IS educators and of business. Forty of the world's most influential IS educators jointly specified the key concepts in IS for business students (Ives et al., 2002). Among the authors are those who, in another forum, sought to limit the scope of the IS discipline (Benbasat and Zmud, 2003)! It is suggested that this list (Table 12.2) comprises the essence of the discipline in its business and organizational contexts. The breadth of scope and the balanced focus on technology, organizational, management and social issues are noteworthy.

Table 12.2 *Key IS concepts – educational perspective*

1	What are information systems?
2	How do information systems influence organizational competitiveness?
3	Why have databases become so important to modern organizations?
4	Why are technology infrastructures so important to modern organizations?
5	What is the role of the Internet and networking technology in modern organizations and how is e-business transforming organizations and markets?
6	What are the unique economics of information and information systems?
7	How do information systems enable organizational processes?
8	How do organizations develop, acquire and implement information systems?
9	What is the nature of IS management?
10	What ethical, criminal and security issues do organizations face when using information systems?

The conclusion of these eminent authors is that:

'We believe that information technology is now the prime driver and enabler of business strategy for many, if not most, organizations'. (Ives et al., 2002)

Irrespective of whether or not this conclusion may be sustained, their unanimous view, at least in this context, is that IS must retain a broad focus on issues at the intersection of technology and business. This may suggest, however, a potential threat to the discipline. This paper, and the related paper of Avison (2003), may be seen as defensive, an attempt to protect the discipline in business schools following the dotcom boom and bust. But we are not pessimists and do not share the concerns of Markus (1999) who postulates that we should consider 'the unthinkable: what happens if the IS field as we know it goes away.' However, we suspect that she is somewhat 'tongue in cheek' here, she is really arguing in the paper for a repositioning of the discipline towards 'an electronic integration of socio-economic activity.'

12.9 Key IS issues – industry perspective

Given that the focus of IS is on applications of technology in organizations and by individuals, then analysis of the key IS management issues confronting business can assist in defining the core focus of IS and IS theory.

Since 1988, the IS services provider, Computer Sciences Corporation (CSC) has conducted periodic international surveys of key issues confronting IS management. The report of the latest publicly available survey (CSC, 2001) is based on responses from more than 1000 IS executives in 31 countries with 34% from North America, 29% from Europe, 24% from Asia, and 12% from Australia. More than 70% of respondents were the top IS executive in their organization.

Table 12.3 *Changes in top five IS management issues over time (a) (CSC, 2001)*

Issues		
Europe	**2001**	**1988**
Optimize enterprise-wide IT services	1	-
Optimize organizational effectiveness	2	-
Update obsolete systems	3	19
Connect with customers electronically	4	-
Optimize and use data	5	12
North America	**2001**	**1988**
Optimize enterprise-wide IT services	1	-
Information security	2	19
Align IT and corporate goals	3	1
Optimize and use data	4	7
Optimize organizational effectiveness	5	-

The organizations were predominantly large, with 36% having annual revenues less than 250 m, 35% 250-1 billion and 28% having revenues greater than 1 billion (all figures US$). Responses came from 22 industries with 11% from financial services.

Table 12.3 identifies the key issues for Europe and North America in 2001 and shows the dynamic nature of key IS challenges confronting organizations by comparing their importance in 1988. Only one of the top five North American issues in 2001 was rated in the top five issues in 1988.

Location also appears to have some significance. None of the 2001 European issues was in the top 10 in 1988. While three of the top five issues in Europe are rated in the top five in North America, with the exception of the top issue, the remainder have differing priorities.

Table 12.4 shows the converse, with the five top issues in 1988 and their relative importance in 2001. This table emphasizes further the dynamic nature of management challenges with only one common issue from 1988 in the top five for 2001 and just two in the top 10. In this case, location appears less significant in 1988 with all five European issues identical to the North American list, although with priorities one and two reversed.

Table 12.4 *Changes in top five IS management issues over time (b)* (CSC, 2001)

Issues		
Europe	**1988**	**2001**
Develop an IT plan	1	-
Align IT and corporate goals	2	13
Educate management on IT	3	19
Use IT for competitive advantage	4	9
Develop and information architecture	5	20
North America	**1988**	**2001**
Align IT and corporate goals	1	3
Develop an IT plan	2	-
Educate management on IT	3	12
Use IT for competitive advantage	4	16
Develop and information architecture	5	18

In their analysis of these tables, CSC suggests that 'develop an IT plan' may no longer be seen as a task to complete but an ongoing project requiring continuous adaptation to the changing environment. Similarly, 'use IT for competitive advantage' and 'align IT and corporate goals' are continual processes that have become part of the accepted role of IT, rather than being considered as particular events. Therefore the table can be seen as somewhat misleading in these cases, unless interpreted carefully.

This analysis of top IS issues in industry is completed with a comparison in Table 12.5 of the top ten issues from the international study (CSC, 2004) and a study of 301 Society of Management and The

Conference Board members in the USA across more than 10 industries (Luftman and McLean, 2004). Although the terminology differs across the two studies (as well as across the CSC studies from 2001 to 2003) and the priorities may vary from year to year, there is a high level of consistency between the studies about the major IS/IT challenges confronting industry.

The later CSC study (2003) examines issues at a more detailed level than in 2001. The top USA issue in 2001, optimizing enterprise-wide IT services, incorporates enterprise architectures (second in the list) and sourcing options (fifth) in 2003. Information security (second in 2001) equates to the third in 2003; alignment (third in 2001) equates to the first in 2001; optimizing data (fourth in 2001) is incorporated in the second in 2003; and organizational effectiveness (fifth in 2001) is part of both the fourth and sixth issue of 2003. The SIM/TCB study (Luftman and McLean, 2004) also reflects differing priorities for issues, but the issues identified and the research themes they reflect are fundamentally aligned.

This high degree of consistency in industry issues across numerous studies helps in defining the core focus of IS and IS theory as well as assisting researchers to identify research themes that will have an impact outside academia for sustained investigation.

Table 12.5 *Comparison of key IS/IT issues for executives 2003*

	CSC international study 2003 (CSC, 2004)	SIM/TCB USA study 2003 (Luftman and McLean, 2004)
1	Maximizing the return on IT for the business	IT and business alignment
2	Enterprise architectures for business agility	IT strategic planning
3	Safeguarding information assets	Security and privacy
4	Driving competitive advantage through innovation	Attracting / retaining IT professionals
5	Selecting and managing sourcing options	Measuring value of IT
6	Structuring for global organizations	Measuring performance of IT
7	Managing business change	Creating information architecture
8	Managing business relationships	Reducing complexity
9	Connecting with CEO and peers	Speed and agility
10	Adopting new roles and responsibilities	IT governance

In contrast to the alignment of industry's challenges with IS/IT over time is its focus on actual technologies. The dynamic IT environment and variability of industry's technology focus are illustrated in Table 12.6. Across three separate surveys in 1991, 1996 and 2000, there was not one common technology or technology issue. The attention given to the Internet by industry leaders is an admittedly extreme example of how industry's attention to a technology can suddenly develop (and decline) in interest.

In 1995, the Internet was No. 20 on Europe's list of important new technologies and No. 24 on North America's. In 1996, it was No. 1 in both regions. (CSC, 2003)

Five years later, the 2000 survey does not mention the Internet directly, although it is concerned about some Internet-related issues: bandwidth, privacy, security, information survivability, knowledge discovery and exploitation and human-computer connection, though most of these apply to other technologies as well.

The tables of top issues confronting IS management are useful for ensuring the relevance of IS research. Prospective IS PhD candidates and supervisors may also be cautioned by the results of these industry surveys since it is apparent that industry issues are highly dynamic with changes from year to year. PhD students, particularly if studying part-time, need to be aware that research which commences when an issue is topical may not be completed until that issue is no longer seen by industry leaders to be significant. They need also to be aware that 'hot' issues tend to be pursued by many PhD students world-wide, so that it might be difficult to verify that they have homed-in on an original aspect. Candidates may, therefore, be reasonably advised by their supervisors to be cautious before committing to long-term research of a topic or issue that suddenly appears to be very topical. Another related problem is that it can be difficult to get published towards the end of the PhD period as many others will be trying to get published when there might be less interest in the topic.

The most striking example of this came following the technology crashes in 2000 and 2001 and the demise of the dotcoms, when e-business as a strategy appeared to have dropped off the corporate agenda. In May 2003, the *Harvard Business Review* published a deliberately provocative paper *'IT doesn't matter'* (Carr, 2003). Yet, in the same month, the reputable US magazine *Business Week* presented market research showing that, notwithstanding poor media reviews and an apparent lack of corporate attention, actual electronic business between corporations in 2003 (and subsequent productivity gains) exceeded even the most optimistic predictions in 1999 (Mullaney, 2003).

Table 12.6 *Changes in top five critical technologies over time and location* (CSC, 2003)

	1991 North America and Europe		**1996 North America and Europe**
1	Case and other software productivity tools	1	Internet and World Wide Web
2	Expert Systems	2	Groupware
3	LANs/networking	3	E-commerce
4	Image systems and processing	4	Broadband networks
5	Client server technology	5	Network security
	2000 North America and Europe		**2000 Australia and Asia**
1	Ubiquitous bandwidth	1	Knowledge discovery/exploitation
2	Knowledge discovery/exploitation	2	Privacy, security, information survivability
3	Net-centric computing	3	Ubiquitous bandwidth
4	Privacy, security, information survivability	4	Net-centric computing
5	Human-computer connection	5	Smart environments

Prospective researchers seeking to make a relevant contribution would, therefore, be well advised to be cautious in selecting a topic that is suitable for sustained investigation while ensuring their work is grounded appropriately in theory.

12.10 Analysis of research categories

Concern has been expressed that the IS discipline suffers from a lack of focus due to excessive diversity in its research. Table 12.7 shows a cross analysis of seven sources that contribute to determining IS research focus and theory compared with the research categories proposed by Barki et al. (1993). The table demonstrates remarkable uniformity in breadth and depth of focus by industry and education over the past 20 years. Despite specific emphasis by one or more sources, taken as a whole, there is a high degree of alignment on core issues.

Table 12.7 *Cross-analysis of sources determining core focus of IS research*

Research categories (Barki et al., 1993)	Reference Discipline	External environment	IT systems	Organizational environment	IS management	IS development and operations	IS usage	IS types	IS education and research
ACS submission, 1992	√	√	√	√	√	√	√	√	√
Benbasat and Zmud, 2003	-	-	√	*	√	√	√	√	*
Baskerville and Myers, 2002	√	√	√	√	√	√	√	√	√
Ives et al., 2002	-	√	√	√	√	√	√	√	√
Key IS management issues, CSC 2001	-	-	√	√	√	√	√	√	-
Key IS management issues, CSC 1988	-	√	√	√	√	√	√	√	-
Key technology issues, CSC 2000	-	√	√	√	√	√	√	√	-
Barki et al., 1993	√	√	√	√	√	√	√	√	√

Key: √ core focus, - not mentioned or excluded; * limited applicability

The outlying categories, reference disciplines and research, could not be expected to be included as issues of concern to industry, but research and education on a specific discipline may reasonably be considered part of that discipline. The IS discipline should engage in a discourse with other reference disciplines as they all seek to cater for technology-enabled transformation of industries and organizations. This appears to be one of the weaknesses of the argument that IS educators and researchers should deliberately exclude potentially relevant theory from other disciplines.

12.11 Methods of research

Chapters 14 and 15 explore the methods of research open to the IS researcher. However, it is appropriate in this chapter at least to consider how accepted methods have changed. The leading IS journal, *MIS Quarterly,* has changed greatly in its editorial policy over the years. In September 1989 it suggested that a paper *'in the Research and Theory category should ... be based on a set of well-defined hypotheses, unbiased and reproducible ... often [involving] the collection of considerable quantitative data through such means as laboratory experiments or survey instruments. The data are then subjected to statistical analysis.'* In the March 1993 issue of *MISQ* there was a broadening of this stance as they welcomed *'research based on positivist, interpretive, or integrated approaches [though] we remain strong in our commitment to hypothesis testing and quantitative data analysis.'* More recently, Allen Lee as editor has bravely opened the methods of acceptable research further, where qualitative research is seen to be the equal of quantitative research (but not without opposition, as recipients on the *ISWorld* list serve looking at the various messages between Allen and his opponents will be all too aware).

12.12 Seminal works in IS

Researchers will be interested in IS papers considered to be exemplary and/or seminal. Walstrom and Leonard (2000) present a list of 61 most frequently cited papers from the IS literature. In many cases, works on this list illustrate the application of theories from reference disciplines to IS situations. Titles include: Porter's 'Competitive strategy: Techniques for analyzing industries and competitors' (1980), and 'How information gives you competitive advantage' (1985); March and Simon's 'Organizations' (1958); Rogers 'Diffusion of Innovations' (1962, 1983); and Galbraith's (1977) 'Organizational Design'. In attaining its current level of maturity the IS discipline has benefited greatly from application of theories from reference disciplines. The list emphasizes the critically important role of theory – from whatever source – in assisting to explain IS phenomena or to predict outcomes of IS activities.

Details of other IS works considered exemplary are presented on *ISWorld* (see resources below).

12.13 IS resources

IS resources of potential interest to prospective researchers are available online from *ISWorld* (www.isworld.org). The *ISWorld* website contains a section on PhD studies, including: getting into a PhD program; getting started; research frameworks; IT management issues and concepts; exemplary works in IS research; the IS dissertation database and details of professional ethics in IS (www.isworld.org/phd/phd.htm). Other options include membership of the *AIS* (www.aisnet.org) and participation in one of the *International Federation of Information Processing (IFIP)* working groups (www.ifip.org). IFIP has a division (Technical Committee 8) with a particular focus on IS that incorporates a range of IS Working Groups.

12.14 Conclusions

This overview of the IS discipline: IS theory, its scope, foundations, major categories, concepts, seminal works and useful resources, can assist prospective IS supervisors and PhD students alike in selecting sustainable research topics that contribute to the development of IS theory and practice. It acknowledges the rapidly developing nature of the IS discipline as it responds to the essential dual roles of IS in enabling organizations to realize potential strategic and operational benefits while facilitating the fundamental transformation of traditional business practice.

The IS discipline is located to assist these organizations and industries through both research and education. The energy that powers organizational innovation fuels the energy and excitement that enthuses IS researchers to contribute to the development and revision of IS theory.

Although this chapter acknowledges different views and orientations of researchers in this comparatively new and exciting discipline, core concepts and issues identified by researchers, educators and industry over the period from 1988 to 2003 display fundamental alignment and agreement in their focus.

IS has reached a level of maturity where it has gone beyond merely incorporating seminal works in other disciplines: it now acts as a reference discipline in its own right. Its status has changed from an emerging to an accepted academic discipline, impacting on teaching, research and practice. Its work is both important and permanent.

13

Quality and Originality

Jan Pries-Heje and David Avison

13.1 Introduction

This chapter will help you to cope with the issues of quality and originality that your students will raise throughout the stages of a PhD study. First we discuss the notion of quality. Then we give examples of how a PhD supervisor can ensure the quality of both process and product in the three main stages of a PhD study:

1 Initiation and proposal
2 Research and course work
3 Finalizing.

At the end of the chapter we discuss originality and give examples of how a PhD can be considered original. The following fictional but not unrealistic student–supervisor exchange gives an introduction to the problems addressed in this chapter.

Student: I've decided to do case study research.
Supervisor: That's interesting.
Student: How many cases need I do for a quality PhD?
Supervisor: That depends.
Student: How long need I spend in each company?
Supervisor: That depends.
Student: How many people need I interview?
Supervisor: That depends.
Student: If I make this observation from the case study, will it be an original contribution to IS research?
Supervisor: That depends.
Student (to himself): My supervisor is hopeless.

13.2 Quality

There are at least six different perspectives to defining the notion of quality. Garvin (1987), for example, identifies the following five definitions:

1   *Product-based* Quality is a precise measurable variable. Differences in quality reflect differences in the quantity of some product attribute.
2   *Transcendent (relative quality)* Quality is universally recognizable; it is related to a comparison of features and characteristics of the product.
3   *User-based* Quality is fitness for intended use.
4   *Manufacturing-based* Quality is conformance to specifications.
5   *Value-based* Quality is defined in terms of costs and prices. A quality product is one that provides performance at an acceptable price or conformance at an acceptable cost.

There is a sixth school of thought, related to manufacturing-based quality, but nevertheless distinctly different. It might be called *process-based quality*. The thinking behind this school is that a good process must lead to quality products. Maturity models, such as the capability maturity model (Paulk et al., 1993), are prominent examples of this kind of thinking.

Again, the use of an information systems development methodology provides another example. It aims to guide the systems developers in their choice of the techniques that might be appropriate at each stage of the project and also help them plan, manage, control and evaluate information systems projects. In so doing, an appropriate IS is developed within an acceptable time limit and cost. Some methodologies give the user an ISO international quality standard for process (Avison and Fitzgerald, 2003).

Product-based quality

In product-based quality, it is assumed that quality can be measured using some carefully chosen attributes. Product-based quality is often used to evaluate information systems research, and research in general. The British government, for example, has initiated a program where university research quality is evaluated on a 7-point scale going from 5* to 1. The main purpose of the UK research assessment exercise (RAE), which takes place every 4 to 5 years, is to enable the higher education funding bodies to distribute public funds for research (£1 billion per annum) selectively on the basis of quality. Table 13.1 lists the ratings and their accompanying descriptions, in descending order.

Table 13.1 *Research assessment exercise (RAE) rankings*

Rating	Definition
5*	Research quality that equates to attainable levels of international excellence in a majority of sub-areas of activity and attainable levels of national excellence in all others.
5	Research quality that equates to attainable levels of international excellence in some sub-areas of activity and to attainable levels of national excellence in virtually all others.
4	Research quality that equates to attainable levels of national excellence in virtually all sub-areas of activity, possibly showing some evidence of international excellence, or to international level in some and at least national level in a majority.
3a	Research quality that equates to attainable levels of national excellence in a substantial majority of the sub-areas of activity, or to international level in some and to national level in others together comprising a majority.
3b	Research quality that equates to attainable levels of national excellence in the majority of sub-areas of activity.
2	Research quality that equates to attainable levels of national excellence in up to half the sub-areas of activity.
1	Research quality that equates to attainable levels of national excellence in none, or virtually none, of the sub-areas of activity.

In this approach, international and national recognition is assessed through measurable attributes, such as the amount of external research funding achieved. Publishing in international journals, and being cited in them is particularly important. However, this product-based definition can be problematic because, for example, there is no common agreement on what is a good journal in information systems.

Recently, there have been a number of surveys attempting to rank good IS journals. Peffers and Ya (2003), for example, identified 326 journals in a variety of fields that published IS research. The ten top-ranked journals for information systems research, ranked by average weighted perceived value rating, are given in Table 13.2. Another source of rankings, more US-centric, can be found at the following website *http://www.isworld.org /csaunders/rankings.htm.*

Table 13.2 *Journal rankings* (Peffers and Ya, 2003)

1	Information Systems Research
2	MIS Quarterly
3	Journal of Management Information Systems
4	European Journal of Information Systems
5	Decision Support Systems
6	Information and Management
7	Information Systems Journal
8	Journal of the Association for Information Systems
9	International Journal of Electronic Commerce
10	Information Systems

The most important feature of these rankings is, perhaps, that they can be used to demonstrate product-based quality. Peffers and Ya (2003) conclude that the results of the survey are '…likely to be most useful [to] IS researchers seeking to provide evidence of journal value in tenure and promotion cases.'

Transcendent, user-, manufacturing- and value-based quality

The transcendent definition of quality is unlikely to be helpful to the less experienced supervisors and their students. Making a statement that 'quality is universally recognizable' does not really help, even if Robert Pirsig

(1984) argues in his book *Zen and the Art of Motorcycle Maintenance* that the quality of something is absolute and we recognize it when we see it.

The user-based definition is interesting in that it raises the question: Who is the user of a PhD thesis? If the user is 'academia in general' then fitness for intended use is some kind of demonstration of 'being academic' enough. That is probably close to what we discussed above; thus being academic means publishing in good journals, and the rankings in the section above tell you what can be considered good journals.

However, if the intended user is industry or society, then we need to discuss the issue of relevance. Any representative from industry will probably ask questions like: 'Who is this useful to? What can its use be? and How do you know it has value in practice?' We have included questions inspired by this need for relevance in the checklist below.

The manufacturing-based definition is only relevant for as long as it is meaningful to talk about specifications. For example, the Ministerial order in Denmark for PhD studies states:

'(1) The PhD degree shall be awarded to candidates who have successfully completed a PhD programme ... (2), and has demonstrated, through a publicly defended thesis, a capacity to carry out a scientific project involving independent use of the scientific methodology of the subject and hereby furthering research at the level equivalent to the international standard of PhD degrees within the subject area.'

Likewise there may be specifications, rules or even a law describing requirements for a PhD in your country. You can also take a look at Part V of this book to get an overview of differences between countries.

Process-based quality
The main idea in process-based quality is that a good process will lead to a good product. A process can be defined as the set of activities, tools, methods, and practices that can be used to guide the flow of production (inspired by Humphrey, 1989). So if you follow a well described and sound process you should have a better chance of producing quality.

In this book we have included two chapters, one on quantitative research methods (Chapter 14) and another on qualitative research methods (Chapter 15). Both chapters prescribe a research process that you can follow, and by so doing you and your research students have a better chance of producing a quality PhD.

13.3 Initiation

What do we do when students ask us to be their supervisor? The first quality issue concerns the student's maturity. Hersey and Blanchard (1987) suggest asking two questions:

1   Is the person ABLE? (Has the necessary knowledge and skill)
2   Is the person WILLING? (Has the necessary confidence and commitment)

The ability of a potential PhD student has to be judged on prior work and experience, and can be divided into three groups: scientific, educational and teaching. A masters-level dissertation, publications, and production, such as a website or a system developed for someone, all evidence scientific experience to some degree.

A bachelor or master's level degree in information systems or a related subject provides evidence of educational experience. The grades achieved are an important indicator, but whether the student achieved the goals set in a timely fashion is equally important.

Another indicator concerns other relevant experience:

> I often consider working experience an advantage. Thus 5 years as a software developer in a company is to me a very important sign of ability. I know that others don't have the same positive attitude towards working experience. But I have seen that students fresh from university often have a very hard time acquainting themselves with the real problems of a research project, such as that involving information systems development. They often end up with something very theoretical – probably rigorous enough but without any relevance. Whereas a PhD student that has work experience often ends up with a dissertation that is both rigorous and relevant.

Another positive attribute concerns teaching experience. The future academic is expected to teach as well as research. Indeed, the PhD student may well be expected to teach or assist a teacher in workshops during the time of the project.

Motivation is much harder to judge. Only an interview for at least 2 hours will help determine that. The main question is of course 'Why do you want to become a researcher?' Answers that the authors have heard include: 'control over my own work,' 'I don't want to work for profit,' 'I want to improve mankind,' 'I am fascinated by this problem' and 'it seems a great way to spend 3 years.' Many, indeed most, of these responses will not be enough to sustain 3 years' hard study with many ups and downs. Some time needs to be spent delving into the real reasons and satisfying both yourself and the student that the motivations are enough.

At least as important is the question: Can we bear each other for the next three or more years? Sometimes we meet people where the 'chemistry' simply does not work. There will be stressful times for both supervisor and researcher ahead so, if that is the case, you should not get into a potentially unhappy supervisor–student relationship. A colleague may be more suitable as supervisor.

An example evaluation

As we see throughout this book, there is a lot of variation in PhD programs. For example, in the US it is usual for the PhD student to pay for the studies. In other countries, PhD students are considered employees and they are paid a salary. That is typical in Scandinavia. We provide an example evaluation from the latter tradition below. Section A, containing personal information such as name, date of birth, social security number, etc., has been removed, and the remainder of the example has been made anonymous. Nevertheless, the example provides an insight into what we could be looking for in a potential candidate for a PhD study.

B – Scientific qualifications

The proposed project concerns the use of IT in modernizing the public sector, and falls within the [University name] competence area IT and Organizations. The project focuses on the strategic and practical implementation of eGovernment, areas that are both central to the competences at [University name]. Possibilities exist to work with other researchers and PhD students at [University name].

The description of the project is interesting and shows that the applicant has a good command of the relevant literature. Also the problems described and the research method suggested seems relevant and has the promise of leading to very interesting results. Furthermore, we find that the plan included with the application will form a solid basis for a 4-year PhD-study.

No publications were included.

C – Educational qualifications

The studies prior to PhD studies are relevant for the proposed projects and give the candidate relevant skills. The studies were finished with high grades and on time. The courses most relevant to the proposed project have especially high grades.

D – Other relevant qualifications

The candidate has, since May 2003, been teaching at university level in [course name] for Professor [teacher name] at [University name]. The Professor has given a personal recommendation that is very positive. Thus the candidate seems to have a good teaching potential. The candidate has held several positions relevant to the project described. The position in [Department in Ministry] will provide good background material for a project studying the use of IT in modernizing the public sector.

| **E – Conclusive general evaluation** |
| The interesting project description and the relevant background for the specific project – both educational and work experience – have lead the committee to find the candidate qualified for a 4-year PhD study at [University name]. |

13.4 Proposal

The proposal should outline the research. It includes a title, a research question, background for the research question, research methodology, and an outline schedule. When we receive an outline of a PhD plan it is important to focus on quality. Will this proposal lead to a quality product? Who is the user of the answer to the research question? Will the user perceive it as fulfilling a need? Is the process outlined realistic in that it can lead to the expected product? Is the timetable realistic?

A number of questions to ask when evaluating a proposal are given below:

| |
| **Research question** |
| 1   Good, short research question? |
| 2.   Discussion of who is interested in the answer to the research question? |
| **Research description** |
| 3   Interesting title? |
| 4   Good argument giving reasons why the topic is interesting? |
| 5   Theoretical framework – does it show command of the existing literature on topic? |
| 6   Are expected results described? |
| **Research method** |
| 7   Discussion of which method best answers the research question? |
| 8.   Is there a reference to other studies using the same method? |
| 9   Does one get a good overview of the data collection and data analysis method? |
| **Schedule** |
| 10   Well-defined deliverables – making it easy to see whether work is done? |
| 11   Milestones – making it easy to see whether student is on schedule? |
| 12   Planned publication outlets? |
| **PhD supervision** |
| 13   Is there an agreement with a potential PhD supervisor? |
| 14   Have PhD student and supervisor co-operated before. Result? What if not? |

13.5 Research and course work

After the proposal or the research plan has been accepted, the research begins. In other chapters of Parts II and V we have given accounts of what that means. One of the inspirations from quality thinking that we strongly recommend in this phase is to conduct quality reviews.

A quality review is a formalized meeting where a document is held up against some requirements or expectations. The meeting can be more or less formalized. It can involve the supervisor and the PhD student only or it can involve other people as well. In the USA and the UK, there is often a committee assigned to ensure the quality of the PhD (see also Part V).

The purpose of a review can be related to one or more of the following:

- To point out potential areas for improvement
- To ensure consistent quality across chapters, papers, etc.
- To approve a product, theory or model
- To educate the PhD student.

It is an important principal in reviews that the reviewers *point out* problems but do not solve them. The same typically goes for a review conducted within the supervisor–student relationship (see Chapter 3).

A possible way to plan and execute a review is to go through the following four steps:

1. Plan the review
2. Prepare the review
3. Conduct the review meeting
4. Correct defects and verify quality.

1 Plan the review

There are three aspects to planning the review:

1. *Gather the review package.* This includes work product (for example, a chapter), checklists (for example, those from this book), and references. The student would normally do this.
2. *Form the review team.* If the review is going to be an informal meeting between the supervisor and the student, then formation is easy. In another situation, for example, a meeting for a whole committee, forming the review team requires more work, and it can become quite difficult to plan the date.
3. *Assign roles.* This will only be necessary if there are more than two persons involved in the review. The supervisor is normally the obvious choice to moderate the meeting. The number of reviewers needs to be resolved. Too many reviewers can cause problems and conflicts.

2 Prepare the review

There are two kinds of preparation that may be needed. There is always a need for the reviewer to read the review package. If the review is about a methodology chapter for a PhD, then the reviewers need to read that chapter and compare it to what they expected. In some situations there is a need for a preparatory meeting, for example, where the reviewers need to have some pre-knowledge before they read or understand the chapter. When reading the material for the review, the purpose is to find the maximum number of non-minor issues. Use checklists and references to focus attention. Note critical, severe, and moderate issues, either separately or in the document itself (today most text editors have a commenting feature that can be used).

3 Conduct the review meeting

At the meeting you should assess each issue together. Determine whether it is a defect that needs to be corrected. Note the decision on what needs to be done, and resolve minor issues where possible. If it is a group meeting, for example (part of) a committee, the moderator chairs the meeting. The purpose is to create a consolidated, comprehensive listing of non-minor issues, and to provide an opportunity for group synergy. The sequence in a review meeting with a group can be:

1   Moderator raises each issue sequentially
2   Reviewers raise further issues
3   Moderator or supervisor notes issues.

4 Correct defects

The next stage is for the PhD student to work on the issues one by one. At some point the student believes that all issues have been resolved. Then it is time for the supervisor to assess and verify the quality of the (reworked) product. If there are major changes, then the review process may be repeated.

What to review?

Reviews can be conducted in three different areas, eventually in combination: literature, research results, and research method. Let us take them one by one.

Literature: A very important principle in all kinds of research is that the PhD student demonstrates knowledge of existing research. Students expect their supervisors to point them to the fundamental literature of the topic, though the student is then expected to develop the search in more depth.

Below you find a number of questions to ask when reviewing the literature selection of a thesis.

Background literature
1 Convincing grasp of relevant literature?
2 Material well-organized? Useful to whom?
3 Trends and patterns within this stream of research identified?
4 Literature only to support argumentation?
Research question literature
5 Clear story line?
6 Linked to literature?
7 Literature on research method?
Results and contribution
8 Contribution described and put in the context of the literature?
9 Clear perspective on significance and limitations?

Research Results: In the first phase – initiation and proposal – the PhD student lays out a plan for the research. While the research is going on, we need to ask whether the results are materializing as expected. The results that we are looking for depend on the research question. Cryer (2000) gives nine different examples of research problems and research outcomes. We have taken the examples that are most relevant to IS research, and for each of them give examples of review questions to ask.

1 **A new or improved product**
  Who needs this product?
  How did you elicit requirements for the product?
  Have all the relevant stakeholders been identified?
  Are stakeholders involved in eliciting requirements?
  How will you ensure a well-designed product?
  How will you build or construct the product?
  Can you build the product alone?
  If help for building is procured, how do you ensure that your contribution is uniquely identifiable?
  How will you test (validate) the product?
  How will you use the package or product after it has been developed?
2 **A new model or theory or interpretation of an existing theory or model**
  When is there a need for this new theory/model?
  How have you ensured that the theory/model is really new?
  How will you design and build the theory/model?
  How do you plan to validate the theory/model?
  What is the publication outlet?
3 **An improvement or interpretation of an existing theory or model**
  Do you know the existing theory?
  What have other researchers used the theory for?
  How will you design and build the theory/model?

> How will you incorporate other researchers' work?
> How do you plan to validate the theory/model?
> What is the publication outlet?

Research Method

The research method is the way it is decided to carry out the research. In this book we have dedicated two chapters to research methods, namely one chapter on quantitative research methods (Chapter 14) and another on qualitative research methods (Chapter 15). Both chapters can be used to organize a review.

Finalizing

Mullins and Kiley (2002) studied how experienced examiners assess research theses. One of the questions they asked was 'what makes an outstanding thesis?' The following responses seemed to characterize a good PhD, though clearly, Mullins and Kiley link a PhD to art:

1. 'An artistic endeavor where the student is designing the work and there is elegance of design, of the synthesis, and executions'
2. Creativity
3. Design – where it all fits together
4. Elegant
5. A well-sculpted piece of work.

> My personal experience is that when we are getting close to finalizing, it is a good idea to insist on a date where everything is written in a first draft. Very often a lot of my comments are not related to a specific chapter or section but to the interplay between separate pieces of the thesis. If we are talking about a full-time student the date should be at least 3 months before final delivery – and probably longer.

13.6 Originality

Most countries have regulations stating something like: 'A PhD is rewarded for an original contribution to knowledge.' But that is easy to say but harder to do. For a new PhD student, one of the major uncertainties is whether their idea or their research problem will lead to an outcome that fulfills the criteria of being original enough.

A PhD thesis can be original in many different ways (see, for example, Phillips and Pugh, 2000).

1   The thesis can be the first to discuss a theoretical concept not treated in writing before
2   It can provide a single original technique, method or observation, often as part of a larger piece of work that is less original
3   It can carry out empirical work that has not been done before
4   It can test something in a specific country that has only been looked at in other countries
5   It can take a particular method or technique and apply it in a new way or in a new area
6   It can be cross-disciplinary, combining things that have not been combined before.

Cryer (2000) argues that originality 'can be in terms of the research design, the research process or the outcomes of research, and it can have a single major aspect or several minor ones.' She continues to compare a PhD to an expedition into uncharted land (like the journey and adventure metaphors in Chapter 3) where you can make discoveries in several ways:

1   Explore the unknown
2   Explore the unanticipated
3   Use of data
4   Outcomes
5   By-products
6   The experience.

One indicator is that the results are (potentially) publishable. However, results can also be so original that they are hard to publish. If the student's findings are contrary to common wisdom, the reviewers may doubt what they are finding. However, this is not usually a concern.

How to ensure that a PhD will be considered original
Many PhD students have unwarranted worries about originality. The key to coping with this worry is to ask the originality question early and often. You can bring it up the first time a research question is proposed: 'How about originality?' Later you can ask: 'Is it reasonable to expect this to turn out original enough?' We have mentioned reviews before in this chapter. Originality is a very important item on the agenda for a review. However, your job may well be to reassure your student that the originality aspect of a PhD thesis need not be at the level deserving a Nobel Prize!

When we discussed different measures of quality, we were rather dismissive of the transcendent definition of quality. We argued that making a statement that 'quality is universally recognizable' does not really help. Yet the experienced supervisor and examiner does exercise elements of this when assessing the thesis:

> Bearing in mind other work I know that gained the award of a PhD, does the thesis seem to evidence around 3 years' research work; do the contributions seem to some extent original; will other IS researchers value to some extent the work achieved; has some other assessor (journal editor or conference program committee) deemed aspects the work of sufficient quality to publish; might the thesis embarrass the university when placed on the library shelf; will the PhD student be OK as an academic; will the student be capable of leading other research projects later; in short, will the student let you as the supervisor and the university down?

These are questions that we ask. We also ask other experienced supervisors what they think, to get the most balanced view possible. We suggest that you do the same. You will need to justify and articulate the decision: a simple statement such as 'it is of the required standard' is required but not enough.

13.7 Conclusion

In this chapter we have looked at the important issues of quality and originality. To the very experienced supervisor, these may be obvious as evidenced in a thesis, but for the rest of us, more help is needed. We have given six general perspectives to the notion of quality, and it is expected that a thesis evidences at least one of these. We have also suggested ways in which quality can be evaluated through peer reviews, journal rankings and the like. A model for evaluating research proposals has been provided, along with models for reviewing progress and contribution. Criteria for assessing the originality of a thesis have also been suggested.

14

Quantitative Research

Detmar Straub, David Gefen and Marie-Claude Boudreau

14.1 Introduction

One of the most time-honored approaches to investigating important IS and organizational phenomena is quantitative research (also known as quantitative, positivist research). Quantitative techniques have been used so often and for so long by the IS academy that a set of standards as to what is acceptable have emerged and are generally expected by knowledgeable reviewers. Some of these are statistical in nature, but others have more to do with best methodological practices of the IS research community.

This chapter addresses the needs of researchers conducting quantitative, positivist research (QPR) in IS – both those just beginning to learn these methods and seasoned veterans. The research tasks that are addressed include all stages in the scholarly process, including literature review and theory development stages, and the later stages of design and execution.

The chapter provides the necessary background for understanding the philosophy behind quantitative statistical methods. It discusses the epistemology and ontology of positivist research. These methods provide a quantitative estimation of hypothesized relationships and their significance and should be applied when assessments of significance and strength of relationships are necessary. These methods are the most widely used in IS research and so understanding them and the assumptions behind them is imperative.

Quantitative, positivist research

QPR is a set of methods and techniques that allow IS researchers to answer scholarly and pragmatic questions about the interaction of humans and artifacts such as computers, systems, and applications. There are two cornerstones in this approach to research. The first is the emphasis on quantitative data. The second cornerstone is the emphasis on positivist philosophy of science.

Regarding the first cornerstone, these methods and techniques tend to specialize in quantities in the sense that numbers come to represent values and levels of theoretical constructs and concepts and the interpretation of the numbers is viewed as strong scientific evidence of how a phenomenon works. The presence of quantities is so predominant in QPR that statistical tools and packages are an essential element of the researcher's toolkit. Sources of data are of less concern in identifying an approach as being QPR than the fact that empirically derived numbers lie at the core of the scientific evidence assembled. A QPR researcher may use archival data or gather data through structured interviews. In both cases, the researcher is motivated by the numerical outputs and how to derive meaning from them.

This emphasis on numerical analysis is also key to the second cornerstone, positivism, one definition of which is the testing of theory that is falsifiable.

Differentiating QPR

QPR is orthogonal to analytical (math) modeling, a scientific method that typically depends purely on mathematical derivations and assumptions for interpreting reality. This difference stresses that empirical data gathering or data exploration is part and parcel of QPR, while the positivist philosophy deals with problem-solving and the testing of the theories derived to test these understandings. It is also orthogonal to conceptual research, research that articulates the important conceptual underpinnings of a phenomenon.

QPR is also not design science research (for further information on this approach, see Vaishnavi and Kuechler's *ISWorld* website at http://isworld.org/Researchdesign/drisISworld.htm) in which IT artifacts are designed to improve processes. Models are among the general outputs resulting from design research (March and Smith, 1995). There are three main differences:

1   In QPR, the models employed are most often causal models, whereas design research places its stress on ontological models.
2   The goal of QPR is truth, whereas the goal in design science research is utility (Hevner et al., 2004).
3   QPR validates its findings through data, whereas design science research can find acceptable validation of a new design to be a mathematical proof of concept.

Nevertheless, it should be noted that design researchers are increasingly using QPR, specifically experimentation, to validate their models and prototypes, so QPR is also becoming a key tool in the arsenal of design science researchers. Hevner et al. (2004) argue that design science research should be combined with behavioral science research (such as QPR), as they complement each other.

To the qualitative researcher, a phenomenon can best be interpreted by studying speech acts, relationships between people and computers, archival documents, diagrams of artifacts in the workplace, and the like. If a qualitative researcher believes that these sources of data, gathered by techniques such as interviewing, can be rendered into useful numbers, then this researcher might be classified as a qualitative, positivist researcher in Myers' classification scheme for qualitative research (see Chapter 15). Given the philosophical predisposition of qualitative researchers, these numbers would likely be viewed as suggestive rather than in any sense definitive.

Qualitative work is an activity that lets the researcher get a better understanding of the phenomena in order to formulate a scientific theory later. It should be noted in passing that this attribution is not a settled matter for many IS researchers. In fact, there have been efforts to combine the techniques and viewpoints of positivists and non-positivists to triangulate on phenomena (Kaplan and Duchon, 1988). Lacity and Janson (1994) argue that both approaches can be viable, and both can be shown to be valid under various conditions.

QPR epistemology and ontology

The underlying view of nature that leads a scholar to conclude that QPR can produce knowledge is that the world has some objective reality that can be captured and translated into testable hypotheses, usually in the form of statistical or other numerical analyses. A seminal inspiration for this came from the scientific epistemology of logical positivism. This was articulated in the *Vienna Circle* of Positivists, primarily by Karl Popper, during the 1920s and 1930s. The 'pure' positivist view of scientific exploration as a search for *the Truth* has been supplanted in recent years with a belief that all measurement is based on theory (rightly acknowledged to be a social construction) and hence capturing an 'objective' truth is ultimately impossible. Even the measurement of a purely physical attribute, such as temperature, depends on the theory of how materials expand with heat. Hence, interpreting the readings of a thermometer cannot be regarded as a pure observation but is itself an instance of implicit theory (Coombs, 1976). Empirical data is thus said to be 'theory-laden.'

At the heart of the positivist mind-frame is the concept of *deduction*. There are four steps in deduction:

1   Testing internal consistency, that is, verifying that there are no internal contradictions
2   Distinguishing between the logical basics of the theory and its empirical, testable, predictions
3   Comparing with existing theory, showing that the new theory advances knowledge. Specifically, it is necessary to show that the new theory has superior empirical substance and hence more predictive power
4   Empirical testing aimed at falsifying the theory with data. When the data do not contradict the hypothesized predictions of the theory, it is temporarily corroborated. The objective of this test, according to Popper, is to falsify, not to verify the predictions of the theory. Verifications, he argues, can be found for almost any theory if one picks and chooses what is looked at.

By way of contrast, the interpretive researcher tends to see the world as being entirely a social construction that will demonstrate large variance depending on the observer and the interpreter of the phenomenon. Hence reality is seen as highly subjective by an interpretive researcher.

It is also critical to note that more recent methodologists like Campbell and Stanley (1963) and Cook and Campbell (1979) are not as enamored as Popper with respect to the need for a theory to be falsified. Cook and Campbell (1979), in particular, go to great lengths to argue that the social sciences will almost never be able to prove deterministically that a cause leads to an effect, as can sometimes be shown in the natural sciences. Statistical relationships can be instructive, however, and this means that one must be more cautious about asserting that a theory has been disconfirmed by a single study. In short, later methodologists are more willing to stress the extent to which a theory has been confirmed, given a cumulative tradition of work and the fact that these researchers found statistically significant relationships between certain causes and certain effects.

Saying that in the epistemology of QPR, the world is seen to have an objective reality, is not equivalent to saying that QPR assumes that constructs and measures of these constructs are moving toward perfection over the years and should set this as the goal. In fact, Cook and Campbell (1979) repeatedly make the point that QPR will always fall short of the mark of perfect representation. For this reason, they argue for a 'critical-realist' perspective, positing that 'causal relationships cannot be perceived with total accuracy by our imperfect sensory and intellective capacities' (p. 29). Moreover, Meehl (1967), pointing out the underlying properties of statistical means and standard deviations, argues logically that measures that approach perfect precision can actually erode our confidence that we are capturing reality.

There are many ontologies or typologies of QPR. In fact, we offer one ourselves in the next section. The important point to remember about these ontologies is that research methods are not naturally occurring artifacts. Distinctions between them will be socially constructed, on the one hand, or based on practice, on the other. Nevertheless, researchers need to know something about the capabilities of these methods so that they can match them to their research problems and evaluate them when they are asked to review for community publications. Otherwise, these are distinctions without a difference.

Other quantitative techniques

This chapter focuses on the most common QPR types within the IS community. There are many other classes of quantitative research that we either omit or can only gloss over here. This is not to suggest in any way that these methods and tools are inferior or to be avoided. Only that they are not as common.

A good example of an omission is the 'scenario creation' or 'policy capturing' method. In this method, data are collected through questionnaires that present hypothetical scenarios (see, for example, Daft and Trevino, 1987; Fedor et al., 1989; Zmud et al., 1990; Straub and Karahanna, 1998). The hypothetical situations (or policy-capturing scenarios) afford large sample sizes by having subjects evaluate numerous, feasible real-world alternatives. One hundred 'subjects,' thus, who evaluate 10 scenarios each, could yield a sample size of 1000. The method allows for quasi-experimental manipulation of the independent variables through variations of scenario wording. Webster and Trevino (1995) offer a critique of the method.

14.2 Philosophical perspectives

A useful perspective on what quantitative positivist research methods conceptually are can be gained by seeing them in the context of Myers' framing in the *ISWorld* qualitative research website (http://www. qual.auckland.ac.nz/; adapted here with permission from Michael Myers), see also Chapter 15.

Figure 14.1 shows how, for qualitative research, the basic epistemological positions are threefold: positivist, interpretive, or critical. In the case of quantitative research, however, the interpretive and critical positions are not applicable; only 'positivist' is. The positivist epistemology (discussed in detail next) relies on a host of scientific methods that produce numerical and alphanumeric data. Accordingly, epistemological assumptions for both quantitative and qualitative research can be represented as in Figure 14.2.

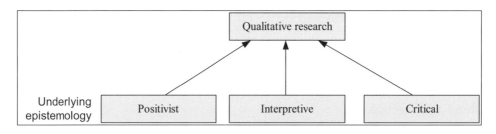

Figure 14.1 *Epistemological assumptions for qualitative research*

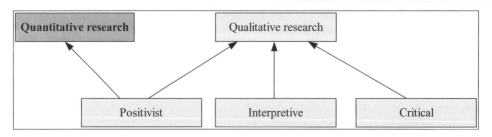

Figure 14.2 *Epistemological assumptions for qualitative and quantitative research*

14.3 Positivism

At the heart of positivism is Karl Popper's dichotomous differentiation between 'scientific' theories and 'myth.' A scientific theory is a theory whose predictions can be empirically falsified; that is, shown to be incorrect. Therefore, proposing a scientific theory is by necessity a risky endeavor; that is, it may be thrown out if not supported by the data. Einstein's Theory of Relativity is a prime example, according to Karl Popper (1959), of a scientific theory. When Einstein proposed it, the theory may have ended up in the junk pile of history had subsequent empirical tests not failed to disconfirm it, despite the enormous amount of work put into the theory and despite its mathematical appeal. The reason Einstein's theory was accepted was because it was put to the test. Eddington's eclipse observation in 1919 confirmed its predictions, predictions that were in contrast to what should have been seen according to Newtonian physics. Eddington's eclipse observation was a confirm-or-break event for Einstein's theory. The theory would have been discredited had the light from stars not appeared to shift during the eclipse because of the sun's gravity.

In contrast, according to Popper, is Freud's psychoanalytical theory, which can never be disproven because the theory is sufficiently imprecise to allow for convenient 'explanations' and the addition of ad hoc hypotheses to explain observations that contradict the theory. The ability to explain any observation as an apparent verification of psychoanalytical theory is no proof of the theory, because it can never be proven wrong to those who believe in it. A scientific theory, in contrast to psychoanalysis, is one that can be empirically falsified. This is the *falsification principle* and the core of positivism. Basically, experience can show theories to be wrong, but can never prove them right. It is an underlying Popperian principle that *theories can never be shown to be correct.*

This *demarcation* of science from the myths of non-science also assumes that building a theory based on observation, otherwise known as *induction*, does not make it scientific. Science, according to positivism, is about solving problems. It is not about fitting theory to observations. That is why introspection is not really science either, in the opinion of 'pure' positivists. Induction and introspection are important, but as a pre-science; that is, as a stage leading to the creation of a scientific theory. In this sense, Popper differs markedly from later commentators like Yin (1994), who argues that qualitative techniques, like case study, are scientific and can be used to both build and test theory.

Central to understanding Popper's principle is the recognition that there is no such thing as a pure observation. Every observation is based on some pre-existing theory or understanding. Furthermore, it is almost always possible to choose and select data that will support almost any theory if the researcher just looks for confirming examples. Accordingly, scientific theory, in the positivist view, is about trying to falsify the predictions of the theory.

It is enough therefore, that one observation that contradicts the prediction of a theory falsifies it and renders it incorrect. Furthermore, even after being tested, a scientific theory is never verified because it can never be shown to be true, as some future observation may yet contradict it. Accordingly, a scientific theory is, at most, extensively corroborated, which makes it accepted until proven otherwise. Of course, in reality, measurement is never perfect and is always based on theory. Hence, positivism differentiates between falsification as a principle, where one negating observation is all that is needed to cast out a theory, and its application in the real world through methodologies that recognize that observations may themselves be erroneous. Hence, it is widely accepted in practice that more than one observation is needed to falsify a theory.

The viewpoint of this chapter is that positivism should be regarded as one of the tools in the arsenal of a researcher. Arguably, recognizing science as a problem-solving endeavor, positivism itself (if it could be separated from the people who articulate or follow this position) would probably endorse this position.

Post-Popperian perspectives

As noted above, Cook and Campbell (1979) present a less stringent and severe perspective with respect to scientific epistemology. While the pure positivist epistemology deals only with observed and measured knowledge, the post-positivist epistemology recognizes that such an approach would result in making many important aspects of psychology irrelevant because feelings and perceptions cannot be readily measured.

In post-positivist understanding – pure empiricism that is, deriving knowledge only through observation and measurement – is understood to be too demanding. Instead, post-positivism is based on the concept of *critical realism;* that there is a real world out there independent of our perception of it and that the objective of science is to try and understand it. This concept is combined with the notion of *triangulation;* that is, the recognition that observations and measurements are inherently imperfect and hence the need to measure phenomena in many different ways. The post-positivist epistemology regards the acquisition of knowledge as a process that is more than mere deduction. Knowledge is acquired through both deduction and induction.

Another commentator who questioned Popper was Imre Lakatos (1970, 1978). Lakatos argues that there is a core set of propositions in a scientific theory, surrounded by a 'protective belt' of hypotheses that are related to the core set, but not requisite for establishing the 'truth' of the core. If the hypotheses in the belt are proven to be untrue, then the core propositions may still be inviolate. The spirit behind Lakatos' scientific epistemology is similar to Cook and Campbell (1979) (which supersedes Campbell and Stanley, 1963) in that there is greater latitude in allowing for exceptions. Popper's scientific epistemology tends to be highly deterministic and this is both its strength and its weakness.

Underlying positivist assumptions

In all QPR research methods, the underlying statistics (mainly T, F, and χ^2 statistics) deal with rejecting the *null hypothesis* of no effect. (The χ^2 statistic in LISREL is an exception, although this method likewise employs the T statistic.) Viewed from a positivist point of view, the objective of statistics employed by the QPR methods is to falsify the null hypothesis, which is the assumption that the data in the dependent variable are not affected by the data in the independent variable or variables. Since each theoretical hypothesis (the hypothesis as stated in the theory) should be the exact opposite of its null hypothesis by predicting a difference in the dependent variable, it follows logically that if the null hypothesis is rejected, then presumably the theoretical hypothesis is supported. The theoretical hypothesis may be supported in this case but not proven because theory according to the positivist philosophy cannot be proven. The essence of the statistics also takes into account the positivist recognition of imperfect measurement; hence, statistics test the *probability* that the results could have been obtained due to randomness in the data given the nature of the sample. It is based on this probability that the null hypothesis is rejected and by implication that the theoretical hypothesis is supported.

14.4 General QPR approach

Type of research

Initially, a researcher must decide what *type of research* is to be conducted: confirmatory or exploratory research. Hair et al. (1995) suggest that confirmatory studies are those seeking to test (confirm) a prespecified relationship, whereas exploratory studies are those which define possible relationships in only the most general form and then allow multivariate techniques to estimate a relationship(s). In the latter case, the researcher is not looking to 'confirm' any relationships specified prior to the analysis, but instead allows the method and the data to define the nature of the relationships.

Classes of general research approaches

Another perspective on QPR is based on Jenkins (1985). Using Stone's (1978) categorization scheme as a basis, he classifies strengths and weaknesses of a wide range of research methods (also referred to as 'research approaches' or 'methodologies'). Evaluating these characteristics, it is possible to sub-divide these methods into QPR and non-QPR methods.

Table 14.1 *QPR versus non-QPR methods*

QPR Methods	Non-QPR Methods
Field experiment	Math modeling (analytical modeling)
Lab experiment	Group feedback
Free simulation experiment	Participative research (action research)
Experimental simulation	Case study
Adaptive experiment	Philosophical research
Field study	
Opinion research	
Archival research	

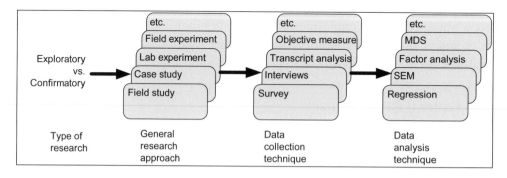

Figure 14.3 *Type of research*

It should be noted that the choice of a type of research and a general research approach does not 'force' a particular data collection technique or data analysis technique. It may, however, influence it, as a general research approach may be better served by a subset of all possible data collection and analysis techniques available. Figure 14.3 distinguishes the four basic choices quantitative researchers will need to make in the conduct of their QPR research.

IS researchers who are not familiar with these techniques should read about them in greater detail using one of the many excellent reference books available. Stone's (1978) book is one of these, but there are a wide variety of choices. An online book of interest is Trochim (2001), published by atomicdogpublishing.com. Students can acquire a one year online access for much less than the printed version.

14.5 Data collection techniques

Within each general research approach, one or many data collection techniques may be used. Typically, a researcher will decide on one or multiple techniques while considering overall appropriateness to the research, along with other practical factors, such as: expected quality of the collected data, estimated costs, predicted non-response rates, expected level of measure errors, and length of the data collection period (Lyberg and Kasprzyk, 1991). It is of course possible that a given research question may not be satisfactorily studied because specific data collection techniques do not exist to collect the data needed to answer such a question (Kerlinger, 1986).

The most popular data collection techniques include: surveys, secondary data sources, observation, objective tests, interviews, and Q-sorting. IS researchers should note that the term 'research instrument' is preferable to 'survey' in many respects in that it is neutral and does not imply a methodology. A research instrument can be administered as part of an experiment, a mailed survey or questionnaire, a semi-structured interview, or a Web survey or questionnaire. Therefore, the gathering of quantitative data directly from respondents should likely not be called a 'survey.' In addition, we prefer the term 'experimental instrument' as a neutral term for capturing data in experiments. 'Questionnaire' is acceptable as well, but, like 'survey,' carries connotations of a mailed instrument.

Another term that needs to be used with more deliberation in the IS literature is *instrumentation*. Instrumentation is a collective term for all of the tools, procedures, and instruments that a researcher may use to test a theory or gather descriptive data. There are no established standards for evaluating all forms of instrumentation, although the standards for assessing measurement validity are evolving (Straub et al., 2004). Experimenters typically pretest their experimental tasks, but what would be the minimal 'tests' that would lend credibility to the tasks as properly manipulating the subjects? Tests for demand characteristics are equally vague, even though it is well-recognized that these can lead to serious consequences (Orne, 1962; 1969; Latham et al., 1988; Judd et al., 1991).

14.6 Data analysis techniques

Before discussing data analysis, it is important to recognize that we are interested in studying research constructs, which are abstractions such as the perceived usefulness of a technology as in the *technology acceptance model* line of work. Perceived usefulness does not have a tangible existence, and, in fact, it is interesting precisely because of this fact. It is said to be a 'latent' construct in that it has a reality that is latent in, and revealed through, the measures that one employs to capture it. Incidentally, researchers typically use the terms 'construct' and 'variable' interchangeably, although 'variable' can also be used, rather ambiguously, to mean 'measure.'

Almost everything of interest studied in IS is a latent construct. Even the variable time may be thought of as an abstraction, in spite of the fact that we have a set of ready-made and widely accepted measures for it. But it is an abstraction, nonetheless. If one were to ask respondents how much time they typically spend working on their computers every day, we could measure this with an 'extent' scale and find that respondents averaged 3.2 on a 4 point scale anchored with 0 as 'to no extent' and 4 as 'to a large extent.' The nature of the measures shows that we can have high or low values on the construct time without having to necessarily retreat to a clock measure such as minutes. Therefore, logically, time is an abstraction. There is not just one highly tangible way of thinking about it.

Data analysis can take the form of simple descriptive statistics or more sophisticated statistical inference. Data analysis techniques include univariate analysis (such as analysis of single-variable distributions), bivariate analysis, and more generally, multivariate analysis. Multivariate analysis, broadly speaking, refers to all statistical methods that simultaneously analyze multiple measurements on each individual or object under investigation (Hair et al., 1995); as such, many multivariate techniques are extensions of univariate and bivariate analysis.

14.7 Issues of measurement

Measurement is, arguably, the most important thing that a quantitative, positivist researcher can do to ensure that the results of the study can be trusted. In this chapter, we refer to the validity associated with measurement as 'instrumentation validity.' This is a change from the term 'instrument validity' used in Straub (1989) and other methodologists. We will discuss later why the validity of other matters besides the instrument itself is important. In an experiment, for example, it is critical that a researcher check not only the experimental instrument, but also the phrasing of the experimental task. This task is part of the instrumentation, but not part of any instrument. Straub et al. (2004) discuss best practices and give examples and guidelines for the researcher.

Figure 14.4 shows how to prioritize instrumentation validity with internal validity and statistical conclusion validity. Depending on which validity(ies) one chooses to perform, three paths are possible. From worst to best, these are the black, the grey, and the white paths.

Black Path: The black path in Figure 14.4 represents poor instrumentation validity, poor internal validity, and good statistical conclusion validity. To illustrate, imagine a situation where a series of statistical tests demonstrate high levels of significance. One may be hopeful that the model is accurate and that the statistical conclusions will show that the posited relationships are true and important. Unfortunately, unbeknownst to the researcher, the specified model is wrong. There are variables that have not been included (rival explanations) that explain even more variance than the model does! To make matters worse, the constructs involved in the posited relationships are potentially unreliable and may not even be measuring the right content.

Grey Path: The grey path in Figure 14.4 represents poor instrumentation validity, good internal validity, and good statistical conclusion validity. In this case, imagine a situation where one is testing constructs to see which variable would or could 'confound' the contention that a certain variable or research construct is a good explanation for a set of effects. But if either the posited independent variable or the confound (rival explanation or construct) is poorly measured, then it is uncertain whether one or the other variable is the true cause. So there is an internal validity problem that is really not simply a matter of testing the strength of either the confound or the theoretical independent variable on the outcome, but is a matter of whether one can trust the measurement of either variable. Without instrumentation validity, it is really not possible to assess internal validity.

White Path: The white path in Figure 14.4 represents good instrumentation validity, good internal validity, and good statistical conclusion validity. This is the best case scenario, where instrumentation validity has shown that constructs are likely real and reliable, and that they are measuring the right content. Internal validity, then, has ruled out rival hypotheses. Statistical conclusion validity, finally, has established that mathematical relationships between constructs are assured with a certain degree of confidence.

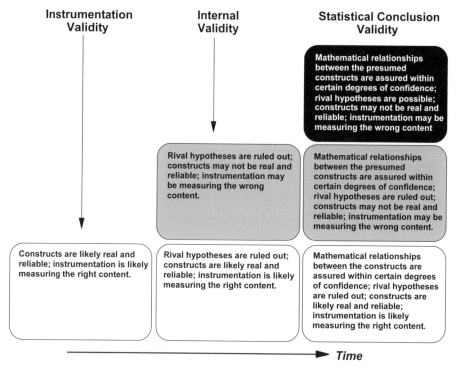

Legend: White is preferred path; grey is cautionary; black is least desirable

Figure 14.4 *Primary and prior importance of instrumentation validity* (modified from Straub et al., 2004 and Straub, 1989)

In summary, because instrumentation validity is a critical first step in QPR, it must be acceptable at a minimal level. If not, then the findings from a study are meaningless, and one cannot trust or contend that either internal validity or statistical conclusion validity has been achieved.

Types of instrumentation validity

Straub et al. (2004) describe the 'ins' and 'outs' of instrumentation validity. The paper presents the arguments for why various forms of instrumentation validity should be mandatory and why others are optional. Basically, there are four types of scientific validity with respect to instrumentation. They are: (1) content validity, (2) construct validity, (3) reliability, and (4) manipulation validity.

1   Content validity

Content validity includes all the ways that a researcher can employ to prove that his or her instrumentation is a not unreasonable drawing from all of the forms that the researcher could have chosen to capture a construct (Cronbach, 1971). Suppose you included satisfaction with the IS staff in your measurement of a construct called User Information Satisfaction (UIS) but you forgot to include satisfaction with the system itself? Another researcher might feel that you have missed the boat and that you did not draw well from all of the possible measures of this construct. This person could legitimately argue that your content validity was not the best.

2   Construct validity

With construct validity, we are interested in whether the instrumentation has truly captured data through operations that will result in constructs that are not subject to common methods bias and other forms of bias. Maybe some of the questionnaire items, the verbiage in the interview script, or the task descriptions in an experiment are ambiguous and are giving the participants the impression that they mean something different from what was intended. This is a construct validity issue.

The problems occur in two major ways. Items or phrases in the instrumentation are not related in the way they should be or they are related in the ways they should not be. If the items do not converge or run together as they should, it is called a *convergent validity* problem. If they do not segregate or differ from each other as they should, then it is called a *discriminant validity* problem.

As Straub et al. (2004), Gefen et al. (2000), and Straub (1989) point out, there are numerous ways to test for construct validity.

We now turn to the issue of *fixing problems with construct validity*. Suppose you test for construct validity and find out that some of your constructs are problematic. What can and should you do? The approach described in Churchill (1979) is to purify the measures. If one follows this approach, including pretesting and pilot testing the instrumentation, the likelihood that there will be no problems to begin with is much better.

Churchill (1979) also justifies a view that holds that measures that do not contribute to the constructs in a factor analysis can be dropped. This would include PCA, PLS, and covariance-based SEM.

3 Reliability

Reliability is the assurance that the items posited to measure a construct are sufficiently related to be reliable (that is, low on measurement error) considered as a set of items (Cronbach, 1951). The difference between reliability and convergent validity is a matter of how one proves that a set of items 'run' together. In convergent validity, this test involves a comparison to other variables. Reliability tests look only at the items in the construct's own scale and do not compare across constructs.

There are many ways in which reliability can be tested. As Straub et al. (2004) show, these include: internal consistency (also known as Cronbach's alpha), composite reliability (PLS and LISREL), split-half reliability, test–retest reliability, alternate forms of reliability, inter-rater reliability, and unidimensional reliability. This article discusses each of these in detail, and so these topics do not bear repeating here.

4 Manipulation validity

This form of validity applies only to experiments and is discussed in greater detail, including statistics for assessing it, in Straub et al. (2004). Suffice it to say at this point that in experiments, it is critical that the subjects are manipulated by the treatments and, conversely, that the control group is not manipulated. One way to do this is to ask the subjects directly. Those who were aware that they were manipulated are subjects producing useful data on the effect of the treatment. Those who were not aware, depending on the nature of the treatments, should have been assigned to the control group or dropped from the data.

Those who were not manipulated add unwanted variance to your sample since you are measuring the effects of a treatment that did not take place. So it is quite legitimate to remove them from the tested samples. On the other hand, if you still get the effects, in between-group studies especially, then you have a very robust test. You could quite rightly argue that the effect is larger than it would have been had you restricted the samples to those who replied in a manner that indicated that they were, indeed, manipulated or control subjects.

14.8 A critical perspective and limitations of QPR

QPR provide a set of powerful tools to analyze numeric data. It provides an objective and replicable set of statistical methods that can examine theories by estimating hypothesized coefficients and assessing their significance. But these inherent strengths of QPR are also its inherent weaknesses. QPR deals with numeric data, typically numbers collected through surveys or observations. On the pro side, this makes the analysis relatively objective. Numeric data make it harder for researchers to see what they are looking for in that it is embedded in the data, and so while QPR results in more valid and believable analysis, this can be deceptive if, for instance, the data itself is not good. Another deceptively reassuring aspect of numbers is that, even though they can be statistically manipulated, they appear to be less ambiguous than language and pictures. But, while these can be, under optimal circumstances, advantageous, they come at a price.

QPR has limitations. QPR is inherently deductive in nature. The methods are geared toward testing theories. They are less suited to building theories because numbers are not as contextually and socially rich as soft data, such as words and pictures might be. This makes QPR somewhat less powerful when it comes to gaining insight from the data. Such limitations can be overcome by incorporating soft data analysis. An example of overcoming this limitation is in Gefen (2002) where the numeric data were analyzed in a QPR manner with LISREL, but triangulated with an analysis of written responses to an open ended question which replicated the QPR analysis. This triangulation added rich social examples to the model.

Another inherent limitation of QPR is the underlying assumptions in the statistical analysis. When applying QPR, it is necessary to recognize that statistical analyses are only indicative of the correctness of the model. Statistics alone cannot absolutely disprove a hypothesis. Statistics at best provides tentative support for the proposed model. There are several reasons for this. First, statistics are based on probability, meaning that hypotheses are only 'probably' rejected (or not). Second, the correctness of the analysis depends on satisfying a set of questionable assumptions in the statistical test. In most statistical tools, it is assumed that the data demonstrate a multivariate normal distribution and that the relationships both in the measurement model and in the structural one are linear. In reality, both these assumptions are questionable. Although this is the acceptable practice, strictly speaking, interval data derived from answers on a 1 to 7 Likert scale, or even a 1 to 11 scale, are not usually normally distributed.

Moreover, statistical analyses assume that the independent variables are insignificantly correlated. When this is not the case – that is, when there is multicolinearity – the results may be ambiguous and open to rival interpretations. Practically speaking, the possibility of rival interpretations means that QPR methodologies may not always live up to their positivist aspirations. Additionally, statistical analyses often assume that the error terms are more or less the same across the whole range of values of the independent variables. When this is not the case – that is, when there is heteroscedasticity – the coefficient estimates and the p-values may be inflated.

Last, but not least, most statistical tools estimate a linear relationship. This is because the mathematical estimations are too complex otherwise and because with interval data estimating other patterns, such as inverted U relationships, are often impractical. Although this is the accepted practice, one should be aware of these limitations and acknowledge them in the study.

14.9 Conclusion

QPR is frequently found to be a highly attractive macro-level methodical choice for IS researchers. The key to rigorous use of this approach is to match the research design to the research problem, but adhering to the well known standards for the method is equally important. Researchers just entering the field will be well advised to practice these techniques according to the thresholds and other heuristics that have been articulated in the literature. The reviewing process for journals will expect this and hold authors and PhD students to this gold standard.

15

Qualitative Research

David Avison and Michael Myers

15.1 Introduction

One of the most difficult tasks of the research supervisor is that of advising the research student on which research method to adopt. Researchers need to justify the research approach used, giving reasons why it was appropriate, why other approaches were not used, and show that it was used correctly. Poor advice from the supervisor early into the PhD can therefore cause the student major problems afterwards. In the previous chapter we provided an overview of quantitative research in information systems. In this chapter we discuss qualitative research approaches with examples of their use. Even now, in some information systems departments, these are less accepted than the more established quantitative approaches, so research students need to be confident in this area so that choices can be justified.

Qualitative research approaches tend to be particularly appropriate for research into IS practice. Whereas much of the early research in information systems had a technical focus (for example, on automating the back office or optimizing decisions), in the 1980s the focus shifted to the *management* of information systems. Then in the 1990s the focus broadened considerably, from the management of information systems to the relationship between IS and *organizations as a whole*. IS, as a field of study, has now expanded to include issues such as communication and collaboration between people and organizations, inter-organizational systems, electronic commerce, and the Internet. Given the tremendous scope of the field, it is perhaps not surprising that there is also great diversity in the research methods and approaches used to study information systems phenomena. Papers in both qualitative and quantitative research are now welcomed in our top journals, as long as the research itself is of a high quality. This was not always the case, as statements from previous editors of the *MIS Quarterly*, for example, make apparent; but it *is* true now. Arguments for the use of various research approaches in IS are also suggested in Galliers and Land (1987). One important point to note is that qualitative research has the potential to be both rigorous and relevant (for a fuller discussion of the rigor versus relevance debate, see Kock et al., 2002).

In this chapter, we first look at three philosophical perspectives to qualitative research: positivist, interpretive and critical. We briefly describe some research methods: action research, case study, ethnography and grounded theory. Following this, we look at two modes of analysis: hermeneutics and metaphor. Finally we provide a brief discussion of qualitative techniques for data collection and suggest ways in which qualitative research can be written up. In all cases we describe briefly and cite exemplars of published research for further study. Many of these exemplars can be found in Myers and Avison (2001), a collection of some of the best qualitative research articles in information systems.

15.2 Overview of qualitative research

Research methods can be classified in various ways; however, one of the most common distinctions is between quantitative and qualitative research methods. *Quantitative research methods* were originally developed in the natural sciences to study natural phenomena. Examples of quantitative methods now well accepted in information systems (and the social sciences generally) include survey methods, laboratory experiments, formal methods (for example, econometrics) and numerical methods such as mathematical modeling. These were discussed in the previous chapter. *Qualitative research methods* were developed in the social sciences to enable researchers to study social and cultural phenomena. They are designed to help us understand people and the social and cultural contexts within which they live. Examples of qualitative methods are: action research, case study research and ethnography. Qualitative data sources include observation and participant observation (fieldwork), interviews and questionnaires, documents and texts, and the researcher's impressions and reactions.

Supervisors and their students are strongly advised to study exemplars of papers illustrating the use of these approaches in action. One of the classic (and most cited) empirical examples of qualitative research in information systems is the article by Markus (1983). In a well-crafted article, she discusses how various theories help to explain power and politics in the implementation of management information systems. In particular, she studies how theories of resistance can explain implementation problems for information systems at a large manufacturing concern. The paper also provides an excellent example of case study research (see below). Mumford et al. (1985), Nissen et al. (1991), Lee et al. (1997) and Kaplan et al. (2004) also provide many excellent examples of qualitative research in IS and Myers (living) provides a source of references which is regularly updated.

15.3 Philosophical perspectives

All research (whether quantitative or qualitative) is based on some underlying assumptions about what constitutes 'valid' research and which research methods are appropriate. These should be made explicit in the thesis. Again, discussions between the supervisor and student should be as much about these issues as the practical task in hand. In order to conduct and/or evaluate qualitative research, it is essential to know what these (sometimes hidden) assumptions are. For our purposes, the most pertinent philosophical assumptions are those that relate to the underlying epistemology that guides the research. Epistemology refers to the assumptions about knowledge and how it can be obtained (for a fuller discussion, see Hirschheim, 1992).

Orlikowski and Baroudi (1991) provide an excellent overview of the various research approaches and assumptions in IS research. Following Chua (1986), the authors suggest three distinct epistemological categories: positivist, interpretive and critical. While these three research epistemologies are *philosophically* distinct (as ideal types), in the practice of social research these distinctions are not always so clear-cut. There is considerable disagreement as to whether these research 'paradigms' or underlying epistemologies are necessarily opposed and there is further debate about whether they can be accommodated within the one study.

Nevertheless, some research studies are multi-method, and researchers need to be aware of this potential trap and have some defense. Research based on more than one underlying epistemology is more difficult to defend.

It should be clear from the above that the word 'qualitative' is not a synonym for 'interpretive.' Indeed, qualitative research may or may not be interpretive, depending upon the underlying philosophical assumptions of the researcher. Indeed, qualitative research can be positivist, interpretive, or critical. It follows from this that the choice of a specific qualitative research method (such as the case study method) is independent of the underlying philosophical position adopted. For example, case study research can be positivist (Yin, 1994), interpretive (Walsham, 1993), or critical, just as action research can be positivist (Clark, 1972), interpretive (Elden and Chisholm, 1993) or critical (Carr and Kemmis, 1986). These three philosophical perspectives are discussed below.

Positivist research

Positivists generally assume that reality is objectively given and can be described by measurable properties, which are independent of the observer (researcher) and his or her instruments. Positivist studies generally attempt to test theory, in an attempt to increase the predictive understanding of phenomena. In line with this, Orlikowski and Baroudi (1991) classify IS research as positivist if there is evidence of formal propositions, quantifiable measures of variables, hypothesis testing, and the drawing of inferences about a phenomenon from the sample to a stated population.

The article by Benbasat et al. (1987) is an excellent example of a positivist approach to doing case study research in information systems. It examines four published research cases and suggests for each how the study could have been shaped to produce more useful insights. Suggestions are provided for researchers who wish to undertake research employing this approach. Several characteristics useful for categorizing the studies are identified. A sample of papers drawn from information systems journals is reviewed. The paper concludes with examples of research areas that are particularly well suited to investigation using the case research approach.

Criteria for the evaluation of case research are also suggested in the paper. Whereas, in quantitative research, such criteria for evaluation are often well established and understood, and it is relatively easy to assess whether the research method has been used appropriately, this is certainly not always the case in qualitative research, particularly that which is non-positivist. Nevertheless, it would be a great pity for research in information systems if all supervisors and their students avoided qualitative research because of the potential risks. The potential benefits in terms of the impact of our research into practice are also great.

Interpretive research

Interpretive researchers start out with the assumption that access to reality (given or socially constructed) is only through social constructions such as language, consciousness and shared meanings. Interpretive studies generally attempt to understand phenomena through the meanings that people assign to them and interpretive methods of research in IS are 'aimed at producing an understanding of the context of the information system, and the process whereby the information system influences and is influenced by the context' (Walsham, 1993, 4:5). Examples of an interpretive approach to qualitative

Table 15.1 *Summary of principles for interpretive field research* (adapted from Klein and Myers, 1999)

1	**The fundamental principle of the hermeneutic circle** This principle suggests that all human understanding is achieved by iterating between considering the interdependent meaning of parts and the whole that they form. This principle of human understanding is fundamental to all the other principles.
2	**The principle of contextualization** Requires critical reflection of the social and historical background of the research setting, so that the intended audience can see how the current situation under investigation emerged.
3	**The principle of interaction between the researchers and the subjects** Requires critical reflection on how the research materials (or 'data') were socially constructed through the interaction between the researchers and participants.
4	**The principle of abstraction and generalization** Requires relating the idiographic details revealed by the data interpretation through the application of Principles 1 and 2 to theoretical, general concepts that describe the nature of human understanding and social action.
5	**The principle of dialogical reasoning** Requires sensitivity to possible contradictions between the theoretical preconceptions guiding the research design and actual findings ('the story which the data tell') with subsequent cycles of revision.
6	**The principle of multiple interpretations** Requires sensitivity to possible differences in interpretations among the participants as are typically expressed in multiple narratives or stories of the same sequence of events under study. Similar to multiple witness accounts even if all tell it as they saw it.
7	**The principle of suspicion** Requires sensitivity to possible 'biases' and systematic 'distortions' in the narratives collected from the participants.

research include Boland (1991) and Walsham (1993). In view of the comments made earlier, Klein and Myers (1999) is a particularly useful contribution as it suggests a set of principles for the conduct and evaluation of interpretive research. These principles are summarized in Table 15.1.

The article by Walsham (1995) is an excellent example of an interpretive approach to doing case study research and therefore makes an interesting comparison with Benbasat et al. (1987). Walsham looks at a number of in-depth case studies that focus on human actions and interpretations surrounding the development and use of computer-based information systems. He addresses philosophical and theoretical issues concerning the nature of such interpretive case studies, and methodological issues on the conduct and reporting of this type of research.

Critical research

Critical researchers assume that social reality is historically constituted and that it is produced and reproduced by people. Although people can consciously act to change their social and economic circumstances, critical researchers recognize that their ability to do so is constrained by various forms of social, cultural and political domination. The main task of critical research is seen as being one of social critique, whereby the restrictive and alienating conditions of the status quo are brought to light. Critical research focuses on the oppositions, conflicts and contradictions in contemporary society, and seeks to be emancipatory; that is, it should help to eliminate the causes of alienation and domination. Examples of a critical approach to information systems research include Ngwenyama and Lee (1997) and Hirschheim and Klein (1994).

The article by Ngwenyama (1991) looks at critical social theory as an approach to information systems research and practice. The language of its discourse and radically different position on scientific enterprise have been significant barriers to the adoption of critical social theory as an IS research method. The paper attempts to open the discourse on critical social theory by presenting a review of its basic concepts and discussing some of the theoretical problems and challenges that must be addressed if progress is to be made in applying it to the practical issues of information systems. The paper focuses on Habermas' critical social theory.

15.4 Qualitative research methods

Just as there are various philosophical perspectives that can inform qualitative research, so there are various qualitative research methods. A research method is a strategy of inquiry which moves from the underlying philosophical assumptions to research design and data collection. The choice of research method influences the way in which the researcher collects data. Specific research methods also imply different skills, assumptions and research practices. The four research methods that are discussed here are action research, case study research, ethnography and grounded theory.

Action research

There are numerous definitions of action research; however, one of the most widely cited is that of Rapoport, who defines action research in the following way:

> *Action research aims to contribute both to the practical concerns of people in an immediate problematic situation and to the goals of social science by joint collaboration within a mutually acceptable ethical framework* (Rapoport, 1970, p. 499).

This definition draws attention to the collaborative aspect of action research and to possible ethical dilemmas that arise from its use.

Action research has been accepted as a valid research method in applied fields such as organization development and education. In information systems, however, it is only within the last decade that action research has started to make an impact. A brief overview of action research is the article by Susman and Evered (1978).

Baskerville and Wood-Harper (1996) review the origins, techniques and roles associated with action research into information systems. The paper proposes what the authors call 'a rigorous approach' to action research and suggests certain domains of ideal use (such as systems development methodology). Avison et al. (1999) emphasize the fact that action research is an iterative process involving researchers and practitioners acting together. They suggest that action research as a research method is especially relevant to practice. Action research encourages researchers to experiment through intervention, to reflect systematically on this, and to modify their views as a result of this reflection.

Avison et al. (2001) look at the process in action research projects, and look at some of the key choices and alternatives in controlling action research. They discuss three aspects of control: the procedures for initiating an action research project, those for determining authority within the project, and the degree of formalization. Mumford (2001) gives general advice to the action researcher. In 2004 *MIS Quarterly* published a special issue on action research. All six articles in the special issue can be considered as exemplars of action research (Baskerville and Myers, 2004).

Case study research

Case study research is the most common qualitative method used in information systems (Alavi and Carlson, 1992; Orlikowski and Baroudi, 1991). There are numerous definitions, but Yin (1994) defines the scope of a case study as follows:

> *A case study is an empirical inquiry that investigates a contemporary phenomenon within its real-life context, especially when the boundaries between phenomenon and context are not clearly evident (p.13).*

Clearly, the case study research method is particularly well suited to IS research, since the object of our discipline is the study of information systems in organizations, and 'interest has shifted to organizational rather than technical issues' (Benbasat et al., 1987).

Case study research can be positivist, interpretive, or critical, depending upon the underlying philosophical assumptions of the researcher.

A standard text for anyone wanting to do positivist case study research is the book by Yin (1994). We have seen that Benbasat et al. (1987) provides a good example of a positivist approach. The article by Lee (1989) suggests a scientific methodology for IS case studies. Frequent debates about case study research leading to a PhD center on how many case studies are necessary. Lee argues that research based on a single case study is able to satisfy positivist criteria for scientific research. We agree with him that one in-depth case study is sufficient, if done well – there should be other, additional reasons, for conducting more than one case.

For interpretive case studies, Walsham (1995) provides an excellent overview. Two good empirical examples of the interpretive case study method in IS are the articles by Myers (1994) and Walsham and Waema (1994). The article by Klein and Myers (1999) suggests a set of principles for the conduct and evaluation of interpretive case studies (and ethnographies) in information systems (see Table 15.1 above).

Ethnographic research

Ethnographic research comes from the discipline of social and cultural anthropology where an ethnographer is required to spend a significant amount of time in the field. The ethnographer 'immerses himself in the life of people he studies' (Lewis, 1985, p. 380) and seeks to place the phenomena studied in their social and cultural context.

After early groundbreaking work by Wynn (1979), Suchman (1987) and Zuboff (1988), ethnography has now become more widely used in the study of information systems in organizations, from the study of the development of information systems (Hughes et al., 1992; Orlikowski, 1991; Preston, 1991) to the study of aspects of information technology management (Davies, 1991; Davies and Nielsen, 1992). Ethnography has also been discussed as a method whereby multiple perspectives can be incorporated in systems design (Holzblatt and Beyer, 1993).

The article by Harvey and Myers (1995) provides an overview of the use and potential use of ethnography in IS research. In this article, the authors concentrate on the conflicts of objectives between scholars and practitioners as stakeholder groups in IS research. They suggest that there is a gap between the process of knowledge generation conducted by researchers and that conducted by practitioners. The authors seek to show how ethnography provides the principles to support both groups, hence bridging the gap. As Avison et al. (1999) show, action research also bridges that gap. Myers (1999) provides an overview of the different kinds of ethnography that are applicable in IS research.

Grounded theory
Grounded theory is a research method that seeks to develop theory that is grounded in data systematically gathered and analyzed. According to Martin and Turner (1986), grounded theory is 'an inductive, theory discovery methodology that allows the researcher to develop a theoretical account of the general features of a topic while simultaneously grounding the account in empirical observations or data.' The major difference between grounded theory and other methods is its specific approach to theory development. Grounded theory suggests that there should be a continuous interplay between data collection and analysis. Grounded theory approaches are becoming increasingly common in the IS research literature because the method is extremely useful in developing context-based, process-oriented descriptions and explanations of the phenomenon under study.

The article by Orlikowski (1993) is an excellent example of the use of grounded theory in IS research. It presents the findings of an empirical study into two organizations' experiences with the adoption and use of computer-aided software engineering (CASE) tools over time. Using a grounded theory research approach, the study characterizes the organizations' experiences in terms of processes of incremental or radical organizational change. The framework and findings suggest that in order to account for the experiences and outcomes associated with CASE tools, researchers should consider the social context of systems development, the intentions and actions of key players, and the implementation process followed by the organization.

15.5 Qualitative techniques for data collection

The use of qualitative techniques for data collection is the same in IS research as it is in other disciplines, so we provide only a brief discussion here and emphasize those concerns that relate to the supervisor–supervisee relationship rather than provide details of the technique. Good discussions of qualitative techniques for data collection can be found in Denzin and Lincoln (1994), Miles and Huberman (1984), Rubin and Rubin (1995) and Silverman (1993).

Once the general research area has been decided (if not before), the researcher will conduct a literature review. The supervisor may suggest the fundamental work to look at, but it will not be long before the research student follows other paths. Along with conventional sources, the Internet provides a huge (but not necessarily wholly accurate) resource. It soon becomes the difficult job of the supervisor to attempt to restrain the student from following too many alternative topics. It might then be difficult to find a focus for the research and a research question to address, which may become apparent following study of the literature (for example, a research question unanswered or a question that seems to have conflicting answers). It is also important to keep good records of the literature looked at. A potentially very useful facility is computer software, such as *Endnote,* which can keep track of full reference details (that can be reformatted for publishing purposes) and hold comments on each of the works. A useful collection of Endnote resources for IS researchers is the *ISWorld* site at http://www.isworld.org/endnote/index.asp

It may soon be apparent that the researcher wishes to find evidence about the research topic in its natural setting. One of the most difficult aspects can be gaining access to the organization or organizations where data can be collected. The student not only needs entry to the organization, but willingness of its employees to help and that requires trust and credibility. Much will depend on the supervisor's own research record and reputation, and the supervisor may be expected to set up the opening. Providing an incentive to the organization, such as a report of the research findings, may also help. On the other hand, damage to that reputation may be the result of the student's poor preparation for interviews, heavy-handedness or disagreement concerning ethical issues; for example, not keeping to confidentiality agreements. At some universities, access needs approval from the university ethics committee before the project can be carried out.

Written evidence provided by subjects, such as completed questionnaires, is normally associated with quantitative studies, but through open-ended questions they can provide narrative data. For example, one of the present authors has used them to obtain negative and positive stories about IT in companies (Avison et al., 1999). Even so, most qualitative studies obtain the bulk of their data through interviews, observation and the like, and questionnaires and other documents might be used more to provide some initial information about the organization or help the researcher to choose which particular organization to study.

Interviews are usually structured or semi-structured. Deciding who should be interviewed, gaining access to them, making a schedule and providing for contingencies can be as challenging as deciding how to make best use of the time through pertinent questions. A pilot study may help in resolving some of these issues. Interviewees may well be biased in some way, and observation can provide corroborative evidence that 'it does or doesn't happen that way.' Such evidence may also be obtained via a group interview or focus group, where the conversation is between the researcher and a number of participants rather than with one interviewee only.

Conversations, including telephone interviews, might be recorded, and again it is important that the student is aware of the protocols and permission has been obtained. The research student also needs to be aware of the time it takes to analyze these recordings following the interview. Help and support may be required if the student feels a sense of 'drowning in data.' But keeping records is crucial in all research work, as well as keeping a diary.

A popular computer package for text analysis is NUD-IST, but there are alternatives. These can help analysis tasks such as categorization, relationship and pattern recognition, coding (following grounded theory) and summarizing. There needs to be formal training courses provided by the academic institution or other means provided for research students to gain the necessary skills. Again, supervisors need to ensure that their students are aware of all the issues either through individual conversations or through a formal research methods course undertaken by all research students. However, although the supervisor can guide the student and the university can provide the infrastructure, in the end it is the student's PhD, not the supervisor's.

15.6 Qualitative modes of analysis

Although a clear distinction between data gathering and data analysis is commonly made in quantitative research, such a distinction is problematic for many qualitative researchers. For example, from a hermeneutic perspective it is assumed that the researcher's presuppositions affect the gathering of the data – the questions posed to informants largely determine what you are going to find out. The analysis affects the data and the data affect the analysis in significant ways. Therefore, it is perhaps more accurate to speak of 'modes of analysis' rather than 'data analysis' in qualitative research. These modes of analysis are different approaches to gathering, analyzing and interpreting qualitative data. The common thread is that all qualitative modes of analysis are concerned primarily with textual analysis (whether verbal or written).

Although there are many different modes of analysis in qualitative research, just two approaches or modes of analysis will be looked at here: hermeneutics and approaches which focus on narrative and metaphor. Other approaches used in IS include semiotics, and Klein and Truex (1995) provide a good example of using such an approach. It could be argued that grounded theory is also a mode of analysis, but since grounded theory has been discussed earlier, that discussion will not be repeated here.

Hermeneutics
Hermeneutics can be treated as both an underlying philosophy and a specific mode of analysis (Bleicher, 1980). As a philosophical approach to human understanding, it provides the philosophical grounding for interpretivism (see above). As a mode of analysis, it suggests a way of understanding textual data. The following discussion is concerned with using hermeneutics as a specific mode of analysis.

Hermeneutics is primarily concerned with the *meaning* of a text or text-analogue (an example of a text-analogue is an organization, which the researcher comes to understand through oral or written text). The basic question in hermeneutics is: 'what is the meaning of this text?' (Radnitzky, 1970). Taylor (1976) argues that:

> *Interpretation, in the sense relevant to hermeneutics, is an attempt to make clear, to make sense of an object of study. This object must, therefore, be a text, or a text-analogue, which in some way is confused, incomplete, cloudy, and seemingly contradictory – in one way or another, unclear. The interpretation aims to bring to light an underlying coherence or sense (p. 153).*

The idea of a hermeneutic circle refers to the dialectic between the understanding of the text as a whole and the interpretation of its parts, in which descriptions are guided by anticipated explanations (Gadamer, 1976). It follows from this that we have an expectation of meaning from the context of what has gone before. The movement of understanding 'is constantly from the whole to the part and back to the whole' (ibid). As Gadamer explains, 'It is a circular relationship…the anticipation of meaning in which the whole is envisaged becomes explicit understanding in that the parts, that are determined by the whole, themselves also determine this whole.' Ricoeur suggests that 'Interpretation…is the work of thought which consists in deciphering the hidden meaning in the apparent meaning, in unfolding the levels of meaning implied in the literal meaning' (Ricoeur, 1974, p. xiv).

There are different forms of hermeneutic analysis, from 'pure' hermeneutics through to 'critical' hermeneutics. However, a discussion of these different forms is beyond the scope of this chapter. For a more in-depth discussion, see Bleicher (1980), Palmer (1969); and Thompson (1981).

If hermeneutic analysis is used in an information systems study, the object of the interpretive effort becomes one of attempting to make sense of the organization as a text-analogue. In an organization, people (for example, different stakeholders) can have confused, incomplete, cloudy and contradictory views on many issues. The aim of the hermeneutic analysis becomes one of trying to make sense of the whole, and the relationship between people, the organization, and information technology.

Boland (1991) is a good example of a research article in IS which explicitly uses hermeneutics. Other examples are those by Lee (1994) and Myers (1994). Boland uses hermeneutics to make an interpretive reading of the way four experienced managers analyze and give meaning to the output from a personnel evaluation information system. The output from an information system is viewed as a text being read and interpreted by the information system user. Some unique features of the user as an active reader of the information system text are identified.

Narrative and metaphor
Narrative is defined by the Concise Oxford English Dictionary as a 'tale, story, recital of facts, especially in fiction, story told in the first person.' There are many kinds of narrative, from oral narrative through to historical narrative. Metaphor is the application of a name or descriptive term or phrase to an object or action to which it is not literally applicable (for example, a 'window' in the Windows PC operating systems).

Narrative and metaphor have long been key terms in literary discussion and analysis. In recent years there has been increasing recognition of the role they play in all types of thinking and social practice. Scholars in many disciplines have looked at areas such as metaphor and symbolism in indigenous cultures, oral narrative, narrative and metaphor in organizations, metaphor and medicine, and metaphor and psychiatry.

A good introduction to the use of metaphor in organizational theory is Morgan (1986). Polkinghorne's (1988) book on narrative has been extremely influential in the social sciences. In IS the focus has mostly been on understanding language, communication and meaning among systems developers and organizational members.

The article by Hirschheim and Newman (1991) is an excellent example of the use of metaphor in information systems development. The authors challenge the commonly-held assumption that information systems development (ISD) can be conceived of as a normative process reflecting conventional economic rationality. They suggest that even the basic assumptions about the rationality of the actors and the social processes they engage in need to be critically appraised, and suggest that symbolism holds more promise as an explanation.

15.7 Writing up qualitative research

Just as there are many different qualitative methods and approaches to qualitative data analysis, so there are many different writing styles and approaches. For a brief overview of some of these styles as they relate to ethnography, see Harvey and Myers (1995) and Myers (1999). It is hard to over-emphasize the importance of good writing.

For writing up qualitative research in general, we highly recommend Wolcott's (1990) book. This book has many practical suggestions. For example, Wolcott points out that many qualitative researchers make the mistake of leaving the writing up until the end, i.e. until they have got 'the story' figured out. However, Wolcott makes the point that 'writing is thinking.' Writing actually helps a researcher to think straight and to figure out what the story should be. The motto of every qualitative researcher should be to start writing as soon as possible.

A common problem for qualitative IS researchers are that IS researchers are expected to publish their work in journal articles. Generally speaking, journal articles are regarded much more highly than books in business schools. However, most types of qualitative research lead to the gathering of a significant mass of data. It can be difficult for qualitative researchers to write up their results within the space constraints of a journal article. Another problem is the expectation that singular findings will be presented in each paper, i.e. each journal article should have just one main 'point.' Often a qualitative doctoral thesis such as an ethnographic study will have many points.

One solution is for qualitative researchers to treat each paper as a part of the whole. That is, a qualitative researcher has to devise a way to carve up the work in such as way that parts of it can be published separately. Then the issue becomes which part of the story is going to be told in one particular paper. A qualitative researcher has to come to terms with the fact that it is impossible to tell the 'whole story' in any one paper, so he or she has to accept that only one part of it can be told at any one time.

One advantage of such a strategy is that there is potential for an ethnographer to publish many papers from just the one period of fieldwork. Usually it is possible to tell the same story but from different angles. A good example of someone who adopted this strategy is Wanda Orlikowski. Orlikowski succeeded in having many papers published based on the one period of ethnographic fieldwork she did for her PhD at MIT.

15.8 Conclusion

We believe that this chapter and the articles discussed draw attention to the tremendous progress that has been made within the field of information systems, particularly within the past decade, due to the adoption of qualitative research approaches alongside quantitative ones. Qualitative research approaches tend to be particularly appropriate for research into IS practice. Research supervisors and their students need to consider these approaches alongside quantitative approaches and choose that which is most appropriate for the chosen subject. We have suggested that there are three philosophical perspectives to qualitative research: positivist, interpretive and critical and we have briefly described some research methods: action research, case study, ethnography and grounded theory. We then looked at two modes of analysis: hermeneutics and metaphor before finally providing a brief overview of techniques used. We hope this small contribution will lead to an even greater interest and appropriate use of qualitative approaches in IS.

Part V:
PhD Models

Part V focuses on different PhD models, for although the degree can be seen as a generally-accepted world 'brand', there are important differences. The four chapters look at what we have termed the US model (written by Duane Truex and Cherie Long), UK model (Guy Fitzgerald), Latin model (João Alvaro Carvalho and Frantz Rowe), which combines the Portuguese and French perspectives, and Scandinavian model (Karlheinz Kautz).

In truth, the descriptions in the chapters are more examples than normative prescriptions, as there are many differences within countries and types. To give an overview, nevertheless, Guy Fitzgerald asked all the authors to complete a table rating key elements on a seven-point scale with *1* very low and *7* very high. Each table is displayed around the introductory section in each of the four chapters.

If you are a supervisor: we recommend that you construct the table for your particular program and reflect on the differences between your model and others. Can you make up for apparent deficiencies in your model? Are there ways in which it might be possible to 'balance' models? For example, if your scheme rates *academic career driver* as *6* or *7*, can you make the PhD program more attractive as a qualification for a non-academic career? Alternatively, if the control points criterion is given a *1* rating, is it possible to add a mid-point control point to test that the research is going according to plan?

If you are a PhD student: construct the table for your particular program and reflect on the differences between your model and others. Does your version of the table match your supervisor's? Can you make up for apparent deficiencies in your model? For example, can you discuss with your supervisor the possibility of a mid-point control point to test that the research is going according to plan, if your scheme gives control points a low rating?

16

United States Model

Duane Truex and Cherie Long

16.1 Introduction

In this and in each of the following three chapters, we assess the particular model from the point of view of seven key elements. Each criterion is assessed on a seven-point scale with 1 very low and 7 very high. The seven dimensions are:

1 *Academic career driver:* The degree to which the model is driven by an assumption of an ongoing career in academia. If so this would be rated as high, whereas if it is driven by a practitioner career then this would be given a low number.
2 *Supervision dependency:* The degree of dependence of the student on the supervisor in obtaining the PhD.
3 *Degree of isolation:* The degree of isolation of the student from others in the department or other PhD students; that is, the degree to which the model assumes that students work independently and on their own. (This

might be considered a little similar to dimension 2, but this assessment does not involve consideration of the supervisor.)

4   **Control points:** The number or degree of control points for assessing the progress of the student during the PhD process. A control point might, for example, include consideration of progress, which might be deemed satisfactory or lead to termination of the PhD. It will be very low where the student is not formally assessed or controlled until the final examination.

5   **Courses and coursework:** The degree of course content and contribution required in the overall PhD program.

6   **Contribution:** The degree of original contribution to knowledge required of the thesis. This rating applies to the thesis alone, it does not include coursework. A high number would mean that the degree of contribution to knowledge required for a PhD is significant, very low would mean that a PhD need not require original contribution but could, for example, consist of a well executed review of a topic area.

7   **External quality control:** The degree of examination of the PhD (thesis and other) performed by external examiners. If the examination of the PhD is done totally by external examiners from outside of the university or institution, then this number would be very high. If the examination is conducted internally, then it would be very low. Examination by someone outside of the department, but not external to the university would be somewhere in the middle, as would an external and an internal examiner working together with equal power.

The comparison table for the United States model is shown as Table 16.1.

In fact, there is no single and uniform model of the PhD in the United States. The breadth of US programs, like their European and Austral-Asian counterparts, ranges from rather apprentice-like models to more standardized 'factory' models. These are discussed in Chapter 1, which should be read in conjunction with this chapter. However, in the main, US programs do adhere to a more standardized form that incorporates three broad stages of preparation with milestone events at the end of each stage. Roughly titled these are:

1   Course work preparation stage
2   Thesis topic preparation stage
3   Thesis preparation stage.

Table 16.1 *Comparison table for United States*

	Dimension	Rating (1-7) 1=very low 7=very high	Comments
1	Academic career driver	7	A general assumption is that the PhD as a research degree leads to conducting and publishing in an academic setting; and that it is a necessary condition of continuing employment for most US accredited programs.
2	Supervision dependency	5	This varies within as well as between programs. There is often close and frequent student/supervisor coordination including co-authoring of papers.
3	Degree of isolation	5	The isolation can be quite high but it is reduced in cases where there are several other PhD students working in the same research center and if the student is also teaching in the department.
4	Control points	7	This varies, but most programs have one or more interim evaluation points before the thesis proposal defense and final defense.
5	Courses and coursework	7	In most US programs coursework is a necessary, but not sufficient, component of the PhD program.
6	Contribution	6	This is the critical component looked for in a thesis. It is also unlikely that a thesis proposal would have been passed unless the likely contribution was clearly seen.
7	External quality control	5	This varies greatly; but most programs require an external examiner from outside the department and often outside the college. Some require external examiners to be from outside the university. In general, the examiner is one member of the final dissertation review committee. Rarely does this person have a veto vote.

For the purposes of this chapter, we will refer to this as the *American (or US) model*. Using a crude analogy, this model is designed to take the intellectual raw material in the form of incoming students and shape that raw material so that it can undertake research and then allow it to specialize into particular research forms. Thus this model expects a requisite mastery of literature and research skills as an entry condition to more advanced research pursuits. Each of the stages is described in this chapter.

The chapter is directed towards full-time PhD programs. Because the process is so demanding and often requires such a major change in the way a student thinks and approaches the discipline, and because part of the task of the PhD program is re-socializing a student into the norms of an academic life, many schools discourage or will not accept part-time PhD students. However, in those environments in which part-timers are allowed, these following stages will still apply. But in this case progress is likely to be slower given the competition for the student's attention and energies.

16.2 Course work preparation stage

This phase is designed to make students familiar with a common literature in IS, aware of the breadth of the field and to provide sufficient background in research design and research methods as is necessary. The degree of formality and inclusiveness of this phase varies widely from program to program.

In full-time programs, this phase will typically last two complete years in which time the student also meets oft-mandated university *residency requirements*. This requirement means that the student is obliged to take coursework and perform other tasks at the physical location of the institution granting the degree. There are several reasons for this requirement, not all of which apply at every institution:

1   It ensures that the student becomes part of the university community, to become 'acculturated'
2   It helps to assure the quality and integrity of the student's work, for while in residency the student may be evaluated by members of the degree granting institution's faculty more readily
3   It is a residue from earlier apprenticeship models where, in exchange for training, the apprentice provides cheap labor for the master craftsman.

In many programs, there is a mixture of required courses which all research students must take along with a few elective courses to compensate for weaknesses, to fill in gaps in the student's previous training (for example, in statistical methods) or to allow specialization in a particular topic. Many US programs expect a student to have a broad knowledge of the discipline before beginning specific research. Thus, the course work requirement is seen as an efficient way to ensure that students have a common disciplinary knowledge base. Nevertheless, there are varying opinions about what constitutes a necessary and common understanding of topics and issues in the field, so that the coursework requirement only reduces the variability.

Where the student arrives with a very good IS knowledge, the university may require the student to complete coursework outside the area to broaden his or her scholarly outlook. Again, in some programs, the student's professional experience is taken into account when developing a plan for required coursework. While in general it could be said that American programs are somewhat more structured than other programs, therefore, they still may allow for a measure of customization.

In recruiting and selecting PhD students, many US programs prefer to admit people who have had experience in the IS workforce. Some programs based in business schools require a number of years in managerial positions; other programs based in engineering settings prefer people with IT experience. A few programs are very selective, only considering applicants with five or more years' executive-level experience. The impetus for this requirement may come from the belief that the PhD program demands a certain degree of experientially gained maturity. But that expectation is also embedded within a context in which *practice* and *relevance* are seen as vital to the discipline.

In general, American programs are designed for students who have completed a masters-level degree, but on occasion a student may enter directly from an undergraduate program. However, in that case, additional coursework will be required. In such circumstances the student may be awarded a masters degree while working toward the PhD.

I recall teaching an undergraduate systems design course and being particularly impressed by a young international student. The depth and maturity of his questions was exceptional. He expressed interest in a PhD. I advised him to explore programs elsewhere, thinking it would broaden his education. But I also warned him that his age and lack of 'real world' work experience might be a deterrent to admission in most PhD programs. Indeed, he was not accepted elsewhere despite having excellent references. Our program also had experience requirements. But an exception was made and he was admitted directly from the undergraduate program. He proved to be an excellent researcher and gained his doctorate.

To his advisor and committee's surprise he elected not to continue an academic career, but choose to enter industry. This was disappointing news to those who had invested so much time and energy in someone whom they expected to have had a continuing research relationship. We wondered whether he would have been more likely to choose an academic career if he had had work experience first.

Coursework Milestone event

One or more comprehensive examinations, which may be written and/or oral, are taken at the conclusion of the coursework, but in any case before proceeding to the next phase. Typically, they assess the student's knowledge of the IS literature and research design options. These exams help the supervision and sponsoring department determine the student's readiness to continue with more independent dissertation work. They may also be seen as a gate keeping procedure for the field given that students may enter the PhD program from a variety of backgrounds and reference disciplines.

16.3 Thesis topic preparation stage

This is the stage during which the student is actively seeking to narrow down a topic of interest. Guidance is offered to the student by faculty and the institution. Sometimes students join established research centers and so the general topic area is known in advance. Only the specifics of the problem to be addressed may be left to determine. But more frequently the topic is one that the student must uncover for himself. In either case this marks a point of demarcation between the previous period in which the review of the literature and exposure to ideas was expansive and growing. Now the work must become more focused and directed. It may also be a time when the student begins to experience the creative isolation of the research experience.

This is the stage that occupied the first third of the movie 'A Beautiful Mind' in which John Nash sought the topic that later would win him the Nobel Prize for original research. It is reflected in the way that Russell Crowe portrays John Nash, the student, having to find a suitable thesis topic. It is depicted as a struggle.

This can be a problem even for the most well prepared and focused of PhD students. I recall the case of one student who arrived on campus for the mandated residency year extraordinarily well prepared. He had several undergraduate and masters-level degrees, along with six years' professional experience. He arrived on campus having read almost all of the 250 articles on the 'suggested' PhD reading list. He also arrived with a clear sense of what he expected to be his topic; one related to problems he faced in industry.

As he was preparing for his comprehensive examination he also completed a plan for his PhD research and had full chapter outlines for a topic he had first developed in his MBA program. After passing the exam he presented his draft plan to his advisor. Following discussions, he was informed that the topic was not satisfactory. This was a shock to him and caused some disillusionment, at least in the short term. Perhaps there was a hidden agenda here, the committee thinking that the student was too set in his ideas and needed to rethink.

This is also a stage where the student's reading narrows and becomes more focused to support the search for a topic. In many institutions this stage may take a year and it can take up to two years to find and sufficiently develop a suitable topic. The deliverable at the end of this stage is a thesis proposal. The proposal delineates the domain of research and topic that will belong uniquely to the student. It defines where the student intends to make a contribution to knowledge. The student must convince the committee that he or she is ready to advance to the next stage. The proposal describes the research problem, the importance of the problem and how, to date, others have tried to address the problem. The committee must be convinced that the topic is significant and that in doing the research project the student will create new work constituting a contribution to knowledge in the field. The proposal deliverable often constitutes the equivalent of what will later become the basis of the first three or four chapters of the student's thesis.

This stage also marks the beginning of the break from the relatively standardized and regimented degree programs that the student has experienced before. The student becomes more independent. It also marks the point when the student begins to narrow the choice of a PhD supervisor and to recruit members of the committee. Committee sizes vary throughout the US, a norm is between three to five members with one or two members serving as 'external examiners', persons drawn from outside the host department or college, who help to assure the integrity of the examination process.

In some US settings this stage is the most important of the PhD. In these institutions, the proposal defense will not be scheduled nor does it pass unless it is sufficiently well developed and much of the work is nearing completion. Thus, the committee's expectation here is that the topic and problem, the research method, the experiment (if experimental work), research setting (if field work or qualitative research) or development project are already largely completed. In these settings, much of the work has been done such that once past the proposal defense, the PhD is itself largely accepted. However, in most programs the completion of the proposal is the event that signals the beginning of the most important stage of the PhD journey.

Thesis topic milestone event
The milestone event at this stage is the proposal presentation and defense to members of the dissertation committee and sometimes one or two external

examiners. There are three typical outcomes of this process. The student may be failed, in which case he may begin the proposal phase again. He may be passed and therefore formally admitted to doctoral candidacy. More often, he may be given advice from the committee as to adjustments to be made and given a provisional acceptance until those adjustments are completed. Once accepted, the student is formally admitted to PhD candidacy.

The selection of a dissertation supervisor (usually called advisor in the US context) and committee chairperson is one of the most important decisions a student can make. In most cases the student and his project are tied to the advisor.

One student had three different advisors. The first advisor died just as the student was finishing course work and was beginning to prepare a dissertation proposal plan. The intended dissertation topic was going to be in an area closely related to the advisor's work. The student was successful in finding another advisor with whom he shared common interests. But this advisor felt he did not have sufficient expertise in the original field of research and the student's work was redirected to a new and significantly different topic. This required additional coursework for the student and as a result, his comprehensive examination was postponed and his whole dissertation process was delayed for almost a year. He worked under this second advisor for nearly a year when a new opportunity called the second advisor to another university abroad and the same process was repeated.

The student did eventually complete the PhD. But for him it became an almost ten year journey.

16.4 Thesis preparation stage

Once the proposal is defended, the candidate is now largely on his or her own. He or she is expected to be able to conduct independent research and to execute the research plan as developed in the research proposal. For fieldwork, if the research site was not previously arranged or selected, that now becomes a priority. Research method and instrument development must be finalized and the more generalized statement of the methods and approaches described in the proposal now need to be particularized for the problem or site. In short, the research must be conducted, the data analyzed and the insights and findings written up according to the norms of the research tradition.

During this stage the student, now sometimes referred to as ABD (all but dissertation – in the US we tend to use the term dissertation rather than thesis), approaches the most intellectually lonely and risky period of the process. Significant numbers of students fail to complete this stage. This is when the student's emotional and intellectual maturity is put to the test.

A proportion of students leave at this stage to take academic positions as ABDs. The routine of the new academic job, with its many structured requirements on fixed deadlines, may have a negative impact on the energy and time planned to be given to the 'unstructured' work and self-enforced deadlines associated with completing the dissertation research, analysis and writing. Many programs enforce completion deadlines to help structure process and motivate the candidate. A maximum of five or six years is a typical period allowed for the completion and defense.

The mean time to completion of a PhD, from start of coursework to completion of defense, varies widely by discipline and university. In some disciplines, eight to 11 years is not uncommon. Many state governments are insisting on much shorter throughput. In one instance, the state provides funding for a maximum of four years. In our own field, five to six years is not atypical.

Thesis milestone event
During the thesis defense, the candidate must present and defend the research and the findings before the full committee, external examiners and others who may be present. The form and structure of this defense varies widely in the US. But in general, the thesis defense is open to anyone who may be interested in attending. Most schools have rules requiring the posting of defense schedules, so that proponents and opponents may attend. It is rare in the US to have an official opponent interrogator appointed. It is the job of the committee to have read and considered the thesis, and to attend the defense and be able to ask substantive questions and to challenge any apparent weaknesses. One job of the committee chairman, typically the student's dissertation supervisor, is to be reasonably certain that the thesis will be well received before scheduling the formal defense. Because passing a defense typically requires consensus approval of all the examiners, the chairman will have determined that likely objections from within the committee will have been dealt with prior to scheduling the defense. There is wide variation as to the role and power of the committee chair, the student's dissertation supervisor, with respect to the committee, and the external examiners. But in general, the committee will defer to the chair regarding the manner and conduct of the defense.

Once sufficiently complete in the chairman's mind, a version will be submitted as a proposed final draft to the examining committee. The supervisor will be unlikely to schedule the formal defense, unless all examiners have had the opportunity to read and comment back on the thesis first and ensured that the likelihood of any major problems being revealed is minimal. Therefore, the formal defense is unlikely to end up in failure.

Nevertheless, as in the case of the proposal defense, there are three possible outcomes. The rarest, a failure, is a completion of sorts. The candidate is deemed to have failed to meet the requirements of significant independent research and is no longer a PhD candidate. The happiest of options is the unqualified acceptance and completion. In the majority of cases, small questions may arise in the thesis defense and discussion period that follows. In these cases the candidate is given advice and instructions to address required changes, and is awarded a provisional pass. This becomes official only when the changes have been made and certified by the committee chairman.

From the candidate's point of view, of course, the deliverable of the successful defense is an official form with the signatures of the supervisor and all members of the examining committee. In the instance of the provisional pass, the signatures may be proffered by all but the examination committee chair who withholds final signature until the requested changes have been made.

16.5 Conclusion

Compared to many European counterparts, the 'typical' US PhD is a relatively structured model. But readers should not imagine it is uniform. For even in the United States, the PhD is a relatively customized and highly personal degree program. The dissertation defense, when successfully defended, is a kind of 'one off' custom graduation. Once the student reaches this stage, the process is not easily controlled. Later, when the student passes the thesis topic defense and is admitted, the PhD student should be able to claim the thesis as a highly personalized research statement.

17

UK Model

Guy Fitzgerald

17.1 Introduction

As is probably the case with most models, there are a number of similarities in PhD programs in the UK to make a UK PhD model identifiable, but there are also many differences between UK PhD programs. However, there are more similarities than differences and this makes the concept of a UK PhD model a viable notion. In this chapter I will concentrate on the similarities but mention important differences. As in many countries, PhD programs in IS are found in both computer science and business (or management) departments. This chapter could be read in conjunction with Chapter 2. The comparison table for the UK model is shown as Table 17.1.

The most common way of obtaining a PhD is by original thesis. Some UK universities also enable the candidate to submit a set of published papers (usually with an original introduction that discusses the overall contribution) that together are deemed to be the equivalent of a PhD thesis. This method is designed for academics, usually advanced in their careers, who have not

Table 17.1 *Comparison table for UK*

	Dimension	Rating (1-7) 1=very low 7=very high	Comments
1	Academic career driver	6	Many students are from overseas and want to return to their home country to pre-existing academic jobs.
2	Supervision dependency	6	Mixed experience here but mainly relatively high.
3	Degree of isolation	4	In some cases the degree of isolation can be high whereas in other places where there are large PhD programs it is probably low as there are often good social arrangements.
4	Control points	4	Typically relatively low in control except in the large PhD programs which tend to be more formalized.
5	Courses and coursework	2	Varies from none to a few courses, typically research methods based. Where courses exist they are in the early years. This is in the process of changing as there is a move towards a formal taught part for most PhD programs.
6	Contribution	6	Some degree of 'unique contribution to knowledge' required. Both theoretical and empirical contributions are normally sought.
7	External quality control	4	Generally low or none throughout the process but one external examiner required for the final assessment/examination. Clear variation in standards applied, depending on individual examiner.

obtained a PhD in the traditional way or at the usual time. However, in this Chapter I will concentrate on the normal 'by thesis' route.

The UK PhD is usually viewed as 'a training' for an academic career. A PhD is now almost essential for any aspiring academic in the UK, certainly at the higher-ranked universities. It is very unusual for anyone to be appointed without one, or at least without being very close to completion.

This was not always the case, and there are quite a number of academics who were appointed without having a PhD, me for example! It has never been a great hindrance to my academic career because once I passed a certain age nobody seemed interested. Appointment boards looked most at my publication record. However, it does come as something of a shock to my PhD students when they find out!

Whilst the PhD is considered an essential training for academia, it is not really regarded as much use for anything else in the UK. It is not a passport to a good job, although it can sometimes be helpful, and there are some significant exceptions in certain subjects and industries; for example, in biology and the pharmaceutical industry, but this is not the case in IS. In our domain, a PhD may even be counterproductive, seen as an over-qualification. However, as training in how to work independently, how to think, how to write, how to evaluate, and especially how to be critical, it should be seen as advantageous in all walks of life.

When I interview potential PhD candidates about their motivation for undertaking a PhD in IS and computing, I feel I have to disillusion those people that see it as a way of getting a better job. The UK IT industry often sees it as an 'over-qualification' and prefers to appoint people with industrial experience. In my view this is a reflection of the wider problem of relatively poor relationships between academia and industry in the UK.

However, those undertaking UK PhDs from outside the UK often come from countries where a PhD is a recognized qualification for senior positions in industry and government, as well as academia. For this and other reasons, overseas PhD students are very common in the UK, indeed in some universities there are almost no home PhD students. Yet the fees charged for overseas students are relatively high compared to UK and European Union fees (fees for UK and for European Union students are the same). Thus, universities get significantly more money for overseas students, and this helps to explain why universities have been very keen, and relatively successful, in attracting overseas students.

PhDs can be either full-time or part-time (see Chapter 6). Full-time is notionally 3 years but typically takes about 4 and sometimes more. Part-time usually requires a minimum of 4 years' registration but again it sometimes takes much more. As the typical PhD project is an individual research activity, the length of time it takes is dependent on a number of factors.

Quite a number of departments have students who have been undertaking their PhD for much longer than four years. There are now growing pressures on universities from the UK Government, via the Funding Councils (Government agencies who provide research funding to universities), to ensure students complete within 4 years.

Funding to support students for 3 to 4 years full-time research comes mainly from the following sources:

- The student themselves or their family; that is, self-funding students
- Research grants obtained from the UK Funding Councils directly to the student
- Research grants obtained from the UK Funding Councils via support of a particular research project in the university
- Research grants obtained from EC initiatives via support of a particular research project in the university
- Research grants paid by the university to the student
- Government schemes for oversees students.

Many students undertake some work for the department in which they are registered in exchange for some funding. Typically they are asked to work for around 150 hours a year. This may involve teaching, seminars, lab supervision, etc.

A PhD is quite different from an undergraduate project or an MSc dissertation. Whilst each university has their own specific criteria, which may involve being expert in some area, they generally all have some requirement that a PhD 'makes a unique contribution to knowledge.' Thus the benchmark is high. It cannot simply be a good piece of research; the PhD must also make a contribution of some kind. Of course the interpretation of what constitutes a contribution varies and is decided by the examiners (see also Chapter 13).

As indicated above, the common route to a PhD is research 'by thesis' and this means that the student has to undertake research in a particular area, make the necessary contribution to knowledge, and to write up the outcome of the research. The thesis is a substantial piece of writing, of between roughly 60 000–10 0000 words. Some universities have limits on the size but many do not.

Students typically work on their own, although they are expected to be guided by their supervisor or supervisory team. An exception is where the PhD is part of a larger funded research project. In this case the student may have to carve out their own research work for their PhD as part of the larger project.

In the UK the PhD is usually focused wholly on the research and there is no, or very little, taught element as part of the process, unlike some other countries that have more formal PhD Programs. Sometimes courses are provided.

My own Department provides a research course with a large research methods component for all first year PhD students in IS. Students might also be encouraged to attend other courses offered by the Department or the University as a whole to fill in gaps, but this is usually treated as optional.

However, the UK appears to be slowly moving towards a more formal approach to its PhD model, away from this very open and individual system. There are a few different schemes. *The New Route PhD,* for example, is a 4-year PhD that includes a formal taught element that is examined, and must be passed, before progressing to the thesis work. Sometimes this is seen as a move to the US model, but this is not really a good comparison as these alternative schemes still involve the traditional thesis to the same UK standard. The student is expected to complete the normal PhD by thesis following this taught element.

17.2 PhD process

The process begins when potential candidates apply to undertake a PhD in a particular university. This may have been in response to an advert placed by the university (university websites are becoming of increasing importance in attracting PhD students) or by word of mouth. If advertised in newspapers, it usually means that some funding is available. If no funding is available the candidate must be self-funding. Many PhD students have already undertaken their undergraduate or MSc courses at that university. This is usually because lecturers are looking for PhD students, and identify and persuade their best students to apply.

Qualifications
Candidates for PhD programs will typically need to have a first degree of good quality and/or a Masters-level qualification. Many PhD students are recruited directly from undergraduate programs providing they have a first class (1st) or an upper second class honors degree (2^{i}) (these are the top two UK degree classes in a system that has five pass grades). Some universities demand a masters-level qualification in addition. The perceived quality and reputation of the university from which the potential students have obtained their degree is important, and the top universities may demand a first class degree in any case. But the topic of the proposed PhD is crucial: a good fit with the research interests of the department is particularly important. There are some exceptions and significant industrial experience may be taken into account and be acceptable. In some cases, self-funding students may be taken on slightly lesser qualifications. Overseas students usually have to provide evidence of English language proficiency.

Topic of PhD

A potential candidate may propose a research topic and then target a suitable lecturer or professor to be their supervisor. Alternatively, potential supervisors may have particular areas in which they want PhD students. There are many relevant factors in the selection process, such as qualifications, research interests, funding, and topic. Supervisors may be limited with regard to the number of students already supervised. Some universities place maxima on this, perhaps between three and six.

As Research Director in the Department at Brunel University, with responsibility for PhD students, I sometimes feel that I run a kind of research 'dating agency' where we match potential students and potential supervisors, and much of it is down to how the parties hit it off together. It is an inexact science but, like any marriage, this reflects the very personal nature of the PhD student/supervisor relationship.

Some universities do not accept students directly into the PhD program but offer a provisional PhD *place,* with the potential of transferring to the PhD program if good progress is made. This is often a ploy for achieving a very high PhD success rate – as anyone who is not going to make it is not transferred to a PhD! Thus success rates are very high.

Many universities operate a two supervisor system. Sometimes they operate as joint supervisors, but more often the first is the main supervisor and the second acts as a kind of backup.

At Brunel we encourage second supervisor involvement, and specify a minimum of two meetings a year between the student and the second supervisor who also participates in the annual review and other formal stages.

Once the student has been accepted, he or she may undertake courses that have been agreed as necessary, but on the individual research itself he or she typically begins by undertaking a literature search of the relevant area and then focuses on the research topic and begins to address the research questions by following appropriate research methods. The supervisor performs a critical function in guiding and shaping this process and ensuring that the research proposed is capable of legitimately achieving the necessary contribution.

The research topic needs to be formally agreed. The topic originally proposed by the student when applying is often quite different from the research that is eventually undertaken. The proposal is agreed by the supervisor and then gets formal approval by the department (or university). This may involve a formal presentation to a research committee. Once the research proposal has been approved, the student can progress. In cases where the student has been accepted on a provisional basis, approval leads to formal transfer to PhD status.

The second year is typically when the research is actually undertaken. This consists of the construction, fieldwork, survey, analysis, cases, evaluation, experiments, or whatever the topic requires. For overseas students this may involve a return to their country of origin to undertake empirical work.

The third year concerns the completion of the research: re-visiting the literature, analysis of findings, conclusions, reflections, writing-up the thesis, examination, and then, hopefully, a successful outcome.

However, there are many variations. It is typically much more of an iterative process and often the agreed research proposal is not tied down until the second year, with consequent knock-on effects.

> We begin with me, as supervisor, being very directive and pushing the PhD in the direction I wish it to go, but over time this changes and the student takes responsibility for his or her own PhD and he or she becomes the dominant force, and uses me merely as a sounding board. This process may involve many discussions and disagreements, but eventually he or she becomes the expert in the area and responsible for his or her PhD. I think this is a very healthy development.

Examination

Once the research has been completed and the supervisor and student are both happy with the write-up of the thesis, then the examination process begins. Examiners are appointed by the university, but recommended by the department, which essentially means recommended by the supervisor. One examiner is from outside of the university, normally from another university or very occasionally from industry, known as the external examiner. The choice of external examiner is crucial. The external should be an acknowledged expert in the area, usually relatively senior, and not involved in the research of the candidate in any way. Clearly, it is important that the external examiner is known to the supervisor and is, in general terms, sympathetic to the candidate's research area and research methods. Assuming the external examiner accepts, the university determines if they are suitable. This decision is based on their experience of supervising and examining PhDs. A second examiner is also appointed. The internal examiner is appointed from within the university, usually from the same department, but neither the first nor second supervisor. Formally both examiners have equal rights and powers in the consideration of the PhD but normally it is the views of the external examiner that carry most weight.

Once the two examiners are appointed, a date for the 'viva' or oral examination is set. In the meantime, the examiners are sent the thesis and they write independent reports and make provisional recommendations as to the outcome. Then the viva is held in which the examiners question the candidate about his or her research and the content of the thesis, and the candidate 'defends' the thesis. The viva may take anything from an hour to three or four hours. The viva formally only involves the two examiners (internal and external) along with the candidate, but the first supervisor is frequently present as well, although the latter does not usually participate in the discussion. In some institutions, but rare in the UK, members of faculty and other PhD students may be invited as observers.

> Some universities have slightly different processes and rules for the examination. For example, some require two external examiners. In others the internal examiner has to be from a different department. At Brunel University a separate chairperson has to be present at the viva, to ensure fair play.

The viva has a number of purposes. The examiners need to ensure that the work is indeed that of the candidate, that the student understands the thesis and its implications, that he or she can discuss the issues rationally to clarify any areas of confusion and, most importantly, that the candidate is given the opportunity to react to, and counter, any concerns that the examiners have.

The period running up to the viva, sometimes a few months, where the work is finished and there is little to do, can be a very worrying time for the candidate. They see it as the culmination of three or more years' work and that the outcome can hang on the views of just one person, the external examiner. The viva has a mystique in the UK education system, partly because of the terminology employed. The candidate 'defends his or her thesis' from attack, indicating a somewhat adversarial meeting. Candidates often feel that it is the quality of their verbal defense in a one hour meeting which is being examined. The viva is rarely open to the public so the student will never have sat in, or experienced, a viva previously. It can thus be a very fraught experience for the candidate. One way of helping the student in this regard is to organize a *mock* viva a couple of weeks beforehand.

> One student was determined not to be daunted by the viva and approached it in a very positive frame of mind! I was surprised, as was the external examiner, when the student started asking very challenging questions of the examiners – a very unusual role reversal! Luckily the student settled down and relaxed and all was well.

> As a supervisor, I find I want to answer the questions asked of my students or at least tell the student what to say, particularly if I feel they are not doing themselves justice! However, I usually manage to keep quiet as required.
>
> My students are usually happily surprised by the viva. Having dreaded the event for months, they often find that it is relatively painless and even quite enjoyable – provided of course that the outcome is right.

However, in practice, although it is a very worrying time, it is usually not quite as bad as the student expects. Most people's experience is of a fair and rational, albeit challenging process. A point that often gets forgotten is that the examiners have already read the thesis independently and formed an opinion. The viva is simply to help confirm their understanding of the work. Unfortunately the odd nightmare viva does happen and, although rare, helps to feed the viva mystique and terror stories.

The outcome

The outcome of the viva can take a number of forms. The ideal scenario is that the two examiners agree that the thesis is of the necessary standard, that original contribution has been demonstrated, and the candidate has defended the thesis adequately in the viva. In this case the examiners sign that the candidate has passed, that the university can award the degree of PhD, and that the person can now be called *Doctor*. This is not the most common outcome. The most common outcome is that the examiners agree that in general terms the necessary standard has been achieved but they require some changes. This is known as *minor changes* which the examiners think can take up to 3 months (the period varies from university to university). The required changes are specified in detail and the candidate goes away and undertakes them. For minor changes, it may be agreed that only the internal examiner need review the changed thesis. Once the changes are approved, the candidate is deemed to have passed. There has just been a short delay in the process.

A more serious outcome might be *major changes*. This is where there is some doubt in the examiners' minds and they recommend that major changes be undertaken. These usually have to be carried out within a year. Once the changes have been made, both examiners will probably review the revised thesis and may or may not request another viva. If the examiners are happy that the revised thesis now meets the standard they will pass the candidate and again, even for major changes, the ultimate outcome is still a pass.

I always tell my students that once they have their PhD no one ever asks if it was a PhD that required minor changes or even major ones. After it is awarded it is a PhD, like any other!

The more problematic outcomes are the award of an MPhil degree or outright failure. The award of an MPhil, rather than a PhD, indicates that there is significant work of a good standard, but that there is not the necessary original contribution to knowledge required for the award of a PhD. Thankfully, these outcomes are rare.

In the UK it is generally felt that it is part of the role of supervisors and departments not to put forward candidates for examination who are not yet ready or whose likelihood of passing is low. Of course there are times when it does happen, but it is relatively rare. A candidate who does fail has access to an appeals procedure within the university. This usually requires them to demonstrate shortcomings in the examination process, rather than just that they disagree with the outcome. Sometimes an appeal can result in the appointment of another examiner, in which case the candidate may have better luck. But this is very unusual.

I usually remain in touch with my PhD students long after they graduate, indeed it may be a lifetime relationship. One of my colleagues calls them 'his family'!

18

Latin Model

João Alvaro Carvalho and Frantz Rowe

18.1 Introduction

The title of this chapter is no more than a comfortable way out from the problem of how to entitle a chapter that describes the doctoral degree models in two Latin countries where such models are similar without making any assumptions regarding what happens in other Latin countries (for example, Italy or Spain) but somewhat different from the two PhD programs described in the previous two chapters on the US and UK models.

The first part of this chapter looks at the Portuguese model and the second part addresses the French model. However, due to the resemblances existing between the two models, only some notable differences in the French system have been included.

Latin countries are experiencing important changes in the way their university studies are structured resulting from agreements that have been

Table 18.1 *Comparison table for Portugal*

	Dimension	Rating (1-7) 1=very low 7=very high	Comments
1	Academic career driver	6	Most candidates are already working in a higher education institution; the PhD will facilitate their career progression.
2	Supervision dependency	5	The degree of dependency on the supervision is high, conditioned only by the candidate's autonomy.
3	Degree of isolation	6	The isolation is high; it is reduced on cases where there are several other PhD students working with the same supervisor.
4	Control points	1	There are few (or no) control points during the process other that the final examination.
5	Courses and coursework	1	Normally these do not exist.
6	Contribution	6	A lot of importance is attributed to the contribution. It is normally recommended that this is well emphasized in the thesis.
7	External quality control	6	Two external examiners should integrate the examination committee that will assess the thesis.

reached amongst European education authorities aiming at a more transparent recognition of academic qualifications and at higher levels of student and teacher mobility within Europe. The comparison table for the Portuguese model is shown as Table 18.1.

18.2 Portuguese model

In Portugal, in the 1980s, only the older and well established universities were able to host PhD students. With a reduced number of PhDs in the country (when compared with other European countries) most PhD candidates (especially in the areas of science, technology and management) would think first about carrying out their doctoral studies abroad. In the last 15 years, doctoral education in Portugal has experienced a dramatic change. Due to an increase in the number of young people seeking higher education, the number of faculty in universities and other higher education institutions started to increase. At the same time, several government initiatives were launched that aimed to increase Portugal's research performance. Such initiatives included programs for funding doctoral candidates, both in Portugal and abroad, directed both to candidates already teaching in universities and to young people interested in research careers. Such careers were also stimulated by many MSc programs launched by that time in most universities.

Doctoral student's aims and typical profile

In Portugal, doctoral education is mainly sought by those who need the doctoral degree in order to pursue an academic career. Normally, candidates are already teaching and researching in higher education institutions and, besides their first degree (normally the result of a five years' graduation program called *Licenciatura),* they also hold a Masters degree, a two years' postgraduate program that includes a one year taught program and one year for preparing a dissertation).

> Many candidates think that the PhD thesis is a kind of long MSc dissertation. I try to alert candidates as early as possible to this misconception and to the many difficulties of a PhD project: research complexity, the need for a contribution to knowledge, financial demands, compatibility with other work duties, family, etc. Most often, instead of frightening them I notice they become enthusiastic about undertaking such a challenging enterprise!

The doctoral degree enables the candidates to go forward one step in the university academic career automatically, or to facilitate them reaching the top level at polytechnic institutions (the latter is not required to exhibit a strong research record and their teaching tends to be more oriented towards practice).

Typically, before starting their doctoral studies, doctoral candidates have served for some years (between three to six years) as teachers and research assistants in the school with which they are affiliated.

For their doctoral studies, most candidates look for research areas that constitute an evolution (perhaps a specialization) from their previous studies (at *Licenciatura* and Masters' level) and try to match the needs of the institutions with which they are affiliated, from the point of view of subject areas for teaching and/or research.

In such a scenario, candidates normally have a good background in the area that they are going to carry out their doctoral research, they already have significant academic experience (including several years of teaching experience), and they have clear ideas about the subject areas that they want to explore during their doctoral studies.

Selecting the place where to do their research is something that relies on word of mouth and on general knowledge about the Portuguese universities and their areas of strength. Many candidates will opt to research in their own universities. In so doing, they will avoid the registration fees that would otherwise cost around three thousand Euros. However, they are likely to take an alternative option if their institution is not strong in the area or is not offering the doctoral degree in the area.

Full-time, part-time and funding
In order to have enough time to dedicate to their doctoral studies, candidates already working in a public university are entitled to three years, full paid, leave of absence. Three years is the official expected duration of a doctoral project. In practice, three years is the minimum time for such a project. The typical duration of a doctoral project is four to five years (in some universities, after five years, candidates have to revalidate the registration of their doctoral project).

Although most universities do not have part-time programs, many students are actually working on their PhDs on a part-time basis. Part-time students take a little longer to finish their PhDs, usually around five to six years.

Funding for carrying out doctoral studies can be obtained from the Portuguese government. Grants cover registration fees and a salary. Research assistants involved in research projects (and funded by those projects) often combine a PhD with their regular research duties.

Another source of funding is aimed at the development of higher education institutions. This program finances institutions so that they can find replacements for colleagues carrying out doctoral studies. The program also finances registration fees. It is not common in Portugal to have industry financing PhD studies.

PhD model
After identifying and contacting the potential supervisor, and after formalizing admission, PhD students start their doctoral projects. In most cases the PhD process does not include any kind of taught courses. Students are therefore working on their own but in contact with their supervisor. Unless there are other PhD students working with the same supervisor, the PhD process is normally a solitary endeavor.

Further, the PhD process does not normally include any kind of formal assessment other than the final thesis evaluation. However, students might be required to present some formal progress reports to their supervisors and their supervisors might be required to write reports to the scientific council of the school and in this way help identify problematic situations.

During the PhD process, students are encouraged to present their work in conferences, and publish in journals. This is viewed as being part of their preparation for becoming researchers. At the end of the process, the publications can be used to demonstrate that the work described in the thesis has already been judged positively in a scientific forum. Normally the supervisor is co-author and his name appears following that of the student.

The final examination involves at least five examiners, two of which have to be external. After the thesis is submitted, but before the final discussion, there is a first meeting of all examiners where they state whether they consider that the thesis can be assessed formally as it is or whether it needs to be revised first. In the case where a revision is recommended, candidates have three months to make the changes required by the examiners and to correct the errors they indicate.

The thesis discussion is a very formal event, taking place in a prestigious room or theatre with the candidate and the examiners wearing their academic robes. The discussion is public and colleagues and family normally show up. Usually it starts with a presentation of half an hour describing the work made by the candidate. This is followed by questions from the examiners. Two of the examiners have been previously appointed as the main examiners, but all of them may ask questions during the discussion that can last as long as three hours. The final result is either a fail or a pass. In some universities there can be a grade associated with the pass: good, very good or distinction.

> The University of Minho has a simple pass or fail classification. However, the examiners can make further remarks in the minutes of the meeting. Candidates giving a particularly good performance are praised. Francisco's thesis was accepted though he defended it poorly. The minutes stated that one of the examiners voted for his failure making it clear that it was not a good pass.

Information systems

Doctoral studies in information systems fit the general scenario described above. In most cases, IS appears as a sub-discipline within either management or information technology (informatics). In the first case it is reasonable to expect a PhD project with its roots in social sciences both in terms of theory and methods (which might be either quantitative or qualitative). In the second case the result will more likely to be centered on the study and development of methods for IS development or focusing on the development of new tools. In this case a *proof-of-concept* approach is often used.

> During an interview with a student with a background on informatics (computer science) who wanted to start a PhD, I was trying to determine what topic he would like to research. His answer was merely information systems. He had not thought further. I realized that we had a long way to go.

Changes in the PhD process

More recently, several changes have been affecting the way PhDs are organized in Portugal. One of these changes is related to the European agreements regarding higher education, normally referred to as the Bologna agreements. As a result, several doctoral programs have been added, some of them integrating a taught year of a masters program in the first year. Advertising doctoral programs in newspapers is now much more common.

The emergence of doctoral programs led to the introduction of taught courses and to different types of intermediate examinations; for example, those associated with taught courses or following the thesis proposal after the first year.

Another change is related to a diversification of doctoral candidates. The number of doctoral candidates with no previous affiliation with higher education institutions is increasing. Most of these candidates are graduates and after finishing their first degrees wish to get involved in research activities. With an increasing number of research projects that Portuguese institutions are involved in, the number of PhD students has increased as well. More recently, a government program has been created to encourage industry to get more involved in research activities by encouraging graduate technicians to register as PhD students.

18.3 French model

Of all models described previously in Part V, the French model is closest to the Portuguese one. Our description of the French PhD shows a striking resemblance to that in terms of the model, the positioning of the discipline and its present evolution, with the introduction of some taught courses at the beginning. On the other hand, funding is more varied (see Chapter 7) and registration costs are still very low in France (200 euros per year). Instead of repeating the above, therefore, we point out some differences in the French system. The comparison table for the French model is shown as Table 18.2.

Preparation to the PhD

The traditional way to enter a PhD program in France has been to have a *Diplome d'Etudes Approfondies* (DEA), now called a Masters of Research, which is a qualification gained after five years' university study following

Table 18.2 *Comparison table for France*

	Dimension	Rating (1-7) 1=very low 7=very high	Comments
1	Academic career driver	5	Important for young graduates in the university system, but lower for 'Grandes Ecoles' graduates. Some people do it for pleasure, but they frequently find out it can be very demanding.
2	Supervision dependency	5	The degree of dependency on the supervision is high, conditioned only by the candidate's autonomy.
3	Degree of isolation	5	The isolation can be high; it is reduced in cases where there are several other PhD students working in the same research center.
4	Control points	1	There are few (or no) control points during the process other that the final examination.
5	Courses and coursework	2	Some, but optional, once you have a Masters in research. In recent years, coursework is spread over the first two years in a doctoral school program.
6	Contribution	6	A lot of importance is attributed to the contribution. It is normally recommended that this is well emphasized in the thesis.
7	External quality control	7	Two external examiners should integrate the examination committee that will assess the thesis. They are considered more important than the others and make separate preliminary reports.

the *Baccalauréat* (the final exam before entering university). It encompasses a set of courses oriented towards research in a particular domain.

Between October and December, the most successful DEA students that defended their Masters' thesis by September attempt to register as PhD students. The issues are to find a research topic, a supervisor, and funding.

There has been some confusion as to whether we should consider this DEA year as part of the PhD program or not. In recent years, as optional courses have been added to PhD programs, the distinction we had between research courses in the fifth year of university studies and the PhD program following has become even more blurred. In any case, it takes more than one year of intense reading of research articles to both understand a domain from a research viewpoint and to focus on a research topic.

At the same time, there are a lot of exceptions to the requirement of having the DEA (or Masters of Research), as a qualification for registering for a PhD. These exceptions are made by the scientific council of the university on a case-by-case basis.

> At the University of Paris-Nanterre, I was allowed to register for the PhD since the university considered my previous research publications, my MSc from the University of Berkeley, and my Engineering degree from a French *Grande Ecole* enough to accept me into their PhD program.

With some years of professional experience and a 5th year university degree, or equivalent, some candidates also begin a doctoral dissertation, after the approval of the scientific council of the university.

> Some DEAs do differ from the norm. For instance at the University of Paris-Dauphine, DEA students have to write seven short papers instead of a Masters dissertation.

For all these reasons the French PhD preparation system appears very varied and it is difficult to speak of a French PhD preparation model.

The masterpiece of a researcher's life
With some naivety, but in the tradition of the PhD programs of established disciplines such as history or literature, the thesis is the masterpiece in the life of a researcher. Therefore, the thesis has had the strong and inefficient trend of being very long, both in time to complete (perhaps 10 years' or so) and in the number of pages. A French PhD Dissertation in IS is normally at least 400 pages long and some are double this size. Despite comments from advisors and examiners, this has not changed in the last 20 years. This might be explained by the inadequate research courses given at the preparation stage. So, as the French are rather anxious people, PhD students try to reassure themselves by including everything in their thesis. However, this does have the advantage of looking at the topic thoroughly rather than merely refining some unimportant issues.

However, it has become clear that it is important to publish and be financed throughout, and more candidates are turning towards quicker and more normative models. At the same time, we are also experiencing new PhD thesis formats like that of an introductory chapter to a collection of papers. In France, we seem to be breaking out of our traditional PhD!

Becoming an assistant professor

Whereas we have presented the university system as being varied in terms of the requirements for doing a PhD, it is very rigid with regard to recruitment. Getting a PhD, even with distinction, is not enough to become an assistant professor in a university belonging to the French Ministry of Education. To enter this career, the young PhD student must be qualified by the National Council of the Universities. The NCU is divided into sections according to discipline. In information systems we either fall under the computer science (n°27) or management science (n°6) section. In the latter, 18 full professors and 18 assistant professors (in France we do not have associate professors), decide each year on about 200 cases of PhDs in management science to see if they are qualified to compete for a position in a university. They make the decision on the basis of the three reports (two from the external examiners and the third from the President of the Committee) following the PhD defense, the publications and the teaching experience of the applicant. Successful candidates are deemed qualified to look for a position for a period of four years. To be qualified in March and compete for positions in universities in May, a PhD student must defend the thesis by the end of December. This explains why most dissertations are examined in December.

18.4 Concluding remarks

Latin countries, and not only Portugal and France, are experiencing many changes in higher education. For example, there are equivalent changes being carried out in Spain and Italy to those discussed above. Their traditional organization of university degrees is being strongly influenced by models used in Northern European countries. The advantages and disadvantages of these changes are still being debated. However, several countries have already made decisions to follow that trend.

We are now going through a very rich experience where imported models co-exist with traditional models and mixed models are emerging. We hope that these emerging models are capable of keeping the advantages of our traditional models whilst, of course improving because of other influences. In globalization, it is important that there is not major cultural loss, and this applies to PhD candidates in general (and IS PhD students in particular) and, dare we say, society at large.

19

Scandinavian Model

Karlheinz Kautz

19.1 Copenhagen Business School model

In Scandinavia, there are as many ways of organizing and conducting a PhD study as there are countries and universities, with a varying degree of compulsory course programs, methods of application, approval, examination and defense, with different performance and financial models, conducted in full-time or part-time mode, based in university or industry, and with university, industry or private funding.

We have therefore chosen to base the chapter on one notable school for information systems, Copenhagen Business School (CBS). At CBS we have chosen to institutionalize information systems research and since 1998 have organized PhD programs in a PhD school. Students normally undertake their PhD in a three year period.

The course of PhD studies in IS at CBS is based on the requirements of the Executive Order of the Danish Ministry of Education (March, 2002) concerning PhD Programs and PhD Degrees.

In this chapter I provide a stage-by-stage overview of the whole process at CBS and I discuss what I do as a supervisor at these times and reflect on some of the issues. The comparison table for the Scandinavian model is shown as Table 19.1.

Table 19.1 *Comparison table for CBS*

	Dimension	Rating (1-7) 1=very low 7=very high	Comments
1	Academic career driver	5	The PhD in Denmark is mainly an academic driver, although at least in the IS field industry has opened up for academics. For a university career a PhD is mandatory. Without a PhD it is nowadays nearly impossible to get an assistant professorship, let alone an associate or full professor position.
2	Supervision dependency	4	When designing the research project the student is dependent on the supervisor; however, in case of conflict the study board protects and supports the student and would even allow a change of supervisor.
3	Degree of isolation	2	The PhD student is part of a PhD school with between 15-20 students at CBS, through Scandinavia numerous PhD schools support the students in networking with peers.
4	Control points	5	There are various control points in the program: the 6 monthly progress report, plus a start-up seminar and an official pre-defense.
5	Courses and coursework	6	Coursework is required corresponding to the workload of half a working year, there are obligatory courses on theory of science and research methodologies and electives from various subject areas of business administration and information systems.
6	Contribution	6	A lot of importance is attributed to the contribution. It is normally recommended that it is well emphasized in the thesis.
7	External quality control	7	Both the pre-defense, the thesis document and the public defense are assessed by a committee consisting of one internal and two external members; at least one of them should be from outside Denmark.

19.2 Aims and structure

The program leading to the PhD degree is set up with the purpose of training researchers at an international level. The PhD program provides mainly active research training under supervision. The PhD program is aimed at meeting present and future needs for qualified people to carry out research, development and teaching tasks at universities and in other educational institutions, in enterprises and other organizations, as well as for other public and private purposes which require a broad knowledge of research.

The PhD degree is awarded in recognition of a student's ability to satisfactorily complete a doctoral program. By writing a thesis, successfully defended at a public defense, the student will have demonstrated an ability to conduct a research project with an independent use of scientific methodology in the subject and thereby furthered research at the level equivalent to the international standard of PhD degrees within the subject area. The goal is to train the PhD student to use an in-depth understanding of a subject area's theoretical, methodological, philosophical and ethical problems in confronting the demands for academic quality that characterize developments in the international research community and the outside world.

19.3 Admission

Admission to a PhD program is based on a previously completed Master's degree course. Enrolment on the program assumes that the student has been awarded a scholarship or has entered into a financial agreement with the School. Scholarships are granted on availability, and the student's application is usually no longer than five to seven pages. The applicant outlines the research question, its background and a preliminary individualized study plan. Prospective students usually make contact with a possible supervisor informally.

> In this phase I typically have a meeting with the candidate to find out whether there is a mutual basis for co-operation for a period of three years, discuss the student's ideas and give feedback on their application.

This application itself is evaluated by an internal committee of two to three academic staff. The final decision whether to permit enrolment on the PhD program is made on the basis of the preliminary individualized study plan by the study board which consists of academic staff usually from the

Department of Informatics and a representative of the PhD students. The plan is usually drafted by the research student together with their possible supervisor.

When processing the enrolment application, the program director checks that:

1. The applicant is deemed to have the necessary academic qualifications to complete the degree program
2. The proposed study plan is feasible within the specified study time
3. The student has secured adequate funding, and
4. One or more supervisors can be appointed.

19.4 Program content

The PhD program itself involves:

- Completing an independent research project under supervision (the PhD project)
- Preparing a written thesis based on a PhD project

> I hold regular meetings with the individual students, to direct their research efforts generally, discuss their research question, their research approach and design, and help them formulate their analytical framework and their research result. This might include the co-authoring of articles dealing with the various aspects of their project.

- Satisfactorily completing PhD courses approved by the study board

> I advise the student on appropriate courses, discuss course proposals with them and approve the attendance of courses

- Participating in active research environments.

> At CBS, the PhD student can spend a six-month period of study at a foreign or Danish research institute or major enterprise. I discuss different possibilities with the student and typically recommend an environment from my personal network which fits the student's research area

- Gaining experience of teaching or other forms of dissemination of knowledge, directly related as far as possible to the PhD project; for example, disseminating research results or providing research assistance in connection with an ongoing project at the department; teaching or other forms of knowledge dissemination.

> I involve myself in the student's dissemination and teaching plan, and advise and approve the student's teaching actions.

19.5 Course requirements

The Informatics PhD School at the Department of Informatics offers courses to its students, but also runs courses in network co-operation on researcher training with other departments at CBS, and with national and international partners. PhD students must take obligatory courses:

1. Scientific theory with a particular focus on business economics
2. Business economics theory as well as one of the following methodology courses:
   * Quantitative research methods
   * Qualitative research methods.

Students may also choose from a variety of courses within the area of Informatics.

The course component is planned according to the study plan by the student in collaboration with the supervisor who regularly assesses the student's progress and is responsible for ensuring that the courses are completed satisfactorily.

With the agreement of the supervisor and the PhD School Director, the PhD student can choose to take a course offered by the PhD School of another institution, possibly abroad. The student's participation, with the supervisor's approval, in both internal and external courses must be documented by a course certificate issued by the respective institution and course teacher.

As a supplement to the supervision provided during their course of study, the PhD student must also present their work at two seminars:

1 Before the end of the first six months, the student must present their research project at a departmental seminar.
2 No later than six months before the end of the PhD program, the student must present a detailed draft of their thesis to one or more opponents who are not part of the supervisory staff; the purpose and course of this seminar is described in more detail in Section 19.8 on the thesis pre-defense.

The supervisor gives approval regarding whether the seminars have been satisfactorily completed. Invitations to the seminars are accepted as documentation relating to attendance.

19.6 Supervision

Every PhD student is supervised by one or sometimes two supervisors. The PhD School allocates a specific number of supervisory hours for the entire course of study. The PhD student is entitled to receive these hours. At the moment these are 150 hours for a three years project or roughly, on average, 1 hour per week.

The Director of the PhD school and the head of department must check that the prospective supervisor is a professor or associate professor at CBS, is an active researcher and has academic insight in the subject area of the student's research project, and can devote adequate time to supervising the student.

> I usually meet my PhD students on a two or three weekly basis to discuss their progress, in the beginning without any documents, but after some months always on the basis of a draft document, be it their research plan, their research design, a literature study or preliminary results. Reviewing and discussing these documents typically takes much more than the allocated 150 hours, but given a certain commitment by the student usually results in stimulating discussions and fruitful research co-operation on the basis of a master-apprentice relationship which often results in joint publications. I have, for example, participated in initial interviews with a PhD student in one of her case organizations and been involved in action research projects with students without, I feel, giving up the necessary distance required to give appropriate feedback on their work.

19.7 Individualized study program: the PhD plan and reporting

The general program content and the course requirements are for the individual PhD student concretized in an individualized study and research program. This is called the PhD plan. This plan typically corresponds to a study period of three years, although students are permitted on application to take up to a maximum of five years. Special agreements can be made for part-time students.

The PhD plan must be prepared as soon as possible and not later than six months after the commencement of the PhD program.

> As supervisor I usually support my PhD students when producing and revising their individual plans. The time schedule ensures that adequate time is set aside for the

> realization of the student's own independent research in accordance with the PhD plan, including the writing of a thesis.

Every six months, the Director of the PhD School assesses whether the PhD student has fulfilled the requirements set out in the PhD plan so far, and makes any necessary adjustments to the plan. The assessment is conducted on the basis of a report from the principal supervisor who, following consultations with the PhD student, confirms in writing that the work is being carried out in accordance with the PhD plan, or reports in writing on any adjustments made to the plan. The PhD student prepares six-monthly reports that are submitted to the principal supervisor for discussion and signature. The declaration is sent to the Director of the PhD School, who gives the PhD student at least two weeks in which to comment on the report before making a decision.

The PhD plan is supported by templates and the document is usually no longer then eight to 10 pages and contains:

1 A time schedule
2 An agreement on the extent of supervision
3 A scheme for the PhD project

> The description must contain the following:
> *   A presentation of the chosen problem and the theoretical contributions that will be used to solve the problem
> *   A presentation of the project's methodology
> *   A list of the relevant literature

4 A scheme for participation in PhD courses
5 A scheme for stays at other research institutions
6 A scheme for the teaching activities and other forms of dissemination of knowledge. Teaching and knowledge dissemination can be planned for one semester at a time
7 An estimate of expected expenses (budget).

19.8 Pre-defense

A pre-defense is conducted for the benefit of the PhD student with the objective to elicit relevant guidance and comments from a select committee of the highest scientific expertise pertaining to the student's research.

The chair of the PhD School appoints the pre-defense committee, which should include at least one 'foreign' member. It is the obligation of the chair, together with the PhD supervisor and the head of department, to suggest a committee that may be a serious candidate for the thesis committee appointed by the dean. Members of the committee take part in the seminar conducted in the spirit of a scientific dialogue rather than as an assessment of a final research contribution. The individual committee members prepare to present constructive criticism of the PhD student's work at the seminar, but be aware that this event is the first intervention for an exchange of perspectives, analyses and suggestions with the student. The purpose of the seminar is to inspire the student to excel in his or her research within the framework of the research project.

The supervisor chairs the pre-defense seminar. The supervisor is obliged to evaluate the pre-defense and inform the chair of the PhD School of his or her evaluation.

The pre-defense seminar is part of the research training of PhD students at CBS and takes place on the basis of a draft of the thesis document in the form of a report written by the PhD student for the occasion. This report, which gives the outline of the final thesis, has to be presented by the PhD student no later than six months before submitting his or her thesis.

The student is obliged to submit material that informs the committee members of his or her objectives and demonstrates examples of analytical approaches and the research conducted. It is in the best interest of the student to ensure that the committee members have ample opportunity to assess the merits of his or her research. Therefore, the report normally should be no longer than 100 pages and include a list of contents divided into a section relating to the submitted report and a section relating to the expected final thesis. The student describes which parts of the research are included in the report and which parts he or she intends to present in the final thesis. In the report, the student must present an outline of the thesis problem followed by a meticulous account of why he or she has chosen the problem and how he or she studied the issue. The report should conclude with an assessment and positioning of the student's research within the relevant research framework, discipline or community. To demonstrate the student's analytic proficiency, the report should include aspects of the major issues to be addressed in the final thesis.

In addition, the report should include choice of models, some of the empirical findings and the most important references in the research. For the purpose of discussing the potential relevance of the research to the overall objective or to select issues, the student should also present contending questions and issues not yet positioned within the thesis.

> As a supervisor I am responsible for giving the PhD student adequate advice about the importance of the pre-defense and for guiding the student on how to benefit the most from this part of his or her research. As part of the preparation of the pre-defense, I therefore discuss the structure and the contents of the report intensively with the students and inform their choices regarding the issues to be included in the report. I do, however, refrain from assessing the report before the committee has done, so as to allow the student to be less biased when discussing the work with the committee.

After the pre-defense, the student considers which advice to follow and which to dismiss, if conflicting with the objectives and means of the thesis work. Such decisions are taken in consultation with the supervisor and only after careful deliberation and assessment of the suggestions raised at the pre-defense seminar.

The seminar is a unique opportunity for the PhD student to receive relevant and serious feedback before the final phase of his or her thesis work. The execution of the seminar is the responsibility of the supervisor in collaboration with the committee and the PhD student. The pre-defense is conducted in such a way that all participants have an opportunity to present their critique and suggestions. This is balanced by the student's opportunity to respond at intervals, rather than only at the end of a series of interventions. In this atmosphere dialogues prevail, not monologues. The supervisor usually facilitates a round of final remarks from the committee members and the student to ensure that conclusions are preliminary and not decisive, since it would be premature to conclude at the end of this seminar. The concluding part of the event takes place after the seminar has been fully considered by the student and typically involves a meeting with the supervisor where the discussions at the seminar and its major results are debated and decisions are made about the final version of the thesis.

19.9 Submission of thesis and preliminary assessment

Officially, the PhD student determines when the thesis is ready for submission and informs the principal supervisor of this date no later than two months before submission. The PhD thesis also has to be submitted together with the principal supervisor's statement regarding whether the student's overall course of study has progressed satisfactorily. Thus, in practice, the supervisor and the students discuss the state of the thesis and commonly determine when the document should be submitted.

On receipt of the thesis, based on the principal supervisor's statement, the Director of the PhD School then determines whether the overall PhD program has been completed satisfactorily. If the Director feels that this is not the case, the PhD student will be given two weeks within which to demand that the matter be brought before the Faculty Council for a final decision.

A thesis cannot be submitted for assessment by more than one person, although a research project that might provide the basis for the thesis may be conducted by several researchers in collaboration.

The principal supervisor may give approval for a PhD thesis to be built around numerous manuscripts or previously published articles related in content and/or methodology. If such manuscripts or previously published articles have been written in collaboration with others, a declaration from each of the authors must be attached stating the extent of the PhD student's contribution to the total work.

> I have not given this approval yet – a PhD thesis based on various publications needs thorough planning and, in my view, an agreement in the IS community which outlets for publications are approved for a manuscript to be counted as a part of a thesis. As long as there is no such agreement it is hard for a supervisor to judge whether a committee will have special requirements, such as the number of individual authored papers and the names of journal and conference submissions.

Once the date for submission has been set, the principal supervisor ensures that the head of department forwards proposals to the Faculty Council regarding the composition of an expert assessment committee. On receiving the proposals for committee members, the Faculty Council will immediately appoint an expert assessment committee composed of three members. The Faculty Council will at the same time appoint a committee chairman, as well as set a deadline with a maximum of two months for the committee's preliminary recommendation.

The committee members must be full professors, full-time associate professors or individuals possessing equivalent academic qualifications. Two of the members must come from outside CBS, preferably from abroad. The supervisor of the PhD student is not permitted to sit on the committee, but can take part in the work of the committee in an advisory role without voting rights.

Within the prescribed deadline of two months, the assessment committee submits a preliminary recommendation which must be unanimous or made by a majority of the committee as to whether the thesis in its current form fulfils the requirements for the award of a PhD degree. If the recommendation is positive, the author is notified and sent a copy of the recommendation.

Provided it does not delay the defense, the chairman of the assessment committee may permit limited changes or supplements to be added to the thesis prior to, or in connection with, the defense of the thesis. It should be feasible, as a rule of thumb, for such changes to be made in about two weeks.

If the recommendation is not favorable, the committee must include a unanimous or majority recommendation that will enable the Faculty Council to decide whether the author may submit the thesis in a revised form within a period of at least three months.

The Director of the PhD School immediately notifies the author that the thesis cannot be recommended for defense, in the form that it has been presented, and of the decision that has been made. The thesis is returned to its author.

19.10 Public defense, assessment and final recommendation

A public defense of the thesis takes place after the assessment committee has submitted its preliminary recommendation and no later than four months after submission of the thesis. The time and venue of the public defense are agreed between the assessment committee, the supervisor and the PhD student, and the defense does not take more than two hours. Announcement of the defense is made on bulletin boards. The thesis must be accessible to the public 10 days before the defense takes place.

The principal supervisor chairs the defense session and facilitates the examination and discussion of the thesis. The defense session is divided into two parts:

1 A lecture based on the thesis, where the author argues the key contributions of the thesis
2 A defense, where the assessment committee's external members act as opponents.

Thereafter, the chairman of the defense proceedings may allow other persons present to ask short supplementary questions. Immediately after the defense session has finished, the assessment committee submits a final recommendation for approval at the Faculty Council regarding whether the degree of PhD should be awarded.

If the members of the assessment committee cannot agree on a positive recommendation that the degree of PhD be awarded, the Director of the PhD School will immediately notify the author.

The degree of PhD is awarded if a positive recommendation has been made by at least two members of the assessment committee and CBS issues a PhD degree certificate.

References and Further Reading

ACS (1992) *Submission to Review of Computing Disciplines,* Australian Computer Society, Canberra.

AHD (2002) *American Heritage Dictionary of the English Language,* 2003.

Alavi, M. and Carlson, P. (1992) A review of MIS research and disciplinary development, *Journal of Management Information Systems,* 8, 4, 45–62.

Alter, S. (2003) A general, yet useful theory of information systems, *Communications of the AIS,* 1, 13.

APA (2001) *Publication Manual of the American Psychological Association,* 5th Edn, American Psychological Association.

Avison, D., Lau, F., Myers, M. D. and Nielson, P. A. (1999) Action research, *Communications of the ACM,* 42, 1, 94–97.

Avison, D. E. (2003) Information systems in the MBA curriculum: An international perspective, *Communications of the AIS,* 11, 6, 117–127.

Avison, D. E., Baskerville, R. and Myers, M. D. (2001) Controlling action research projects, *Information Technology & People,* 14, 1, 28–45.

Avison, D. E., Cuthbertson, C. and Powell, P. (1999) The paradox of information systems: strategic value and low status, *Journal of Strategic Information Systems,* 8, 4, 419–445.

Avison, D. E. and Fitzgerald, G. (2003) *Information Systems Development: Methodologies, Techniques and Tools,* 3rd Edn, McGraw-Hill, London.

Avison, D. E. and Myers, M. D. (1995) Information systems and anthropology: An anthropological perspective on IT and organizational culture, *Information Technology & People,* 8, 3, 43–56.

Avison, D. E. and Wood-Harper, A. T. (1990) *Multiview: An Exploration in Information Systems Development,* McGraw-Hill, Maidenhead.

Bagozzi, R. P. (1980) *Causal Methods in Marketing,* John Wiley and Sons, New York.

Barki, H., Rivard, S. and Talbot, J. (1993) A Keyword classification scheme for IS research literature: An update, *MIS Quarterly,* 17, 2, 209–226.

Baskerville, R. and Myers, M. (2002) Information systems as a reference discipline, *MIS Quarterly,* 26, 1, 1–14.

Baskerville, R. and Myers, M. D. (2004) Foreword to special issue on action research in information systems: Making is research relevant to practice, *MIS Quarterly,* 28, 3, 329–335.

Baskerville, R. L. and Wood-Harper, A. T. (1996) A critical perspective on action research as a method for information systems research, *Journal of Information Technology,* 11, 1, 235–246.

Benbasat, I., Goldstein, D. K. and Mead, M. (1987) The case research strategy in studies of information systems, *MIS Quarterly,* 5, 4, 369–386.

Benbasat, I. and Zmud, R. W. (2003) The identity crisis within the IS discipline: Defining and communicating the discipline's core properties, *MIS Quarterly,* 27, 2, 183–194.

Bleicher, J. (1980) *Contemporary Hermeneutics: Hermeneutics as Method, Philosophy and Critique,* Routledge & Kegan Paul, London and Boston.

Boland, R. J. (1991) Information system use as a hermeneutic process, in Nissen, H.-E., Klein, H. K. and Hirschheim, R. A. (Eds), *Information Systems Research: Contemporary Approaches and Emergent Traditions,* North Holland, Amsterdam, 439–464.

Bollen, K. A. (1989) *Structural Equations with Latent Variables,* John Wiley and Sons, New York.

Boudreau, M., Gefen, D. and Straub, D. (2001) Validation in IS research: A state-of-the-art assessment, *MIS Quarterly,* 25, 1, 1–23.

Boufis, C. (1999) Strange bedfellows: Does academic life lead to divorce? *Salon Magazine,* http://www.salon.com/it/feature/1999/03/24feature.

Campbell, D. T. and Stanley, J. C. (1963) Experimental and quasi-experimental design for research, in Campbell, D. T. and Stanley, J. C. (Eds), *Experimental and Quasi-Experimental Design for Research,* Sooner Text Books.

Carr, N. (2003) IT doesn't matter, *Harvard Business Review,* May, 1–10.

Carr, W. and Kemmis, S. (1986) *Becoming Critical: Education, Knowledge and Action Research,* Falmer Press, London.

CGS (1995) *A Conversation about Mentoring: Trends and Models,* Council of Graduate Schools, Washington, D.C.

Checkland, P. B. (1999) Systems thinking, in Currie, W. L. and Galliers, R. G. (Eds), *Rethinking Management Information Systems*, OUP, Oxford.

Chicago (2003) *The Chicago Manual of Style,* 15th Edn, University of Chicago Press, Chicago.

Chua, W. F. (1986) Radical development in accounting thought, *The Accounting Review,* 61, 4, 601–632.

Churchill, G. A., Jr. (1979) A paradigm for developing better measures of marketing constructs, *Journal of Marketing Research,* 16, 1, 64–73.

Clark, P. A. (1972) *Action Research and Organizational Change,* Harper and Row, London.

Cook, T. D. and Campbell, D. T. (1979) *Quasi Experimentation: Design and Analytical Issues for Field Settings,* Rand McNally, Chicago.

Coombs, C. H. (1976) *A Theory of Data.* Mathesis Press, Ann Arbor, MI.

Cronbach, L. J. (1951) Coefficient alpha and the internal structure of tests, *Psychometrika,* 16, 297–334.

Cronbach, L. J. (1971) Test validation, in Thorndike, R. L. (Ed.) *Educational measurement,* American Council on Education, Washington, D.C., 443–507.

Cryer, P. (2000) *The Research Student's Guide to Success,* Open University Press.

CSC (1988) *Survey of IS Management Issues,* Computer Sciences Corporation, El Segundo, California.

CSC (2000) *13th Annual Survey of IS Management Issues,* Computer Sciences Corporation, El Segundo, California.

CSC (2001) *14th Annual Survey of IS Management Issues,* Computer Sciences Corporation, El Segundo, California.

CSC (2003) *Critical Issues of IS management: A look back,* Computer Sciences Corporation, El Segundo, California.

CSC (2004) *16th Annual Survey of IS Management Issues,* Computer Sciences Corporation, El Segundo, California.

Daft, R. L. and Trevino, L. K. (1987) The relationship among message equivocality, media selection, and manager performance, *MIS Quarterly,* 11, 3, 355–366.

Davies, L. J. (1991) Researching the organisational culture contexts of information systems strategy, in Nissen, H.-E., Klein, H. K. and Hirschheim, R. A. (Eds) *Information Systems Research: Contemporary Approaches and Emergent Traditions,* North Holland, Amsterdam, 145–167.

Davies, L. J. and Nielsen, S. (1992) An ethnographic study of configuration management and documentation practices in an information technology centre, in Kendall, K. E., Lyytinen, K. and DeGross, J. (Eds), *The Impact of Computer Supported Technology on Information Systems Development,* Elsevier/North Holland, Amsterdam.

Davis, G., Karahanna, E., Mukkhpadhayay, T., Watson, R. and Weber, R. (2003) Panel: Defining the core of the discipline, in *Proceedings of International Conference in Information Systems 2003,* Eds, Massey, A., March, S. and Degross, J., Seattle, Washington.

Davis, G. B. and Parker, C. A. (1997) *Writing the Doctoral Thesis: A Systematic Approach,* 2nd Edn, Barrons Educational Series, Hauppauge, NY.

Delamont, S., Atkinson, P. and Parry. O. (1997) *Supervising the PhD: A Guide to Success,* Open University Press, Maidenhead.

Denzin, N. K. and Lincoln, Y. S. (Eds) (1994) *Handbook of Qualitative Research,* Sage, Thousand Oaks.

Diamantopoulos, A. and Winklhofer, H. M. (2001) Index construction with formative indicators: An alternative to scale development, *Journal of Marketing Research,* 38, 2, 269–277.

Dickson, G. W., Benbasat, I. and King, W. R. (1980) The management information systems area: Problems, challenges and opportunities, in *Proceedings of the First International Conference in Information Systems,* McLean, E.R. (Ed.), 1–8.

Elden, M. and Chisholm, R. F. (1993) Emerging varieties of action research: Introduction to the special issue, *Human Relations,* 46, 2, 121–142.

Emory, W. C. (1980) *Business Research Methods,* Irwin.

Evans, J. and Lindsay, W. (1999) *The Management and Control of Quality,* South-Western.

Fedor, D. B., Eder, R. W. and Buckley, M. R. (1989) The contributory effects of supervisor intentions on subordinate feedback responses, *Organizational Behavior and Human Decision Processes,* 44, 396–414.

Fornell, C. R. and Larcker, D. F. (1981) Structural equation models with unobservable variables and measurement error, *Journal of Marketing Research,* 18, 39–50.

Freeman, L. A., Jarvenpaa, S.L. and Wheeler, B.C. (2000) The supply and demand of information systems doctorates: Past, present, and future, *MIS Quarterly*, 24, 3, 355–380.

Gadamer, H.-G. (1976) The historicity of understanding, in Connerton, P. (Ed.) *Critical Sociology, Selected Readings*, Penguin Books, Harmondsworth, 117–133.

Galbraith, J. (1977) *Organizational Design,* Addison-Wesley, Reading, MA.

Galliers, R. D. and Land, F. F. (1987) Choosing appropriate information systems research methodologies, *Communications of the ACM,* 30, 11, 900–902.

Galliers, R. G. and Meadows, M. A. (2003) Discipline divided: Globalization and parochialism in information systems research, *Communications of the AIS,* 11, 5.

Garvin, D. (1987) Competing on the eight dimensions of quality, *Harvard Business Review,* 65, 6, 101–109.

Gefen, D. (2002) Nurturing clients' trust to encourage engagement success during the customization of ERP systems, *Omega: The International Journal of Management Science,* 30, 4, 287–299.

Gefen, D. (2003) Unidimensionality through LISREL: An explanation and example, *Communications of AIS,* 12, 2, 1–26.

Gefen, D., Karahanna, E. and Straub, D. W. (2003) Trust and TAM in online shopping: An integrated model, *MIS Quarterly,* 27, 1, 51–90.

Gefen, D., Straub, D. and Boudreau, M. (2000) Structural equation modeling techniques and regression: Guidelines for research practice, *Communications of AIS,* 7, 7, 1–78.

Giddens, A. (1987) *Social Theory and Modern Sociology,* Polity Press, Cambridge.

Gillenson, M. and Stutz, J. (1991) Academic issues in MIS: Journals and books, *MIS Quarterly,* 15, 4, 147–452.

Gregor, S. (2003) A theory of theories in information systems, in Gregor, S. and Hart, D. (Eds), *Information Systems Foundations: Building the Theoretical Base*, Australian National University, Canberra, 1–20.

Habermas, J. (1979) *Communication and the Evolution of Society,* Beacon Press.

Hair, J. F. Jr., Anderson, R. E., Tatham, R. L. and Black, W. C. (1995) *Multivariate Data Analysis with Readings,* Prentice Hall, Englewood Cliffs, NJ.

Hardgrave, B. and Walstrom, K. (1997) Forums for MIS scholars, *Communications of the ACM,* 40, 11, 119–124.

Harvey, L. and Myers, M. D. (1995) Scholarship and practice: The contribution of ethnographic research methods to bridging the gap, *Information Technology & People,* 8, 3, 13–27.

Hersey, P. and Blanchard, K. (1987) *Management of Organizational Behaviour: Utilizing Human Resources,* Prentice Hall, Englewood Cliffs.

Hevner, A. R., March, S. T., Park, J. and Ram, S. (2004) Design science in information systems research, *MIS Quarterly,* 28, 1, 75–105.

Hirschheim, R. (1992) Information systems epistemology: An historical perspective, in Galliers, R. (Ed.) *Information Systems Research: Issues, Methods and Practical Guidelines*, Blackwell Scientific Publications, Oxford, 28–60.

Hirschheim, R. and Klein, H. (1994) Realizing emancipatory principles in information systems development: The case for ETHICS, *MIS Quarterly,* 18, 1, 83–109.

Hirschheim, R. and Klein, H. (2004) Crisis in the IS field? A critical reflection on the state of the discipline, *Communications of the AIS,* 4, 10.

Hirschheim, R. and Newman, M. (1991) Symbolism and information systems development: Myth, metaphor and magic, *Information Systems Research,* 2, 1, 29–62.

Holsapple, C., Johnson, L., Manakyan, H. and Tanner, J. (1994) Business computing research journals: A normalized citation analysis, *Journal of Management Information Systems,* 11, 1, 131–140.

Holzblatt, K. and Beyer, H. (1993) Making customer-centered design work for teams, *Communications of the ACM,* 36, 10, 93–103.

HSV (2003) Utvärdering av ämnet data- och systemvetenskap/informatik vid svenska universitet och högskolor, *Högskoleverkets rapportserie* :10 R, Högskoleverket.

Hu, L.-T. and Bentler, P. M. (1999) Cutoff criteria for fit indexes in covariance structure analysis: Conventional criteria versus new alternatives, *Structural Equation Modeling,* 6, 1, 1–55.

Hughes, J. A., Randall, D. and Shapiro, D. (1992) Faltering from ethnography to design, in *CSCW '92. ACM 1992 Conference on Computer-Supported Cooperative Work: Sharing Perspectives*, ACM Press, New York, 115–123.

Humphrey, W. S. (1989) *Managing the Software Process,* Addison-Wesley.

Introna, L. and Whittaker, L. (2004) Truth, journals and politics: The case of the MIS quarterly, in Kaplan, B., Truex, D., Wood-Harper, T., Wastell, D. and DeGross, J. (Eds), *Information Systems Research: Relevant Theory and Informed Practice*, Kluwer Academic Publishers, Boston, 744.

Ives, B., Valacich, J.S., Watson, R. T. and Zmud, R. W. (2002) What every business student needs to know about information systems, *Communications of the Association for Information Systems,* 9, 467–477.

Jarvenpaa, S. L., Tractinsky, N. and Vitale, M. (2000) Consumer trust in an internet store, *Information Technology and Management,* 1, 45–71.

Jenkins, M. (1985) Research methodologies and MIS research, in Mumford, E., Hirschheim, R., Fitzgerald, G. and Wood-Harper, T. (Eds), *Research Methods in Information Systems*, North-Holland, 103–117.

Judd, C. M., Smith, E. R. and Kidder, L. H. (1991) *Research Methods in Social Relations,* Holt, Rinehart, and Winston, Inc., Orlando, FL.

Kaplan, B. and Duchon, D. (1988) Combining qualitative and quantitative methods in information systems research: A case study, *MIS Quarterly,* 12, 4, 571–586.

Kaplan, B., Truex, D., Wastell, D., Wood-Harper, A. T. and DeGross, J. L. (Eds) (2004) *Information Systems Research: Relevant Theory and Informed Practice,* Kluwer Academic Publishers, Boston.

Karahanna, E., Straub, D. W. and Chervany, N. L. (1999) Information technology adoption across time: A cross-sectional comparison of pre-adoption and post-adoption beliefs, in *MIS Quarterly*, 23, 2, 183–213.

Kautz, K. and Pries-Heje, J. (2000) Systems development education and methodology adoption, *ACM Computer Personnel,* 20, 3, 6–26.

Keen, C. D. (1999) *Australasian Information Systems Survey 1998*, University of Tasmania, Hobart, Tasmania.

Kerlinger, F. N. (1973) *Foundations of Behavioral Research,* Holt, Rinehart and Winston, New York.

Kerlinger, F. N. (1986) *Foundations of Behavioral Research,* CBS College Publishing, New York.

Klein, H. K. and Myers, M. D. (1999) A set of principles for conducting and evaluating interpretive field studies in information systems, *MIS Quarterly, Special Issue on Intensive Research,* 23, 1, 67–93.

Klein, H. K. and Truex III, D. P. (1995) Discourse analysis: A semiotic approach to the investigation of organizational emergence, in Andersen, P. B. and Holmqvist, B. (Eds), *The semiotics of the workplace*, Walter De Gruyter, Berlin.

Kling, R. E. (1996) *Computerization and Controversy,* Academic Press, San Diego.

Kock, N., Gray, P., Hoving, R., Klein, H., Myers, M. D. and Rockart, J. (2002) IS research relevance revisited: Subtle accomplishment, unfulfilled promise, or serial hypocrisy? *Communications of the AIS,* 8, 330–346.

Kram, K. (1985) *Mentoring at Work: A Developmental Network Perspective,* Scott, Foresman, Glenview, IL.

Lacity, M. C. and Janson, M. A. (1994) Understanding qualitative data: A framework of text analysis methods, *Journal of Management Information Systems,* 11, 2, 137–155.

Lakatos, I. (1970) Falsification and the methodology of scientific research programmes, in *Criticism and the Growth of Knowledge*, Oxford University Press, 91–196.

Lakatos, I. (1978) *Mathematics, Science, and Epistemology,* Cambridge University Press, Cambridge, UK.

Lamb, R. and Kling, R., (2003) Reconceptualizing users as social actors in information systems research, *MIS Quarterly,* 27, 2, 197–235.

Latham, G. P., Erez, M. and Locke, E. A. (1988) Resolving scientific disputes by the joint design of crucial experiments by the antagonists: Application to the Erez-Latham dispute regarding participation in goal setting. *Journal of Applied Psychology,* 73, 753–772.

Latour, B. (1987) *Science in Action: How to Follow Scientists and Engineers through Society,* Harvard University Press, Cambridge, Mass.

Lee, A. S. (1989) A scientific methodology for MIS case studies, *MIS Quarterly,* 13, 1, 33–52.

Lee, A. S. (1994) Electronic mail as a medium for rich communication: An empirical investigation using hermeneutic interpretation, *MIS Quarterly,* 18, 2, 143–157.

Lee, A. S. (2001) Editorial, *MIS Quarterly,* 25, 1, iii–vii.

Lee, A. S. and Baskerville, R. (2003) Generalizing generalizability in information systems research, *Information Systems Research,* 14, 3, 221–243.

Lee, A. S., Liebenau, J. and DeGross, J. I. (Eds) (1997) *Information Systems and Qualitative Research,* Chapman and Hall, London

Lewis, I. M. (1985) *Social Anthropology in Perspective,* Cambridge University Press, Cambridge.

Lindman, H. R. (1974) *Anova in Complex Experimental Designs,* W. H. Freeman, San Francisco, CA.

Loch, K., Straub, D. W. and Kamel, S. (2003) Diffusing the internet in the Arab world: The role of social norms and technological culturation, *IEEE Transactions on Engineering Management,* 50, 1, 45–63.

Luftman, J. and McLean, E. R. (2004) Key issues for IT executives, *MISQ Executive,* 3, 2, 89–104.

Lyberg, L. E. and Kasprzyk, D. (1991) Data collection methods and measurement error: An overview, in Biemer, P. P., Groves, R. M., Lyberg, L. E., Mathiowetz, N. A. and Sudman, S. (Eds), *Measurement Errors in Surveys*, Wiley, New York.

March, S. T. and Smith, G. (1995) Design and natural science research on information technology, *Decision Support Systems,* 15, 4, 251–266.

March, J. G. and Simons, H. A. (1958) *Organizations,* Wiley, New York.

Marcus, N. (2004) *Women in Math, Science and Engineering,* Florida State University, Miami.

Markus, M. L. (1983) Power, politics, and MIS implementation, *Communications of the ACM,* 26, 6, 430–444.

Markus, M. L. (1999) Thinking the unthinkable: What happens if the IS field as we know it goes away, in Currie, W. L. and Galliers, R. G. (Eds), *Rethinking Management Information Systems*, OUP, Oxford.

Martin, P. Y. and Turner, B. A. (1986) Grounded theory and organizational research, *The Journal of Applied Behavioral Science,* 22, 2, 141–157.

McKenzie, G., Powell, J. and Usher, R. (1997) *Understanding Social Research: Perspectives on Methodology and Practice,* Falmer Press, London.

Meehl, P. E. (1967) Theory-testing in psychology and physics: A methodological paradox. *Philosophy of Science* (June), 103–115.

Miles, M. B. and Huberman, A. M. (1984) *Qualitative Data Analysis: A Sourcebook of New Methods,* Sage Publications, Newbury Park, CA.

Mingers, J. and Stowell, F. (Eds) (1997) *Information Systems: An Emerging Discipline,* McGraw-Hill, Maidenhead.

Morgan, G. (1986) *Images of Organization,* Sage Publications, Newbury Park, Cal.

Mullaney, T. J. (2003) E-biz surprise, *Business Week,* 60, 3832.

Mullins, G. and Kiley, M. (2002) It's a PhD, not a Nobel Prize!: How experienced examiners assess research theses, *Studies in Higher Education,* 27, 4, 369–386.

Mumford, E. (1995) *Effective Requirements Analysis and Systems Design: The ETHICS Method,* Macmillan, Basingstoke.

Mumford, E. (2001) Advice for an action researcher, *Information Technology & People,* 14, 1, 12–27.

Mumford, E., Hirschheim, R. A., Fitzgerald, G. and Wood-Harper, T. (Eds) (1985) *Research Methods in Information Systems,* North-Holland, Amsterdam

Myers, M. D. (1994) A disaster for everyone to see: An interpretive analysis of a failed IS project, *Accounting, Management and Information Technologies,* 4, 4, 185–201.

Myers, M. D. (1999) Investigating information systems with ethnographic research, *Communication of the AIS,* 2, 1–20.

Myers, M. D. (living) Qualitative research in information systems,

Myers, M. D. and Avison, D. E. (Eds) (2002) Qualitative Research in Information Systems: A Reader, Sage, London.

Mylonopoulos, N. and Theoharakis, V. (2001) On-site: Global perceptions of IS journals, *Communications of the ACM,* 44, 9, 29–33.

Ngwenyama, O. K. (1991) The critical social theory approach to information systems: Problems and challenges, in Nissen, H.-E., Klein, H. K. and Hirschheim, R. A. (Eds), *Information Systems Research: Contemporary Approaches and Emergent Traditions*, North Holland, Amsterdam, 267–280.

Ngwenyama, O. K. and Lee, A. S. (1997) Communication richness in electronic mail: Critical social theory and the contextuality of meaning, *MIS Quarterly,* 21, 2, 145–167.

Nissen, H.-E., Klein, H. K. and Hirschheim, R. A. (Eds) (1991) *Information Systems Research: Contemporary Approaches and Emergent Traditions,* North Holland, Amsterdam.

OECD (2001) *The Internet and Business Performance,* OECD, Paris.

Orlikowski, W. J. (1991) Integrated information environment or matrix of control? The contradictory implications of information technology, *Accounting, Management and Information Technologies,* 1, 1, 9–42.

Orlikowski, W. J. (1993) CASE tools as organizational change: Investigating incremental and radical changes in systems development, *MIS Quarterly,* 17, 3, 309–340.

Orlikowski, W. J. and Baroudi, J. J. (1991) Studying information technology in organizations: Research approaches and assumptions, *Information Systems Research,* 2, 1, 1–28.

Orne, M. T. (1962) On the social psychology of the psychological experiment: With particular reference to demand characteristics and their implications, *American Psychologist,* 17, 11, 776–783.

Orne, M. T. (1969) Demand characteristics and the concept of quasi-controls, in Rosenthal, R. and Rosnow, R. L. (Eds), *Artifact in Behavioral Research*, Academic Press, New York, 143–179.

Pairin, K., Han, B. and Hong, S. (2003) Objective quality ranking of computing journals, *Communications of the ACM,* 46, 10, 111–114.

Palmer, R. (1969) *Hermeneutics: Interpretation Theory in Schleiermacher, Dilthey, Heidegger, and Gadamer,* Northwestern University Press, Evanston.

Paulk, M., Curtis, B., Chrissis, M. and Weber, C. (1993) *Capability Maturity Model for Software Version 1.1.,* The Software Engineering Institute, Carnegie Mellon University, Pittsburgh.

Peffers, K. and Ya, T. (2003) Identifying and evaluating the universe of outlets for information systems research: Ranking the journals, *The Journal of Information Technology Theory and Application,* 5, 1, 63–84.

Phillips, E. M. and Pugh, D. S. (2000) *How to get a PhD – a Handbook for Students and their Supervisors,* Open University.

Piantanida, M. and Garman, N. (1999) *The Qualitative Thesis,* Corwin Press, Thousand Oaks.

Pirsig, R. (1984) *Zen and the Art of Motorcycle Maintenance: An Inquiry into Values,* Bantam.

Polkinghorne, D. E. (1988) *Narrative Knowing and the Human Sciences,* State of New York University Press, Albany, NY.

Popper, K. R. (1959) *The Logic of Scientific Discovery,* Basic Books, New York.

Porter, M.E. (1980) *Competitive Strategy: Techniques for Analyzing Industries and Competitors,* The Free Press, New York.

Porter, M. E. and Miller, V. E. (1985) How information gives you competitive advantage, *Harvard Business Review,* 63, 4, 149–160.

Postman, N. (1988) *Conscientious Objections: Stirring up Trouble about Language, Technology and Education,* Vintage Books, New York.

Preston, A. M. (1991) The 'problem' in and of management information systems, *Accounting, Management and Information Technologies,* 1, 1, 43–69.

Purao, S. and Truex, D. (2004) Supporting 'engineering' of information systems in 'emergent' organizations, in *Relevant Theory and Informed Practice: Looking Forward from a 20 Year Perspective on IS Research,* Kaplan, B., Truex, D., Wastell, D. and Wood-Harper, A. T. (eds.), Kluwer, Boston, 2004, 175–194.

Radnitzky, G. (1970) *Contemporary Schools of Metascience,* Scandinavian University Books, Goteborg.

Rapoport, R. N. (1970) Three dilemmas in action research, *Human Relations,* 23, 4, 499–513.

Ricoeur, P. (1974) *The Conflict of Interpretations: Essays in Hermeneutics,* Northwestern University Press, Evanston.

Robertson, M., Newell, S., Swan, J., Mathiassen, L. and Bjerknes, G. (2001) Gender within the field of information technology: A comparison of the UK and Scandinavian experience, *Information Systems Journal,* 11, 2, 111–126.

Robey, D. and Markus, L. (1998) Beyond rigor and relevance: Producing consumable research about information systems, *Information Resources Management Journal,* 11, 1, 7–15.

Rogers, E. M. (1962, 1983) *Diffusion of Innovations,* The Free Press, New York.

Rowe, F., Truex, D. and Kvasny, L. (2004) Cores and definitions: Building the cognitive legitimacy of the information systems discipline across the Atlantic, in Kaplan, B., Truex, D., Wastell, D. and Wood-Harper, A. T. (Eds), *Relevant Theory and Informed Practice: Looking Forward from a 20 Year Perspective on IS Research*, Kluwer, Boston, 83–102.

Rubin, H. and Rubin, I. (1995) *Qualitative Interviewing: The Art of Hearing Data,* Sage Publications.

Ryan, S. D. (1999) The motivational reengineering of the information systems graduate teaching assistant's positions, *Journal of Computer Information Systems*, 39, 4, 88–92.

Sambamurthy, V., Bharadwaj, A. S. and Grover, V. (2003) Shaping agility through digital options: Reconceptualizing the role of information technology in contemporary firms, *MIS Quarterly,* 27, 2, 237–263.

Segars, A. H. (1997) Assessing the unidimensionality of measurement: A paradigm and illustration within the context of information systems research, *Omega,* 25, 1, 107–121.

Shannon, C. E. and Weaver, W. (1949) *The Mathematical Theory of Communication,* University of Illinois Press, Chicago.

Silverman, D. (1993) *Interpreting Qualitative Data,* Sage Publications, London.

Simon, H. A. (1981) *The Sciences of the Artificial,* MIT Press, Cambridge, Mass.

Stamper, R. (1997) Organisational semiotics, in Mingers, J. and Stowell, F. (Eds), *Information Systems: An Emerging Discipline*, McGraw Hill, Maidenhead.

Stewart, T. A., Brown, J. S., McFarlan, W., Nolan, R., Strassmann, P. A., Alter, S., Zwass, V., Carr, N., Broadbent, M., McDonald, M., Hunter, R. and Gurbaxani, V. (2003) Does IT matter? The HBR debate, *Harvard Business Review*, May, 1–16.

Stone, E. F. (1978) *Research Methods in Organizational Behavior,* Scott, Foresman & Company, Glenview, IL.

Straub, D. W. (1989) Validating instruments in MIS research, *MIS Quarterly,* 13, 2, 147–169.

Straub, D. W., Boudreau, M.-C. and Gefen, D. (2004) Validation guidelines for IS positivist research, *Communications of the AIS,* 14, 380–426.

Straub, D. W. and Karahanna, E. (1998) Knowledge worker communications and recipient availability: Toward a task closure explanation of media choice, *Organization Science,* 9, 2, 160–175.

Strauss, A. (1987) *Qualitative Analysis for Social Scientists,* Cambridge University Press, Cambridge.

Suchman, L. (1987) *Plans and Situated Actions: The Problem of Human-Machine Communication,* Cambridge University Press, Cambridge.

Susman, G. I. and Evered, R. D. (1978) Assessment of the scientific merits of action research, *Administrative Science Quarterly,* 23, 582–603.

Taylor, C. (1976) Hermeneutics and politics, in Connerton, P. (Ed.) *Critical Sociology, Selected Readings*, Penguin Books, Harmondsworth, 153–193.

Thomas, D. M. and Watson, R. T. (2002) Q-sorting and MIS research: A primer, *Communications of AIS,* 8, 141–156.

Thompson, J. B. (1981) *Critical Hermeneutics: A Study in the Thought of Paul Ricoeur and Jurgen Habermas,* Cambridge University Press, Cambridge.

Trochim, W. (2001) The Research Methods Knowledge Base, 2nd Edn, atomicdogpublishing.com, Cincinatti, OH USA.

Urquhart C (1999), Report of Outcomes from Part Time PhD Workshop at the 1998 Australasian Conference on Information Systems, distributed to the Australian Council of Professors and Heads of Information Systems, April 1999.

Wajcman, J. (1991) *Feminism Confronts Technology,* Polity Press, Cambridge.

Walsham, G. (1993) *Interpreting Information Systems in Organizations,* Wiley & Sons, Chichester.

Walsham, G. (1995) Interpretive case studies in IS research: Nature and method, *European Journal of Information Systems,* 4, 2, 74–81.

Walsham, G. and Waema, T. (1994) Information systems strategy and implementation: A case study of a building society, *ACM Transactions on Information Systems,* 12, 2, 150–173.

Walstrom, K., Hardgrave, B. and Wilson, R. (1995) Forums for management information systems scholars, *Communications of the ACM,* 38, 3, 93–102.

Walstrom, K. A. and Leonard, L. N. K. (2000) Citation classics from the information systems literature, *Information & Management,* 38, 2, 59–72.

Ward, H. (2001) Hewitt calls for more IT women, *Computer Weekly* (http://www.computerweekly.com/article106951.htm).

Webster, J. (1996) *Shaping Women's Work: Gender Employment and Information Technology,* Longman, London.

Webster, J. and Trevino, L. K. (1995) Rational and social theories as complementary explanations of communication media choices: Two policy-capturing studies, *Academy of Management Journal,* 38, 6, 1544–1572.

Wheeler, B. C. (2002) Nebic: A dynamic capabilities theory for assessing net-enablement, *Information Systems Research,* 13, 2, 125–146.

Whitman, M., Hendrickson, A. and Townsend, A. (1999) Research commentary. Academic rewards for teaching, research and service: Data and discourse, *Information Systems Research,* 10, 2, 99–109.

Wilkinson, R. K. and Regets, M. C. (2002) Science and Engineering Indicators – 2002: Profile of the US, *S&E workforce,* 1, National Science Board, Arlington, VA.

Wilson, M. (2002) Making nursing visible? Gender, technology and the care plan as script, *Information Technology and People,* 15, 2, 139–158.

Wolcott, H. F. (1990) *Writing up Qualitative Research,* Sage Publications, Newbury Park, CA.

Wynn, E. (1979) Office Conversation as an Information Medium, PhD thesis, University of California, Berkeley.

Yin, R. K. (1994) *Case Study Research: Design and Methods,* Sage Publications, Newbury Park, CA.

Zmud, R., Lind, M. and Young, F. (1990) An attribute space for organizational communication channels, *Information Systems Research,* 1, 4, 440–457.

Zuboff, S. (1988) *In the Age of the Smart Machine,* Basic Books, Inc., New York.

Authors

David Avison is Distinguished Professor of IS at ESSEC Business School, Paris and part-time Research Professor at Brunel University, England. He is joint editor of the *Information Systems Journal*. He has published over twenty books and a large number of research papers in learned journals, edited texts and conference papers. He is vice chair of *IFIP* technical committee 8 and represents France and was past Chair of *IFIP 8.2*. He was past President of the *UKAIS* and also past chair of the *UK Heads and Professors of IS*. He has been chair of many international conferences and will be joint program chair of *ICIS* 2005 in Las Vegas and joint PhD consortium chair for *ICIS* 2006 in London. He also acts as consultant and has most recently worked with a leading manufacturer developing their IT/IS strategy. He researches in IS development and on IS in their natural setting using action research, though he has also used a number of other qualitative research approaches.

Richard L. Baskerville is professor and chairman of the CIS Department in Georgia State University. He is a former chair of *IFIP* Working Group 8.2, and a program co-chair of two *IFIP* working conferences. His research and authored works regard security of information systems, methods of information systems design and development, and the interaction of information systems and organizations. Baskerville is the author of *Designing Information Systems Security* (J. Wiley) and more than 100 articles in scholarly journals, practitioner magazines, and edited books. He is an editor of the *European Journal of Information Systems,* and associated with the editorial boards of the *Information Systems Journal* and *Journal of Database Management.* He is a Chartered Engineer, holds a B.S. *summa cum laude*, from The University of Maryland, and the MSc and PhD degrees from The London School of Economics.

Marie-Claude Boudreau has been an Assistant Professor of MIS at the University of Georgia since 2001. She received a PhD degree in Computer Information Systems from Georgia State University, a Diplôme d'Enseignement Supérieur Spécialisé from l'École Supérieure des Affaires de Grenoble (France), and an MBA from l'Université Laval in Québec (Canada). Dr. Boudreau has conducted research on the implementation of integrated software packages and the organizational change induced by information technology. She is a researcher associated with the Open Tourism Consortium (www.opentourism.org), and within this group, has been investigating the open source movement with other colleagues. She has authored articles published in many journals, such as *Information Systems Research, MIS Quarterly, Journal of Management Information Systems, Academy of Management Executive, Information Technology & People, Communication of the AIS,* and many conference proceedings. Her teaching interests include data management, enterprise-wide integrated software packages, and globalization of IS.

João Alvaro Carvalho is professor at the University of Minho, Portugal, where he currently serves as head of department and coordinates the IS research group. He holds a PhD in IS from UMIST, UK. His research and teaching interests include: the foundations of information systems, information systems development, meta-modeling, requirements engineering and knowledge management. He is the national representative of Portugal in *IFIP* TC 8 and coordinator of the Portuguese academic society for information systems and editor of *Sistemas de Informação* a Portuguese information systems journal. He has supervised nine PhD students and is currently supervising five other students. He acts as examiner in PhD discussions in information systems, computer science and management at University of Minho and in several other Portuguese universities.

Gordon B. Davis is the Honeywell Professor of Management Information Systems in the Carlson School of Management at the University of Minnesota. In 1967, he and two colleagues started the academic degree program in MIS at the University of Minnesota. He headed the doctoral program in MIS for 25 years and has served as advisor, co-advisor, or committee member to well over 100 doctoral students. His monograph, *Writing the Doctoral Dissertation*, has been used by more than 50 000 doctoral students around the world. He has lectured in 25 countries, held visiting appointments in Europe and Asia, and published 21 books and over 200 articles, monographs and book chapters. He is an *ACM* Fellow, *AIS* Fellow, and recipient of the *AIS* LEO award for lifetime achievement in the field of information systems. He has a PhD from Stanford University and honorary doctorates from the University of Lyon, University of Zurich, and the Stockholm School of Economics.

Robert Davison is an Associate Professor of Information Systems at the City University of Hong Kong. His research interests span the academic and business communities, examining the impact of collaboration technologies on communication and decision making in face-to-face and virtual groups, particularly in cross-cultural settings. He also actively applies an action research perspective to research in organizational contexts. Robert has recently completed editing special issues of the *Communications of the ACM* (Global Applications of Collaborative Technologies) and *IEEE Transactions on Engineering Management* (Cultural Issues and IT Management). Robert is the Editor-in-Chief of the *Electronic Journal of Information Systems in Developing Countries,* and Associate Editor of the *Information Systems Journal* and *Information Technology & People.* Robert's work has appeared in the *Information Systems Journal, Information Technology & People, Information & Management, MIS Quarterly, IEEE Transactions on Engineering Management, Group Decision & Negotiation* and the *Communications of the ACM.*

Steve Elliot is Professor and Head of Business Information Systems at The University of Sydney. He has previously been Head of the School of Business at the University of Newcastle and Director of the IT Research Centre at the University of New South Wales. Steve has worked with information systems extensively in industry with major international firms including Unilever and Caltex, and with the United Nations. He gained his PhD at the University of Warwick, UK. His research has been directed toward the development of theory in the strategic management of technology-enabled business innovation. His research is published in international journals, refereed conference proceedings and an internationally acclaimed book examining successful B2C electronic commerce initiatives in six countries. His current projects focus on the impact of e-business in the B2B banking sector and IS-enabled innovation in procurement. Steve chairs *IFIP* Working Group 8.4 on E-business information systems: multidisciplinary research and practice.

Guy Fitzgerald is Professor of Information Systems at Brunel University and is Director of Research in the Department of Information Systems and Computing. Prior to this he was at Birkbeck College, University of London, Templeton College, Oxford and Warwick University. He has also worked in the computer industry with companies such as British Telecom, Mitsubishi and CACI Inc., International. His research interests are concerned with the effective management and development of information systems and he has published widely in these areas. His most recent work is concerned with the development of more flexible information systems. He is co-author, with David Avison, of an influential book *Information Systems Development: Methodologies, Techniques and Tools* and is co-editor, also with David Avison, of the *Information Systems Journal (ISJ)* from Blackwell Publishing.

David Gefen is Associate Professor of MIS at Drexel University, Philadelphia USA, where he teaches Strategic Management of IT, Database Analysis and Design, and VB.NET. He received his PhD in CIS from Georgia State University and a Master of Sciences in MIS from Tel-Aviv University. His research focuses on psychological and rational processes involved in enterprise resource planning, CMC, and e-commerce implementation management. David's wide interests in IT adoption stem from his 12 years of experience in developing and managing large information systems. David is a Senior Editor of *Data Base*. His research findings have been published in *MIS Quarterly, Journal of Management Information Systems, Journal of Strategic Information Systems, IEEE TEM, EM, DATA BASE, Omega, JAIS, CAIS,* and *JEUC,* among others. David is also first author of the textbook *Advanced VB.NET: Programming Web and Desktop Applications in ADO.NET and ASP.NET.*

Anita Greenhill is a lecturer in Information Systems and Technology Management at the Manchester Business School, Manchester University. She received her PhD from the Engineering and Information Technology Faculty, Griffith University. Anita has over 50 published articles in various fields of interest and expertise. Anita's research interests include social, cultural and organizational aspects of information systems. Adopting social shaping and critical approaches to IS research, she researches a diversity of topics including ICT-enabled work practices, space, virtuality, Web information systems development, and gender, information technology policy and education, and qualitative research methods. In addition to her academic interests Anita actively participates online via a social hub which can be found at http://www.spaceless.com.

Muhammadou M.O. Kah is Assistant Professor of e-commerce and information technology in the School of Business-Camden, Rutgers University. He completed his PhD at Stevens Institute of Technology, Hoboken, NJ; and also has a Masters of Science in finance from The George

Washington University, Washington, DC. He was in the faculty at Howard University and taught as an Adjunct at George Washington University, and Saint Mary's University, Halifax, Canada. Dr. Kah's current research focuses on how businesses and governments can effectively use information technologies (ex. e-government) and the Internet, in particular, to add value; ICT Strategy and Policy and the applications of real options in IT strategic decision making; ways in which advances in ICTs contribute to poverty reduction, economic growth and development, and enhances quality of life for developing economies and communities.

Jainaba M.L. Kah is Assistant Professor of Public Policy and Administration and Director of the International Public Service and Development Program (MPA) at Rutgers University. Dr. Kah has a PhD in urban planning from the Bloustein School, Rutgers University; and a Masters in Development Economics from Dalhousie University. Dr. Kah has extensive practitioner experience working for the World Bank as an Urban/Transport Specialist. She also taught at Strayer University in Virginia, and Saint Mary's University, Halifax, Canada's Extension Program in The Gambia. Her research interests focus on development economics and administration, transportation/urban planning and policy in developing/transition economies, GIS, and the use of information communication and technology in public administration and management, decentralization and capacity building in municipal/local governments and micro-finance.

Karlheinz Kautz is professor of Systems Development and Software Engineering at the Department of Informatics at the Copenhagen Business School, Denmark and Director of Studies for the course program on Computer Science and Business Administration. Previously he has been employed as a senior researcher at the Norwegian Computing Center and as a lecturer at universities in Germany, Norway, England and Denmark. He is the chair of the *IFIP* working group 8.6 on Diffusion, Transfer, and Implementation of Information Technology. His research interests are in systems development and system development methodologies for advanced application areas, the diffusion and adoption of information technology innovations, the organizational impact of IT, knowledge management and software quality and process improvement. He has published in these areas in journals like *Information and Software Technology, Information, Technology & People, the Scandinavian Journal of Information Systems, Software Process: Improvement and Practice, IEEE Software, Journal of*

Knowledge Management, Information Systems Journal and is a member of *ACM* and *IEEE.*

Lynette Kvasny is an Assistant Professor of Information Sciences and Technology, and a founding member of the Center of the Information Society at the Pennsylvania State University. She earned a PhD in Computer Information Systems from the Georgia State University Robinson College of Business where she was a KPMG Doctoral Scholar. She received the National Science Foundation's Faculty Early Career Development Grant. Her research interests include digital divide, IT workforce diversity, and community informatics. She has published her research in publications including the *Data Base for Advances in Information Systems*, the *Journal of Computer Mediated Communication* and the *International Journal of Technology and Human Interaction.*

Cherie Long is assistant professor at Clayton State College and University in Morrow, Georgia. Her research focuses on Women in IT, and Information Security. She has received grants from the *NSA, NSF,* and the States of Texas and Florida for Information Security. She has published in numerous MIS journals and books including *The DataBase for Advances in Information Systems.* At Clayton State she is the coordinator for the Information Security Lab and the Information Security Program in the College of Information Technology and Mathematical Sciences. She has worked with doctoral students at The University of Texas at Austin, Georgia State University and Florida International University.

Björn Lundell has been a staff member at the University of Skövde, Sweden since 1984. He received his MSc (1991) in Computer Science from the University of Skövde, and his PhD (2001) from the University of Exeter. He has co-authored a book on the process of undertaking research-oriented final year projects. He has a general interest in qualitative methods, and is a co-developer of the *2G* method. He has acted as method user and mentor in a variety of company contexts. His research is published in a variety of international conferences and journals, and centers on the issues: database modeling, technology evaluation, method development, and theoretical and practical aspects of method transfer into real organizational usage. To this end he has established active links with a number of Swedish companies.

Ramiro Montealegre is the Chair of the Systems Division and an Associate Professor of Information Systems at the University of Colorado, Boulder. He is also a Visiting Professor at Instituto de Empresa in Madrid. He received his doctorate in management information systems from the Harvard Business School. His master's degree in computer science is from Carleton University, Canada. He holds a Bachelor in Engineering degree from the Francisco Marroquín University, Guatemala. Dr. Montelegre is a recipient of five consecutive annual teaching excellence awards for outstanding teaching at the University of Colorado: the Boulder Faculty Assembly Excellence in Teaching, the Tony Tisone Teaching Excellence Award, the Joseph Frascona Excellence Award, the Graduate Professor of the Year Award, and the MBA Professor of the Year Award. His research focuses on the interplay between new information technology, such as the Internet, and organization transformation in highly uncertain environments. He has been involved in studying projects of organizational change in the United States, Canada, Spain, Mexico, and the Central and South American regions.

Michael D. Myers is Professor of Information Systems and Associate Dean (Postgraduate and Research) at the University of Auckland Business School, New Zealand. He currently serves as Senior Editor of *MIS Quarterly Discovery,* Associate Editor of *Information Systems Research*, Editor of the *ISWorld Section on Qualitative Research,* and Editor in Chief of the *University of Auckland Business Review*. His research articles have been published in many journals and books. He won the Best Paper award (with Heinz Klein) for the most outstanding paper published in *MIS Quarterly* in 1999. He also won the Best Paper Award (with Lynda Harvey) for the best paper published in *Information Technology & People* in 1997.

Jan Pries-Heje is Associate Professor at The IT University of Copenhagen, Denmark. Since 2002 he has also been part-time full professor in software engineering and management at the IT University of Gothenburg, Sweden. Jan Pries-Heje holds MSc and PhD degrees from Copenhagen Business School, Denmark. He is certified ISO 9000 auditor and BOOTSTRAP assessor, and has been project manager for a number of Multi Media and IT-related change projects. He worked as a Consultant 1997-2000 in IT quality and software process improvement. He is Chairman of the *Information Systems Research in Scandinavia (IRIS)* Steering Committee. He is the Danish National Representative to *IFIP* Technical Committee 8 (TC8) on Information Systems, and Secretary for TC8 since 1999. His research interests include information systems development, software engineering, and software process improvement. He focuses on organizational and managerial issues. He has published more than 100 papers in these areas in journals and conferences.

Frantz Rowe gained his PhD from the University of Paris following his Masters' at University of California, Berkeley. He has been Professor of IS at the University of Nantes, France, since 1995. Previously he was a Professor at Ecole Nationale Superieure des Télécommunications, Paris, and an Assistant Professor at Ecole Nationale des Ponts et Chaussées. His major research areas pertain to information and communication systems use and their effects on organizations, and to IS project dynamics and change. He has recently directed research projects on change management with ERP projects and the structure of call centers and their performance. He has published over 30 articles in scientific journals and numerous books, and is editor of *Faire de la recherche en systèmes d'information*. He is the Editor-in-Chief of *Systemes d'Information et Management*, http://revuesim.free.fr. He has directed 14 PhD students. He is currently directing the joint PhD program in Management between the University of Nantes, the University of Angers and Audencia. He co-founded the *Association Information et Management* in 1991.

Nancy L. Russo received her PhD in Management Information Systems from Georgia State University in 1993. Since 1991, she has been a member of the Operations Management and Information Systems Department at Northern Illinois University and is currently the Chair of that Department. In addition to on-going studies of the use and customization of system development methods in evolving contexts, her research has addressed web application development, the impact of enterprise-wide software adoption on the IS function, IT innovation, research methods, and IS education issues. Her work has appeared in *Information Systems Journal*, *Journal of Information Technology*, *Information Technology & People*, *Communications of the ACM* and other publications. Dr. Russo serves as secretary of the *IFIP* Working Group 8.2 on Information Systems and Organizations. She is Associate Editor of the *Information Systems Journal*.

Abimbola Soriyan is a lecturer at the Computer Science and Engineering Department, Obafemi Awolowo University, Ile-Ife, Nigeria. She completed her PhD on information systems development in the Nigerian software industry at the same university in 2004. Her research interests include information systems development with emphasis on healthcare. Her present investigations include the reasons why many developing countries have not embraced IT despite the success stories in the West.

Detmar Straub is the J. Mack Robinson Distinguished Professor of Information Systems at Georgia State University. Detmar has conducted research in the areas of Net-enhanced organizations (e-Commerce), computer security, technological innovation, and international IT studies. He holds a DBA in MIS from Indiana and a PhD in English from Penn State. He has published over 110 papers in journals such as *Management Science, Information Systems Research, MIS Quarterly, Journal of AIS, Journal of MIS, Journal of Global Information Management, Organization Science, CACM, Information & Management, CAIS, IEEE Transactions on Engineering Management, OMEGA, Academy of Management Executive,* and *Sloan Management Review.* Former Senior Editor for *Information Systems Research* and Co-Editor of *DATA BASE for Advances in Information Systems,* he is currently Senior Editor for *Journal of the AIS (JAIS)* and DATA BASE. He is also an Associate Editor for *Management Science* and has served in the past as Associate Editor/Associate Publisher for *MISQ Quarterly.*

Duane Truex is Associate Professor of computer information systems at Georgia State University, and researches the social impacts of IS and emergent IS development. He is Associate Editor for the *Information Systems Journal,* has co-edited *The Database for Advances in Information Systems* and is on the editorial boards of the *Scandinavian Journal of Information Systems,* and the *Journal of Communication, Information Technology & Work.* He has published in the *Communications of the ACM, Accounting Management and Information Technologies, the Database for Advances in Information Systems, the European Journal of Information Systems, le journal de la Societé d'Information et Management, the Information Systems Journal, the Journal of Arts Management and Law, IEEE Transactions on Engineering Management,* and forty-four assorted IFIP transactions, edited books and conference proceedings. Truex was co-program chair of the *IFIP* WG 8.2 2004 conference on IS research methods. Truex has served on eighteen PhD thesis committees and has supervised several successful dissertations.

Cathy Urquhart is a Senior Lecturer in Information Systems at the Department of Management Science and Information Systems at the University of the Auckland, New Zealand. She has a PhD in Information Systems from the University of Tasmania. Her other research interests include methodologies for web based development, and the impact of IT on developing countries. She has a strong interest in qualitative data analysis, especially the use of grounded theory in information systems, publishing on this subject in *Qualitative Research in IS: Issues and Trends* (edited by Eileen Trauth). She is on the Editorial Board for *Information Technology* *and People* and reviews regularly for international journals and conferences. She won the award for *Outstanding Paper* for *Information Technology and People* in 2000. She was appointed an Associate Editor of *MIS Quarterly* in 2004.

David W. Wilson holds an appointment at Birkbeck College, University of London as Lecturer in Management Information Systems in the School of Computer Science and Information Systems. His research students, focusing on Information Systems Strategy and Development mainly use interpretative Social Science rooted methods, such as Actor Networks and Grounded Theories to demonstrate their promulgations. David entered academic life on moving to Hong Kong after a prolonged period developing information systems in various UK Government Departments. Amongst more mundane systems developments he was involved in the development of an inverted file database to hold personnel data for the entire UK Civil Service. The constructs being developed were the pre-cursor to much that was later found in relational databases. After 15 years teaching information systems developers in Hong Kong he has developed an interest in cross-cultural studies which is reflected in his student's work. He holds a PhD from Warwick University and was one of the second cohorts on the Civil Service IS course at the LSE.

Index